Helping Skills for Counselors and Health Professionals

Helping Skills for Counselors and Health Professionals provides a model of foundational helping skills that is grounded in a multicultural framework. The chapters in this book explicitly examine implicit bias and the role of culture and systems of oppression and marginalization within the lives of individuals and communities alike. The text also uses ecological systems theory to assist readers in conceptualizing the ways in which culture influences communication styles, perceptions of professional helpers, and individual needs.

Readers will be introduced to concepts that increase awareness of micro and macro-level influences on helping skills, communication, and the patient's life. Within the book's multicultural framework, readers will also find tools for increasing self-awareness to improve communication skills and cultural humility.

Stephanie S.J. Drcar, PhD, is an assistant professor of counselor education at Cleveland State University, where she trains students to become professional counselors.

Kathryn C. MacCluskie, EdD, is a counselor educator with expertise in clinical skill development. In addition to her academic appointment, she sees clients in a small private practice.

Dakota King-White, PhD, is an associate professor and coordinator of school counseling at Cleveland State University. Her research focuses on developing mental health models in systems through a trauma-informed lens.

"In a world in which we often assume people skills cannot be taught, this text provides an evidence-based overview of how to build, maintain, and optimize relationships in health professions education and practice."
Aimee K. Gardner, PhD, *professor and associate dean, Baylor College of Medicine*

"This book should be added to every graduate course seeking to grow culturally competent and self-reflective mental health practitioners. Guided by Bronfenbrenner's ecological systems theory, this text delivers a culturally accountable framework that enhances self-awareness and supports practitioners' efforts to integrate cultural considerations as they develop their helping style and counseling skills."
Layla Kurt, PhD, *associate professor, University of Dayton*

"In a decade ushered in by a pandemic and honed in an active crucible that exposed the impact of systemic racism, trauma, and disregard for science, this textbook is a timely antidote and a classic primer for helping skills instruction. This collection of eleven chapters is written clearly and authentically, with expert integration of trauma informed care, cultural humility, and ethical practice into the presentation of evidence-based empathic helping skills. Sophisticated enough for graduate classes and clinical settings, this book is also a valuable gem to reach undergraduates seeking skills in how to build relationships. It offers a rare and buffet of theories and applications, from Rogers to Prochaska to Bronfenbrenner. This is a truly comprehensive and accessible text, perfect for use in college, in clinics, and by anyone wishing to learn how to better connect with people across settings, populations, and histories."
Anne Sullivan-Soydan, ScD, *clinical associate professor, Boston University, Sargent College of Health and Rehabilitation Sciences*

Helping Skills for Counselors and Health Professionals

Building Culturally Competent Relationships

Stephanie S.J. Drcar,
Kathryn C. MacCluskie and
Dakota King-White

NEW YORK AND LONDON

Cover image: © Getty Image

First published 2024
by Routledge
605 Third Avenue, New York, NY 10158

and by Routledge
4 Park Square, Milton Park, Abingdon, Oxon OX14 4RN

Routledge is an imprint of the Taylor & Francis Group, an informa business

© 2024 Stephanie S.J. Drcar, Kathryn C. MacCluskie, and Dakota King-White

The right of Stephanie S.J. Drcar, Kathryn C. MacCluskie and Dakota King-White to be identified as authors of this work has been asserted in accordance with sections 77 and 78 of the Copyright, Designs and Patents Act 1988.

All rights reserved. No part of this book may be reprinted or reproduced or utilised in any form or by any electronic, mechanical, or other means, now known or hereafter invented, including photocopying and recording, or in any information storage or retrieval system, without permission in writing from the publishers.

Trademark notice: Product or corporate names may be trademarks or registered trademarks and are used only for identification and explanation without intent to infringe.

Library of Congress Cataloging-in-Publication Data
A catalog record for this title has been requested

ISBN: 978-1-032-10885-8 (hbk)
ISBN: 978-1-032-10884-1 (pbk)
ISBN: 978-1-003-21758-9 (ebk)

DOI: 10.4324/9781003217589

Typeset in Garamond
by Taylor & Francis Books

This book is dedicated to our students and clients, who helped us learn to be educators and therapists. And to all aspiring helpers: we know that the journey will be enlightening and profound

Contents

List of illustrations viii
Preface ix
About the Authors xi
Acknowledgments xiii

SECTION I
Helping in a Complex World   1

1 Introduction to Helping   3

2 Ethical Helping Relationships   27

3 Helping in a Pluralistic Society   38

4 Human Development and the Helping Process   60

SECTION II
Techniques for Helping   87

5 Helping Behaviors: Nonverbal and Paraverbal Skills   89

6 Helping Behaviors: Verbal Skills to Encourage   107

7 Helping Behaviors: Verbal Skills to Understand and Connect   125

8 Helping Behaviors: Verbal Skills to Invite Exploration   150

SECTION III
Putting Helping Skills to Work   165

9 Basic Mental Health Assessment   167

10 Evidence-Based Practice   196

11 Helping Skill Integration   210

Index   232

Illustrations

Figures

1.1	Bronfenbrenner's Ecological Model	15
3.1	Bronfenbrenner's Ecological Model	48
5.1	Universal Emotions	95
7.1	The Affect Circumplex	131
7.2	Emotion Wheel	134
7.3	Satisfied Emotions	136
7.4	Unsatisfied Emotions	137
10.1	Empirically Based Practice Components	198
10.2	Levels of Self	200

Tables

3.1	ADDRESSING Framework	42
4.1	Dialogue and Patient Maturity Level	66
8.1	Alternatives to Why Questions	158
9.1	Mental Status Exam	182
9.2	Suicide Risk Factors	186
9.3	Suicide Warning Signs	187

Preface

This book will teach you how to build relationships. The goal is for you to learn how to build strong relationships with your future patients. However, the skills in this book are applicable to most of the relationships in your life. So, what do we hope these relationships look like? We hope, and intend, for you to learn how to have authentic, responsive, and compassionate rapport with all types of people. The patients we serve come from all walks of life and deserve our care and attention. Some readers may feel that "people skills" come naturally to them, and they may wonder if they need to invest their energy into learning these helping skills. Other readers have the motivation and intellect to help but feel that their interactions with others don't come easily. Regardless of your starting point, we feel confident that you can learn how to connect with others in a way that is mutually satisfying: your patients will feel understood and helped and you will feel satisfied in your ability to know and care for them. A common adage is, that people forget what you say, but remember how they felt in your presence. Think about your own experiences with health care providers – you most likely do have recollections of negative interactions, and hopefully other recollections of positive ones. Our intent is for this book to provide you with all the tools you need to make positive impressions and build supportive, impactful, relationships from a trauma-informed lens when working with people you intend to serve.

There are many books of this nature in publication, and they all have their unique merits. This book encapsulates the tried-and-true format of the microskills teaching model while also integrating in two vital frameworks for working in our modern, pluralistic world: cultural competency and trauma-informed care. Additionally, this book is written with a diverse array of providers in mind, because helping skills are not just for the counselors, psychologists, and social workers of the world. Helping skills that build strong relationships are needed for all health providers. Indeed, healing comes in many forms, and most of us know that the attention and compassion of another human, is a vital component of the healing process.

We hope that you find the writing style to be both professional and also accessible, and that you gain some tangible tools and skills that support you being as effective as you have the potential to be. This is important work you are doing, and we applaud your professional goals to contribute to improving people's lives.

About the Authors

Dr. Stephanie Drcar earned her Ph.D. in counseling psychology at The University of Akron and completed her doctoral internship at the University of Oregon's Counseling and Testing Center where she focused on culturally competent clinical work within the multicultural student services rotation. She is an assistant professor of Counselor Education at Cleveland State University. Her primary professional interest is teaching counseling skills to a diverse student population in order to serve a diverse world of clients. Outside of the professional sphere, she enjoys cooking, being in nature, being with her loved ones, and not taking life too seriously.

Dr. Kathryn MacCluskie completed her doctoral work in counseling psychology at West Virginia University, and she has been a counselor educator at Cleveland State University since 1994. In the time since becoming a faculty member and therapist, she has had the privilege to observe major shifts in the helping professions, with huge strides in the visibility and promotion of health and well-being for many under-represented groups of people. Her primary area of professional interest and expertise is student development and pedagogy in teaching clinical skills. Her focus is upon preparing students to serve diverse clients in a variety of settings, with an emphasis on strength-based, culturally responsive strategies to promote positive change. In her leisure she enjoys travel, time with loved ones, and a wide variety of outdoor activities.

Dr. Dakota King-White is an associate professor in counselor education and the program coordinator of the school counseling program at Cleveland State University. Dr. King-White is licensed as a professional counselor and a school counselor. She is a community engaged scholar who engages various partners to ensure that people succeed within their various settings. Dr. King-White gives back to her profession by serving on the Ohio Department of Education (ODE) Whole Child Advisory Board, the ODE Trauma-Informed Schools Committee, and the Ohio School Counseling Association Board as the Chair of the Equity and

Inclusion Task Force. Her broad area of research focuses on developing mental health models in systems from a trauma-informed lens. Through her research she has partnered with various organizations where they have sought and secured funding for research projects locally and internationally. Dr. King-White also serves as a research affiliate with the Center on Trauma and Adversity at Case Western Reserve University. She has collaborated with numerous organizations using her background as a school counselor, mental health therapist, and an administrator in K-12 schools. Dr. King-White has helped schools and other organizations identify resources, develop mental health services and models to support faculty, staff, and youth to thrive within the academic setting and beyond. For her research and achievements, she was named one of Crain's 40 under 40 in 2018.

Acknowledgments

Thank you to our Cleveland State colleagues who made this book possible: Daphyne Durda, Sarah Henley, Mitch Conrad, and Ella Wlodarsky. Thank you to Krystel Chenault for your editing and Anna Moore for your guidance. Thank you, Drs. Gardner, Kurt, and Sullivan-Soydan for your helpful feedback.

Dr. Stephanie Drcar is thankful for the encouragement and support from J, Ellen, Coda, Jackie, and Aimee. She is also thankful to her mentors from across the years, Kathie, Elliott, Avery, Tracy, Jerry, Brooks, Liz, Ron, and Elizabeth. Thank you also to her original helping skills professors from The University of Akron: Drs. Linda Subich and Sue Hardin.

Dr. Kathryn MacCluskie is especially thankful for the support from David, Alex, and David, all of whom hold space for her to flourish.

Dr. Dakota King-White is grateful to collaborate on this project with her colleagues Drs. MacCluskie and Drcar. She is appreciative of the mentorship pertaining to trauma and its impact from Dr. Bruce Perry and Steve Graner from the Neurosequential Network. Thank you also to her mentors, Dr. Jo-Ann Lipford-Sanders and Dr. Daniel Cruickshanks who were her professors from Heidelberg University who provided significant guidance and support throughout her journey of becoming a counselor.

Section I

Helping in a Complex World

Chapter 1

Introduction to Helping

You are on an educational journey to become a culturally competent and trauma-informed healthcare provider. Being a healthcare provider requires a unique balance of discipline-specialized knowledge *and* strong interpersonal skills. Much of your educational journey will focus on gaining the specialized knowledge for practice in your field. However, all that knowledge will be minimally effective if you cannot form strong and authentic rapport with your patients. Thankfully, you might be attracted to your healthcare field because you enjoy interacting with people, and specifically, interacting with people to help them with a challenge they are facing. Even if you enjoy interacting with others, it is still important to develop your interpersonal skills specific to working with patients, so that you can form effective helping relationships with them. This text will take you on an intentional journey of developing helping skills through a trauma-informed lens with patients. This will be a journey that allows you to learn more about yourself; hopefully it is a journey that also strengthens other relationships in your life beyond those you form with patients.

This process of learning helping skills is necessary in a variety of healthcare professions because the provision of the specialized care of your field also requires close interpersonal connection and contact. This textbook is intended for a variety of healthcare professionals, including those in the mental healthcare fields, such as counseling and social work, so we will use the universal terms "patient" and "provider." We will provide examples and dialogue scenarios that use discipline-specific terms at times too, such as "client" or "therapist." Our hope is that you read this book in conjunction with a course that provides you with opportunities to practice these foundational helping skills. Learning foundational helping skills requires practice, and ideally, feedback from others, such as practitioners in your field, fellow students, and real patients. Feedback can be obtained from real-time observation as well as recorded sessions that can be watched by others. Watching oneself in video recordings while practicing these new skills can be uncomfortable, and many students experience anxiety and embarrassment. Please take comfort in knowing that you are in good

DOI: 10.4324/9781003217589-2

company among your peers - this is a common emotional reaction. Over the years, we have consistently found that recorded practice opportunities are an ideal way to improve self-awareness and implement new skills.

Like its predecessors, the approach taken in this text is called the microskills model. The microskills approach emerged in the late 1960s and early 1970s as a means of teaching basic counseling skills to psychotherapists. The microskills model teaches discreet helping skills that build upon one another in their level of complexity and provider directiveness (Ivey, 1971; Truax & Carkhuff, 1967). This text also takes a person-centered approach for using microskills with patients; that is, the provider allows the patient to direct the conversation under the assumption that the patient will discuss what is of importance to them. Being able to use basic helping skills in this person-centered manner will facilitate your rapport building with patients, and strong rapport can improve patient satisfaction (Oliveira et al., 2015). The ability to connect with a patient also allows for meaningful human connection between you and the people you are serving. In addition, the model used throughout the text will focus on the microskills model from a trauma-informed perspective when serving patients in the various fields. Throughout the text, we will integrate trauma-informed principles that support providers in ensuring that patients are able to get the help that they need without providers traumatizing or retraumatizing patients.

Patients are often in a vulnerable position when they seek our help; they may be ill, injured, depressed, scared, or anxious. As healthcare providers, we are in positions of expertise and power - this makes it even more important that we interact with our patients through a trauma-informed lens that is gentle and facilitates healing. The providers hold the power in the helping relationship because they are the expert and have the authority to provide treatment and care. Acknowledging the impact of the power dynamic in the helping relationship is just one of many complexities inherent in using basic helping skills. This text will also introduce you to other important influences in the helping relationship, such as patient cultural identities and their associated experiences and practices as well as the impact of oppression and discrimination on the provider and/or the patient.

Understanding and responding to all these factors require provider self-awareness. Throughout this text we will ask you to self-reflect in the hopes that we enrich your insight into your understanding of the actions, thoughts, and emotions of yourself and others. We encourage you to self-reflect in a curious and non-judgmental manner: avoid assigning labels like "good" or "bad" or "right" or "wrong" to one's own behavior, thoughts, and emotions. A more kind and accurate way to self-assess your efforts is to think in terms of degrees of effectiveness; some responses are significantly more effective in helping a patient than other types of responses. Sometimes self-evaluation is necessary though, and when doing so, it is usually more effective for your growth as a provider to consider if behavior, thoughts, and emotions are "helpful" or "unhelpful" in pursuit of your goal at that given moment. And now, let us begin the journey!

Self-Awareness

In this text, when we discuss self-awareness, we are referring to the process of being attuned and observant of oneself, both what we are feeling and noticing internally, as well as being aware of what others can observe about ourselves. Aspects of our internal experience include thoughts, emotions, motivations, desires, and internal proprioceptive awareness (i.e., detection of internal bodily states, functioning, movement, etc.). The outward experience is perceivable by others and oneself and includes displayed emotions, speech, and behavior. Self-awareness allows for monitoring and adjusting oneself in response to the circumstance, environment, or goals. Self-awareness allows us to adapt and change ourselves to better suit our own needs and/or the needs of others. Imagine that a person visits a friend's house and meets their toddler-aged child for the first time. Given this person's self-awareness of their tall height and loud, booming voice, they might drop to one knee and lower their voice volume as they introduce themselves to the child because their goal is to present themselves as friendly and approachable. This is the type of nearly unconscious self-adjustments a person makes when they act on their self-awareness; that is, they adjust themselves to the needs of the circumstance.

"Demand characteristics" refer to circumstances in which social norms suggest particular behaviors. Being interpersonally effective needs to include observation of ourselves and our internal experiences as well as attentive observation of the person we are helping. In any given interaction, the demand characteristics are somewhat shaped by the behavior of the other person. For example, if we are having a casual in-person conversation with someone and we notice that they are fiddling with their car keys, looking away as we are speaking, or moving their body away from ours, demand characteristics would suggest they are closing the conversation and the appropriate response would be to bring the conversation to a conclusion so they can move on.

Thus, the second important skill needed in the dance of interpersonal interactions is the ability to observe and interpret the behavior of others. Since we cannot know the internal experience of others (i.e., their internal thoughts, emotions, bodily experiences, motivations, desires, etc.) unless they tell us, we must make inferences based on what is observable to us. In Chapter Five of this book, you will learn about how to observe other's speech and behavior so that you can draw reasonable inferences about the meaning of others' behavior. The dance of interpersonal interactions requires this back-and-forth attunement to oneself and others as well as adjustment of oneself to meet one's goals for the interaction. Of course, humans are not robots, so missteps, misunderstandings, and awkwardness can happen! These types of awkward moments and missteps will also occur in your practice of basic helping skills – and that's okay! The goal is not to achieve an unrealistic standard of being "perfect" in social interactions, but of achieving a reasonable degree of authenticity, rapport, and connection in helping relationships.

One valuable and important aspect of increasing self-awareness involves becoming aware of our own cognitive distortions (everyone has some), and then becoming aware of how those distortions are impacting the way we think about other people. The term arises from Cognitive Behavioral Therapy (CBT) and refers to the process by which our expectations, pre-existing beliefs, and style of thinking influence the way we perceive other people. If we are unable to identify our distortions, then those distorted thought processes become a confounding variable, meaning that we run the risk of missing or misperceiving important information. The term "self-fulfilling prophecy" has relevance here. Perhaps you've had the experience of being in an irritable mood one day and finding most people you interact with to also be irritable. When viewing that pattern from a distance, it might be apparent that in communicating with others pessimistically or in an annoyed tone of voice, we elicit negative reactions from other people that we see as supporting our world view that others are rude and annoying. Without actively working at our self-awareness around how we are coming across to others, we run the risk of missing important information about the other person because we've already made assumptions that we mistakenly believe to be accurate. Developing self-awareness takes effort; aspects of our interpersonal style that may be readily obvious to an observer can be difficult for us to see for ourselves until someone points them out.

The importance of self-awareness in various types of interpersonal interactions varies though, and the focus of this text is on developing an effective helping relationship in the healthcare field, not in romantic or work relationships (although these helping skills are somewhat generalizable and you may see a positive impact on other relationships in your life when you use the skills taught in this text). In a helping relationship in the healthcare field, the provider holds a greater level of power and authority over the patient, given the provider's role and expertise, and the patient's position, given their vulnerable status. There may be other factors that add additional layers of privilege or disempowerment to the provider-patient relationship, such as those related to social and cultural variables, of which we will discuss shortly. Given the inherent power that the provider holds, the provider must take responsibility for their interpersonal behavior in professional interactions with patients, which requires self-awareness. Any potential need to increase your self-awareness will depend on your starting point, and in Chapter Five, we will introduce self-reflection questions to support your exploration of this aspect of yourself. The remainder of this chapter will review the major areas of focus in this textbook that will prepare you for developing effective relationships with patients: ethical practice, social and cultural diversity, human development, and the communication skills. First though, let us introduce the concept of trauma-informed care within the helping professions.

Trauma-Informed Principles in Helping Professions

An unfortunately high number of people will experience trauma in their lives, such as abuse, neglect, violence, systemic discrimination, and other adverse events, heightening their risk for adverse physical and mental health outcomes in their lifetime. Healthcare providers should engage with patients in a manner that is trauma-informed. Trauma-informed care is "grounded in an understanding of and responsiveness to the impact of trauma, that emphasizes physical, psychological, and emotional safety for both providers and survivors, and that creates opportunities for survivors to rebuild a sense of control and empowerment" (Hopper, Bassuk, & Olivet, 2010, p. 82)." The Substance Abuse & Mental Health Services Administration (SAMHSA) has identified six principles that should be considered when creating trauma-informed systems of care. The six principles are safety, trustworthiness & transparency, peer support, collaboration & mutuality, empowerment voice & choice, and cultural, historical, and gender issues. According to SAMHSA (2014), trauma-informed systems focus on realizing the impact of trauma, identifying the symptoms, and responding with the intent not to re-traumatize. As providers, when we are working from a trauma-informed perspective, we are integrating the principles from SAMHSA into our everyday practices with the goal of not traumatizing or retraumatizing vulnerable patients. One of the key principles in trauma-informed practices is ensuring that the environment is safe physically and emotionally for the patients we serve. A key element of emotional safety is building trusting relationships.

Building Effective Interpersonal Relationships Through a Trauma-Informed Lens as a Healthcare Provider

This text takes the approach that simply learning basic communication skills inadequately prepares healthcare providers for the myriad of complex people and circumstances they will encounter in their careers. Rather, healthcare providers must:

1   have ethical frameworks to guide their practice to protect their patients;

2 understand and act upon their understanding of the complexities of cultural and social identities and associated experiences; and
3 understand the ways in which basic helping skills should be adjusted when working with people across the lifespan.

Given these three foundational areas, this text will provide a chapter on each of these topics. Your professional education program will also likely provide you additional coursework or training on ethics, multicultural competence, and lifespan development, so we hope that what you learn in this text will help you better understand the implications for this knowledge with regard to your helping skills. Let us now discuss why knowledge of these topics is important as you develop foundational helping skills to better serve your future patients.

Ethics

The first core tenet of this text is the view that effective interpersonal relationships are only possible in professional settings when providers behave in an ethical manner. Ethics are the morally based principles that guide behavior because they establish what is deemed "right" and "wrong." Codes of ethics exist within many professions, but have you ever considered why codes of ethics exist across so many professions? *Take a moment to consider the profession you are training to join; what are the possible implications if there was no unified code of ethics for professionals?* You likely recognize that ethical codes can provide protection for vulnerable patients by providing guidance for professionals on how to provide services to patients while also respecting their inherent human rights. Ethical codes establish professional values that guide providers when a quandary arises in which consideration needs to be given to the implications of various actions. Ethical dilemmas can occur in abstract, hypothetical circumstances and in actual, day-to-day work situations. Some of the day-to-day circumstances that are relevant to our discussion in this text are those that occur in our helping relationships with our patients.

Relationships with patients are just one of many different types of interpersonal relationships in our lives, and different interpersonal relationships serve different purposes. The purpose of friendships is often to provide companionship, belonging, and mutual support. The purpose of relationships with work colleagues is often more transactionally based – that is, working together to accomplish work tasks and goals. The relationships that you build with your patients are based on the explicit purpose of rendering a service that can help them; however, the ongoing and intimate nature of helping and care usually requires authentic rapport and emotional disclosure on the part of the patient. This is where professional relationships in healthcare fields can begin to differ from the professional relationships in other fields, the providers in a

Introduction to Helping 9

healthcare setting must communicate in a manner that is holistically caring and empathic, not simply render helpful services in the absence of tenderness and compassion. Plumbers and automotive mechanics are professionals with specialized skills; successful work in those fields does not require empathy though. In healthcare, being a compassionate and tender provider means being empathic, and being empathic means being connected to the emotional experiences of others. This is where things might feel "messy" for people who recognize the power and influence of emotions on our thoughts and behaviors.

Emotions often motivate the choices we make and our behaviors. For example, emotions of inadequacy can lead to avoidance behaviors, whereas emotions of confidence can lead to action. Emotions of self-righteousness can lead to dismissing others, whereas emotions of compassion can lead to seeking to understand others. Self-awareness of one's emotions as a provider can support the provider in making ethical decisions in their interactions and care of a patient. Providers must be aware of their emotions and motivations because they may feel inclined to take actions that feel intuitive but could actually be harmful to their patient. Dr. Atul Gawande, a surgeon and author, has written about the difficulties that medical professionals often face when working with patients with terminal diagnoses. Gawande (2014) notes that when physicians focus on extending painful and difficult treatment, despite the negative consequences and unavoidable death, they end up forgoing discussion of end-of-life care that acknowledges their imminent death (even though it is scary and upsetting for both the physician and the patient) that could provide meaningful and holistic care in their final days and weeks. When a provider can acknowledge their internal emotional drives, they can recognize that their patient care decisions may not be optimal if they don't balance their emotions with other information. This concept of seeking a balance of emotions and so-called "rationality" is known as using one's "wise mind" from Dialectical Behavior Therapy (Linehan, 2014). Professionals have an obligation to behave ethically in their interactions with patients, and this is usually supported by the ability to inhabit wise mind.

The other reason why ethical codes are beneficial when learning basic helping skills is because they generally establish the need for practitioners to respect the autonomy of their patients. Respecting patient autonomy is just one of the ethical themes that are common across a variety of professional ethical codes that will be discussed in more detail in Chapter Two. The patients we work with will hold diverse social and cultural identities, and thus, their values and goals will vary in response to their diverse identities. What this means is that providers cannot operate from an etic perspective; etic perspectives assume universality of culture, whereas emic perspectives recognize intrinsic distinctions across cultures. Providers who interact with their patients from an emic perspective can more easily recognize the need for respecting patient autonomy, which sometimes means that patients will have goals, values, preferences, and motivations that differ from one's own.

Diversity

A second core tenet of this text is that providers can only build effective helping relationships with their patients when they have a broad understanding and respect for people of a variety of diverse cultural and social identities. Understanding the experiences and practices of people who hold a variety of diverse cultural and social identities allows providers to expand their understanding of all the "unique manifestations of the human spirit," as anthropologist Wade Davis says. It is of crucial importance that providers avoid pathologizing behavior that is unfamiliar but normative for an individual. The term pathologizing is related to ethnocentrism – that is, using one's own cultural norms and values as a basis for judging others' behavior. Pathologizing in the health care professions can be especially detrimental because it distances us by diminishing our ability feel and express empathy; it also reduces the other person's suffering to a diagnosis, which can itself be invalidating and toxic to trust development. We create an authentic connection with those we want to help by engaging with them and accepting their unique context, including many intersecting identities that impact their lives. In addition, understanding the experiences of other cultures can elucidate a patient's potential context for entering a helping relationship with you. As we will discuss shortly, some cultural and social groups have experienced oppression, discrimination, and marginalization from the healthcare systems and providers, and as such, they may meet new providers with skepticism and reservation. A provider who can recognize this potential reservation from their new patients can approach that interpersonal interaction with empathy and respect, all of which are usually communicated via the foundational helping skills taught in this text.

The Nature of Discrimination and Oppression

Discrimination and oppression can impact helping relationships in the healthcare fields. This influence may not always be consciously recognized by the patient or provider; however, the provider has an obligation to recognize and consider the potential influence of historical and recent experiences of discrimination and oppression that the patient has faced. As a healthcare provider, you may represent a larger healthcare system to some of your patients, and therefore, your patient's previous experiences with the healthcare system may loom in the background and set the stage for their interactions with you. If you understand the ways in which healthcare systems and providers have historically failed, marginalized, hurt, and oppressed various groups of people, then you can approach patient interactions with sensitivity and attunement to potential distrust. Chapter Three will provide an in-depth exploration of these topics; however, we want to share some foundational information to set the stage for later learning.

The Pervasive and Multifaceted Nature of Oppression

A multitude of social and cultural groups in the United States and elsewhere experience oppression, that is, unjust treatment from those who hold power. Social and cultural groups refer to those related to ability status, race, ethnicity, religion, socioeconomic status, sexual and gender identity, nationality, and indigenous status. Minority groups sometimes refer to the numerical size of a group. However, in the context of this book, the term "minority group" is primarily referencing any group that experiences differential treatment compared to a majority group that holds greater power within a society (and often is smaller in numerical size compared to the majority group as well). The nature of oppression for diverse groups is pervasive; it exists in structural and systemic ways, in historical treatment, interpersonally, and in everyday "subtle" ways. Those who hold characteristics aligned with the majority, or privileged, social and cultural identities, may be unaware of the pervasive nature of such oppression. It is of tremendous importance for providers with many privileged identities to become fully aware of and sensitive to the inherent inequities that others face and cope with regularly. These inequities will inevitably be variables in the equation determining how successfully you are able to help them, regardless of your discipline.

Here are some examples of oppression that pertain to the world of healthcare to illustrate the nature of multifaceted oppression. As an example of structural oppression, the African American infant mortality rate is twice that of White infants, even when the mother's education levels are equal. Infant mortality rates are influenced by a multitude of factors (including individual factors); however, researchers find that individual factors alone do not account for this difference and acknowledge that long-standing structural racism (e.g., segregation, institutional racism) appear to play a factor in these differential rates (Matoba & Collins, 2017). As a historical example, African American men with syphilis were lied to and withheld treatment in one of the most notorious examples of racism in health research, known commonly as the Tuskegee Syphilis study (Centers for Disease Control and Prevention, 2021). In both examples, the legacy of racism and the devaluing of African Americans have contributed to a poorer health outcomes and justified distrust of the medical system, respectively.

Oppression also manifests within the microlevel too, such as the interactions between patients and their healthcare providers. For example, transgender patients report experiencing blaming, shaming, othering, and discrimination related to their status as a transgender person in their healthcare encounters. Some healthcare providers openly acknowledge the ways in which their biased views negatively impact their work with their transgender patients (Poteat et al., 2013). The manifestation of biased views of diverse groups can also be experienced in indirect ways, which are called microaggressions in some cases. Microaggressions are understood as the subtle ways in which biased and stereotyped views, consciously recognized as unacceptable, emerge unconsciously into interactions with people from diverse groups (Sue, Capodilupo, et al., 2007; Swim et al., 1995). Although the name would imply that microaggressions are "small," ongoing and subtle slights have been described as "constant, low-level background noise" (Landrine & Klonoff, 1997, p. 15), lifting a ton of feathers (Caplan, 1992), and as "slow death by a thousand cuts" (Sue, 2010, p. 66). When mental health therapists act in microaggressive ways with their clients, clients perceive a decreased level of safety in therapy, which can impact the working alliance and therapy outcomes (Davis et al., 2016).

Healthcare Disparities

The majority of the world population live in countries where healthcare disparities exist (Dorling et al., 2007). The Agency for Healthcare Research and Quality (2022a) defines healthcare disparities as the differences that groups face in *access and availability* of healthcare as well as *differences in rates of disease and disability*. AHRQ studies healthcare disparities impacting groups defined by age, race/ethnicity, economic resources, gender, and geographic location. The AHRQ has published the *National Healthcare Quality and Disparities Report* every year for the past 19 years, as mandated by Congress. The 2021 Report found that, although decreasing, disparities continue to exist for all racial and ethnic minority groups in American compared to White, non-Hispanic Americans. The 2021 Report also denoted that people who are poor or low-income and those under 65 with public insurance also experience greater healthcare disparities compared to those who are higher-income and those with private insurance, respectively (Agency for Healthcare Research and Quality, 2022b). Healthcare disparities also exist for groups that are not specifically studied by the AHRQ, such as the LGBTQ+ population (Office of Disease Prevention and Health Promotion, 2022), people with disabilities, and some religious groups (Penner et al., 2013).

Healthcare disparities exist within a broader system of social and economic inequality for minorities (Nelson, 2002). Healthcare disparities stem from multiple factors that are systemic, intrapersonal, and interpersonal in nature (Penner et al., 2013). Deep exploration of the systemic causes of these disparities, such as structural differences in healthcare systems and how they are financially supported (Institute of Medicine, 2002), are beyond the scope of this textbook. Intrapersonal factors, that is, attributes of the patients or the provider, can influence interpersonal interactions between patients and providers. Patient intrapersonal factors may have systemic and historical causes behind them, including low socioeconomic status, low language proficiency, and low health literacy (Penner et al., 2013). Given that the focus of this text is on improving your helping skills as the provider, we will focus on *your intrapersonal factors* and *interpersonal factors* (i.e., the interactions between you and the patient). Addressing the intrapersonal factors of you, the provider, will require work beyond the scope of this text. These intrapersonal components include the stereotypes and biases held by providers that are activated and expressed in interactions with patients. Many professional training programs include coursework to assist trainees in expanding their knowledge and skill with diverse populations and we hope that you can integrate what you learn in this text with that learning.

Improving the variable of interpersonal behavior, often driven by the provider, is within the scope of this text, however. It is important to emphasize that a provider behaving in a culturally competent manner in their interpersonal interactions with their patients will not eliminate the possibility for healthcare disparities given the multitude of contributing factors. We hope though that you will learn approaches in this text that align with the goals of patient-centered communication that aims to help you: 1) understand patient perspectives; 2) consider the impact of the patient's psychological and social context; 3) hold a shared understanding of the concern with the patient; and 4) empower patients to have meaningful involvement in healthcare decisions (Epstein & Street, 2007). As will be discussed later, patients may come to us with negative past experiences with healthcare providers. Learning basic helping skills can assist you in providing validating, open, and empathic communication, which can positively impact patient medical mistrust (Commonwealth Fund, 2021).

Implicit Bias

A finding of the congressionally requested report from the Institute of Medicine, *Unequal Treatment: Confronting Racial and Ethnic Disparities in Health Care*, was that healthcare provider bias, stereotyping, and prejudice may contribute to healthcare disparities (Nelson, 2002). Biases and stereotyped views of others can be in our conscious, explicit awareness or they can unconscious, so-called implicit biases. Researchers have explored the impact of healthcare provider implicit bias and found impacts on treatment recommendations, expectations of therapeutic bonds, pain management, empathy, and patient-provider communication. Researchers suggest that professionals should begin the process of reducing their biases as early in training as possible (Maina et al., 2018). Approaches that have been helpful in reducing implicit bias include approaches that will be emphasized in this text via the use of foundational helping skills, such as seeking specific information from patients versus relying on assumptions, and the ability to engage in perspective taking with patients who hold different identities than the provider (Maina et al., 2018).

The implications are clear: providers cannot simply hope that unexamined or unacknowledged biases will not impact their work with patients. Although you enter this professional journey with the best of intentions, to learn how to help others, you are also responsible for exploring how your existing views of diverse groups can impact your care and interactions with patients. Ensuring that your interactions and care of patients is culturally competent is important given that clients with diverse identities are facing added stress in their lives given their intersecting identities (Meyer, 2003).

Human Development

The approach taken to teaching helping skills in this text rests upon the foundational understanding that people are complex and shaped by the environments where they have grown, lived, and worked. The reason it is important to understand the impact of these environments on people is because it influences their values, personality, preferences, and styles of interaction and communication and therefore, our interactions with them! As mentioned previously, part of the responsibility of a healthcare provider is making reasonable adaptations in their interpersonal behavior to suit the needs of the patient. Although it is not possible to expertly understand all the potential intersections of each patient's social and cultural identities and backgrounds, if a provider has some foundational understandings, then they can recognize that reasonable and subtle adaptations are needed to meet the needs of their diverse patient caseload.

Ecological systems theory is a widely utilized theory created by Urie Bronfenbrenner to understand the influence of social environments on human development. Bronfenbrenner conceptualized five systems that influence a developing person:

- Microsystem: groups that have direct contact with a person
- Mesosystem: relationships between the microsystem groups
- Exosystem: groups and factors that impact a person's life but don't have a direct relationship with the person

- Macrosystem: cultural components of the environment that impact the person and others around them
- Chronosystem: the developmental impact of both time and personal lifespan development

In Figure 1.1, you can see how these systems are visually represented as concentric circles around an individual. The ecological systems theory provides a framework for conceptualizing how a person has developed given the unique interactions between themselves and the cultural and social environments in which they have lived. Spencer (1997, 2006) recognized, too, that beyond the identified nested systems, there are demographic and contextual variables that potentially modify the degree of influence any system level exerts upon an individual. Those contextual variables include race, gender, ethnicity, socioeconomic status, immigration status, faith, skin color, and nativity. We will explore these variables

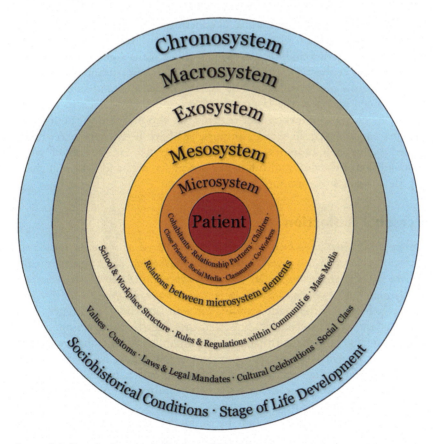

Figure 1.1 Bronfenbrenner's Ecological Model

in more depth later, but for the moment, you can recognize that these variables have shaped each of us and our patients.

In addition, it is not only important to understand how cultural and social variables impact our patient's communication patterns, but also how it influences their values, goals, and expectations for care. As providers, we cannot assume that we share the same values, goals, and expectations for care; rather, we must be curious and open to understand what they hope will result from our care and treatment of them. In essence, this allows for a non-judgmental understanding of what is important to our patients. Getting to know our patients in this way helps us understand the *"why"* behind their goals. A physical therapist might ask a new patient about their goals, and the patient might reply that they want to hold their infant grandchildren again confidently and safely (a goal related to connection). A school counselor's client might share that their goal is to reduce their social anxiety so that they can return to expressing themselves artistically in their high school's show choir ensemble (a goal related to self-expression). A nutritionist's patient might report a goal of adhering to a nutrition plan to assist them in achieving their goals in competitive power lifting (a goal related to achievement). Understanding the "why" behind patient goals allows us to form a deeper connection with our patients, and it's important to recognize that these goals can be influenced by aspects of identities and values.

As we consider how the layers of systems and their social and cultural environments have influenced our patients, we also must think about those systems and contexts in which we ourselves have been shaped. As mentioned before, self-awareness supports our internal exploration of what motivates our behaviors and influences our preferences and values, including those related to communication.

Personal Reflection

Do you prefer direct or indirect communication, transactional or interactional communication, slow or fast-paced communication? How do these preferences vary between different circumstances, say in work communication versus communication with friends? Where do you think those preferences originated from?

If you have a better understanding of your "baseline" preferences and patterns, then you can consider how well these function in the professional healthcare environment with patients. As a reminder, generally we do not expect our patients to alter *their* communication approaches because they are the person we are serving as the provider, but rather, as the person with authority and power, *we* have the responsibility to monitor and adjust our communication to meet their needs.

Given the aspects of bias and discrimination discussed earlier in this chapter, and the paramount importance of multicultural responsiveness, we will take just a moment to ponder what "culturally responsive" approaches might look like. Essentially, cultural responsiveness means recognizing that the dominant group's expectations for behavior are not necessarily the definitive yardstick to which all people's behaviors should be compared. For example, many cultures have different views and beliefs about death and grieving, based on their spiritual traditions or other culture-specific orientations (Thanasiu & Pizza, 2019). In some cultural groups, the deceased family member is experienced as continuing to be present in the family, and people speak to the deceased.

Hall et al. (2016) conducted a meta-analysis of studies comparing treatment outcomes when the strategies represented culturally responsive adaptations of empirically validated treatments. One compelling finding was that studies investigating culturally adapted strategies did observe a greater magnitude of symptom reduction than another intervention or no intervention. There are many ways and times in the life cycle of a family where there may be substantial differences in how landmark events are perceived, addressed, and metabolized. Considering that there is as much individual variation in these processes as there is variation across cultural groups, it once again points to the primacy of listening carefully and understanding each person's unique situation and presentation throughout the helping process.

Skills

The "heart" of this book is basic helping skill development through learning microskills. The term was first created by Allen Ivey as he developed a strategy that involved identifying and teaching discrete components of effective active listening. These microskills will be taught in Chapters Five through Eight and include non-verbal and paraverbal skills, paraphrasing and summarizing skills, and emotion and meaning reflection skills. The microskills approach to teaching basic helping skills breaks down communication with patients into its component parts and encourages you to consider the benefits and impacts of each skill. In our years of teaching basic helping skills, we have found that learning and using the individual skills is not terribly difficult, but what *is* challenging is deciding *which* skill to use in a given moment based on what the patient just said. Students will sometimes describe having two simultaneous foci of their attention when interacting with a patient: one is listening to the patient speak and the other is their own internal decision process considering what to say next. This can be distracting because one's attention is divided and may lead to missing key information that the patient is expressing, particularly if it is subtle. This is a normal experience for novice providers and will generally dissipate with time and experience. Sufficient practice and experience will allow you to use these microskills in a thoughtful and integrated fashion that allows patients to express themselves and to be understood and validated by you.

As you can see, part of this learning process is developing and refining new communication skills. Another part of this learning process is *unlearning* unhelpful communication behaviors; such behaviors might be unconscious and common when interacting with friends and family members. What you may come to realize is although such behaviors are common, they still might negatively impact interactions with patients. For example, a common communication pattern in friendships is self-disclosure of one's personal circumstances. If a friend told you that she was in a minor car accident and that she is having issues with her insurance company, you might communicate empathy by telling her about a similar situation that occurred in your life. Many people use this type of sharing as a means of conveying understanding, as if to say, "I understand how that feels because that happened to me too." The drawback to this behavior is that it can pull the focus of conversation from the friend and onto yourself. Sometimes the circumstance in one person's life isn't comparable to the other situation and the disclosure may minimize or invalidate what is being expressed. Other times you may not have a comparable life circumstance, so you might not be sure what to say beyond something vaguely sympathetic. What you also might consider is that self-disclosure of personal life circumstances may not be appropriate as a means of showing understanding when working with patients. In this textbook we will teach you how to use other skills (e.g., paraphrasing, summarizing, emotion reflection, meaning reflection) that convey understanding and validation without disclosure of your own personal circumstances. You will also find that these new skills will positively impact your communication with a patient because they convey understanding without pulling the conversation toward one's own life circumstance.

Beyond self-disclosure, there will be other communication behaviors you may come to observe in yourself, and you'll need to evaluate their potential impact on communication with patients. Some other behaviors we have seen students unlearn, in the context of patient communication, include: not allowing for moments of silence, expressing incongruent emotions (i.e., smiling when talking about sad topics), and pretending to understand what someone is sharing even if they don't understand fully. What makes these communication behaviors difficult to unlearn is that they serve a purpose. For example, not allowing for silence can reduce moments of ambiguity in conversation and give the speaker control, which can provide relief from anxiety. Expressing incongruent emotions can allow for emotional distance from upsetting and unpleasant emotions. Faking understanding can protect someone from being seen as confused or unknowledgeable. The problem is that each of these examples are temporary avoidance strategies, and they often negatively impact communication with a patient. When there is inadequate silence, the patient doesn't have time to process what you're saying or to speak freely. When the provider expresses incongruent emotions, they communicate their discomfort with the topic, which can lead the patient to talk less about the topic. When the provider fakes understanding, they risk responding to an inaccurate understanding of the situation or simply ignoring aspects of the patient's experience. Learning and using new microskills is just as important as reducing use of these types of unhelpful communication behaviors.

You may find that some of these new communication skills will benefit your communication with others in your life. Students in our classes commonly remark to us that they are using their "new skills" with their friends, partners, and family and find them to positively impact their relationships because they now have deeper and more meaningful conversations. The skills outlined in this text have the effect of slowing down the pace and deepening the emotional content of communication. The slower pace and focus on emotions allow for greater intimacy and authentic connection. Deepened intimacy might evoke feelings of apprehension from people who are emotionally guarded and reluctant to build authentic connection with others. If the prospect of greater authentic connection with others, including patients, evokes unpleasant emotions for you, then you will likely benefit from exploring these concerns further via your own self-reflection. Connecting with patients and their emotional experience usually requires us to connect to our own emotions, and this can be unnerving for people who avoid their emotions. Some questions you might reflect on include: *What am I afraid will happen if I'm connected to the emotions of others? What emotions feel scary to me and why? What are the drawbacks to authentic and deep connections with others? What are the benefits of authentic and deep connections to others?*

Learning basic helping skills is not a linear process but rather will be a mixture of learning more about yourself, increasing insight into the impact of your current communication patterns, and integrating new learning into your identity as a professional helper. The other foundational insight that you'll likely come to as you learn these skills is that helping others doesn't always mean finding a "solution" to the so-called "problem." In fact, calling these skills "basic *helping* skills" is somewhat of a misnomer if you conceptualize "helping" as "problem solving." Rather, these are skills that deepen communication without explicit focus on problem solving per se, but instead on making authentic and validating connections with others. At times there will be no precise solution to the challenges that our patients face; however, providing genuine emotional connection will itself be comforting and healing. It might be more accurate to call these *basic communication skills for connection,* but that is a mouthful, so we'll stick to calling them basic helping skills or microskills.

Reconceptualizing the Purpose of Communication with Patients

An adage that has been misattributed to different authors over the years serves as our starting point: *people will forget the specifics of what you say, but they will remember how they felt in your presence.* We have established that learning basic helping skills requires foundational understanding in the realms of ethics, diversity, and human development. And as we just discussed, basic helping skills are communication skills that assist you in developing authentic rapport and connection with your patients. Taken together, the approach taught in this text will assist you in developing a skill set that is adaptable to a variety of patients and circumstances. There is no singular "correct" way to develop a helping relationship with a patient, and as you move further through this text, you will learn how to consider the patient's social and cultural identities, their values, and their needs into how you can use these helping skills. Individualizing your approach to helping patients might sound like a daunting task, and you might wonder if you could simply take the less taxing method of using the same style of communication with all your patients. The drawback of such an approach is that patients are being asked to accommodate *you* and *your* preferences for communication, even though they are in a position of vulnerability. What this text is asking you to do is to reconceptualize your understanding of the purpose of communication with patients. Communication is not simply transactional, that is, sharing factual information back and forth like two emotionless robots, but rather is an opportunity for authentic connection that is healing in and of itself.

Research on the effectiveness of psychotherapy approaches has emphasized the importance of the common factors that are present across most psychotherapy experiences. These common factors include: a shared belief in the rationale for treatment, the healing context, the therapeutic alliance, and the provider instilling hope in the patient (Ahn & Wampold, 2001). The adage at the beginning of this section references the importance of common factors in treatment outcome. There is a big difference between a professional helper responding to the content (i.e., story details) of a person's concerns, and responding to the expressed emotions and subjective experience of that person as they share the story details. Therapeutic rapport and establishment of trust are essential components of positive outcomes in counseling – and, we would argue, positive outcomes in other helping disciplines. Norcross (2010) observed the high frequency with which clients, when asked about the biggest influences on their positive outcome in counseling, attribute their counseling success to the relationship they had with their therapist. The helping relationship itself, in any discipline, is a valuable, if not essential, aspect of developing trust. A patient's willingness to engage in the process of keeping appointments, following through on suggestions that arose during an appointment, and trusting the helper by taking the risk of engaging in new behaviors and thinking, hinge to some extent on the rapport and trust that arise from the helping relationship.

Another crucial element to patient/provider relationships is the requirement of confidentiality. Across most health professions, providers adhere to confidentiality requirements from both professional ethical codes and state and federal laws. Confidentiality generally requires providers to maintain patient privacy by not disclosing information about patients to others unless the patient has consented or in an emergency. The assurance of confidentiality increases the likelihood that patients will share important and sensitive information with us, but it does not guarantee it. Even though patients may trust that their disclosures are private with their provider, they may still withhold information, owing to fears of judgement or concerns regarding what the provider may do in response to such knowledge of the patient. Providers make it easier for patients to disclose sensitive information to them when they demonstrate a non-judgmental attitude. Being non-judgmental does not mean that providers "approve" of all patient behavior or view all behavior as healthy or helpful. Rather, being non-judgmental means that providers do not apply *their own moral beliefs* in assessment of the actions and beliefs of the patient. A non-judgmental stance recognizes that patients have the right to autonomy of their body, their thoughts, their emotions, and their choices. Providers can provide *clinical* judgement, however; clinical judgement is the accumulation of skill and specialized knowledge and assists providers in making determinations about consequences of actions, both their own and the patient's actions.

Clinical judgement allows providers to give feedback and guidance to their patients about what is healthy or unhealthy for them, based on specialized knowledge from their discipline. It objectively considers the extent to which a person's action results in undesired consequences or contributes to diminished functioning in some aspect of their lives. On the contrary, *personal* judgement is simply applying one's own values, preferences, and morals to someone else without any basis in specialized, discipline-specific knowledge. Let's consider a scenario where a therapist is exercising their clinical judgement and compare that to when they inappropriately provide their own personal judgement.

Scenario 1: A client is telling their mental health therapist about their difficulties with social anxiety.

CLIENT: I've really been struggling with getting out of the house lately. My job lets me be pretty socially removed from people, but I still have to interact with some people and that takes a lot of energy out of me. By the time I get home I feel like I don't have any energy left to deal with being around others.

THERAPIST: I hear that the social anxiety that stems from your workplace seems to be exhausting for you to the point that you struggle to engage in other social experiences.

CLIENT: Yeah, it's like, I know my family wants me to come to more family get togethers, but those make me so anxious. The entire time I'm at a get together, I'm thinking about what they're thinking of me and like, monitoring everything I say... it's so tiring. Then when I get home from the event, I just replay different things again and again in my head and reanalyze them. It's so consuming that I've really just started lying and making excuses for why I can't go to these events, and it is helping because now some people have just stopped inviting me altogether, so I don't have to deal with even saying that I can't come. But even if they do invite me, I still lie about why I can't come. I don't tell them it's because I get all anxious. Instead, I tell them that I'm sick, or that my cat is sick, or that I have car problems.

THERAPIST: It sounds like telling them the truth about why you don't want to come might be too vulnerable for you?

CLIENT: Well, I don't know, I never thought about why I lie to them. I guess I think that they'll tell me I'm being crazy and they'll pressure me into coming since my anxiety isn't a "real" reason to not come, from their perspective. Lying is just easier.

THERAPIST: I see what you're saying. It sounds like these might be some *avoidant* coping strategies, which sort of work. However, avoidant coping strategies can tend to make the existing problem even worse, unfortunately.

CLIENT: (*sigh*) I know. It's like, in the short term I feel relief that I got out of another event but in the long-term, I'm spending less and less time with people, and it makes it even worse when I finally do have to go to something. Then people haven't seen me in a long time, so they ask a bunch of questions and I've also psyched myself out and overthought the whole thing... it's a mess.

In scenario one, the therapist provides *clinical* judgement of the client's behavior (i.e., lying to avoid going to social gatherings). The therapist may *personally* view lying as immoral or unacceptable behavior; however, the therapist does not apply their own moral values onto the client's behavior. Rather, the therapist applies clinical judgement, and in this case, the therapist's response is based on awareness that avoidant coping strategies can exacerbate the symptoms of an anxiety disorder. The last response from the therapist represents a paraphrase and a supportive challenge. Both are microskills you will learn in this text.

Here is a second scenario in which a mental health therapist inappropriately applies their *personal* judgement to a client's behavior.

Scenario 2: A client is telling their mental health therapist about their difficulties with social anxiety.

CLIENT: I've been struggling with spending time with people lately, even when it's my friends. My social anxiety used to only be this bad when I was at school or work, you know, being around people who don't know me that well, but now it's bad with my friends too.

THERAPIST: Tell me more about this.

CLIENT: Okay, so here's an example: I went out to the wine bar with my friends last weekend. That used to be something that was fun for me, but I found myself feeling really anxious before going out because I kept wondering to myself, "Do my friends even like me or do they just tolerate me?" Of course, then I was fixated on the idea that they all find me annoying the entire night. I kept interpreting everything they said or did in my mind as a sign that they hate me. I eventually couldn't stand the anxiety anymore and kept going outside to hit my vape... which was weed... which made everything more tolerable. That's the only way I made it through that evening without going home early.

THERAPIST: It sounds like you felt like you needed to disconnect from the emotional discomfort and stepping outside to use cannabis was an option for you.

CLIENT: I guess so, it's not like it was even a conscious thought at the moment, you know? I just felt like I wanted to escape, and I remembered I had my vape with me and then I was like, "oh yeah, weed, that'll help."

THERAPIST: Yeah, it was an option, but it's kind of a trashy option.

In this second scenario, the client discusses using cannabis to cope with social anxiety. At first, the therapist encourages the client to continue sharing however they eventually provide a *personal* judgement of the client's cannabis use that is informed by their values and biases, not clinical judgement. The therapist describes vaping cannabis as "trashy," which suggests that the therapist holds a negatively biased, potentially classist, view of cannabis use. A clinically informed judgement of the client's cannabis use could have been expressed, such as research that finds cannabis use a means of experiential avoidance in social anxiety disorders (Buckner et al., 2014). However, the impact of the therapist's projection of their own values and bias onto the client's behavior very likely may keep the client from talking further about their cannabis use.

When a provider engages in *clinical judgement* of a patient's behavior, even if the judgement suggests they would benefit from changing, then the patient can recognize that the provider is hoping to help them achieve their goals. However, when a provider engages in *personal judgement* of a patient's behavior, the patient is likely to feel judged in a way that is not necessarily linked to helping them achieve their goals, but rather being compared to the provider's views of what is "good/bad" or "right/wrong." This textbook will assist readers in identifying their own personal values and biases. Providers who have raised their insight into their own values and biases can monitor and avoid the potential that these to be expressed in their helping relationships with their patients. In addition, we hope that providers engage in a lifelong effort to reduce biased and stereotyped views of social and cultural groups as a long-term solution as well.

Providers need to both withhold personal judgement and adhere to ethical and legal obligations regarding patient confidentiality. Providers who combine these capacities along with an altruistic motivation to help their patients are generally experienced as trustworthy and having integrity. A provider who is trustworthy and of sound integrity can create opportunities for patients to share openly, honestly, and fully. These are the foundational building blocks of meaningful clinical relationships, where the patient trusts that their provider is guided by clinical knowledge (not their own personal judgement) and that their actions are aligned with their words. Take a moment to consider who you consider trustworthy in your own life. *What leads you to view them as trustworthy? How do you behave and feel with that person compared to someone else that you don't view as trustworthy?*

Conclusion

Becoming a healthcare provider is an exciting and demanding journey. It will require you to get to know yourself and your patients in a manner that requires vulnerability and openness to change and feedback from both parties. Providers who retain their humanity and do their jobs well sometimes seem rare across helping fields; however, we hope to support your process of becoming one of these types of providers. We hope that you will enter this process with a readiness to explore your own inner thoughts and emotions and build skills that will allow you to truly connect with people in your life, including your future patients.

Small Group Discussion Questions

1. What experiences have you had with providers of the profession for which you are currently training? What aspects of those experiences were positive and helpful, and what aspects were distracting or unhelpful? What impact do these experiences have on your expectations for training?
2. What basis do you believe people in your profession should use to differentiate clinical judgement from personal judgement? What steps does someone need to take in order to consistently make that differentiation?

References

Agency for Healthcare Research and Quality. (2022a, January 10). Disparities. www.ahrq.gov/topics/disparities.html.

Agency for Healthcare Research and Quality. (2022b). *National Healthcare Quality and Disparities Report*. www.ahrq.gov/research/findings/nhqrdr/nhqdr21/index.html.

Ahn, H.& Wampold, B.E.(2001). Where oh where are the specific ingredients? A meta-analysis of component studies in counseling and psychotherapy. *Journal of Counseling Psychology*, 48, 251–257. doi:10.1037/0022-0167.48.3.251.

Buckner, J.D., Zvolensky, M.J., Farris, S.G., & Hogan, J. (2014). Social anxiety and coping motives for cannabis use: The impact of experiential avoidance. *Psychology of Addictive Behaviors*, 28(2), 568–574. doi:10.1037/a0034545.

Caplan, P.J. (1992). *Lifting a ton of feathers: A woman's guide to surviving in the academic world*. Toronto Press.

Centers for Disease Control and Prevention. (2021). The U.S. Public Health Service Syphilis Study at Tuskegee. www.cdc.gov/tuskegee/timeline.htm.

Davis, D.E., DeBlaere, C., Brubaker, K., Owen, J., Jordan, T.A. II, Hook, J.N., & Van Tongeren, D.R. (2016). Microaggressions and perceptions of cultural humility in counseling. *Journal of Counseling & Development*, 94(4), 483–493. doi:10.1002/jcad.12107.

Dorling, D., Mitchell, R., & Pearce, J. (2007). The global impact of income inequality on health by age: An observational study. *British Medical Journal*, 335, 833–834. hdoi:10.1136/bmj.39349.507315.DE.

Epstein, R.M. & Street, R.L. (2007). *Patient-centered communication in cancer care: Promoting healing and reducing suffering*. National Cancer Institute.

Gawande, A. (2014, October 6). No risky chances: The conversation that matters most. *Slate*. https://slate.com/technology/2014/10/end-of-life-medical-decisions-a tul-gawande-book- excerpt-on-no-risky-chances.html.

Hall, G.C.N., Ibaraki, A.Y., Huang, E.R., Marti, C.N., & Stice, E. (2016). A meta-analysis of cultural adaptations of psychological interventions. *Behavior Therapy*, 47(6), 993–1014. doi:10.1016/j.beth.2016.09.005.

Hopper, E.K., Bassuk, E.L., & Olivet, J. (2010). Shelter from the storm: Trauma-informed care in homelessness services settings. *The Open Health Services and Policy Journal*, 3, 80–100.

Institute of Medicine. (2002). Smedley, B.E., Stith, A.Y., & Nelson, A.R. (Eds), *Unequal treatment: Confronting racial and ethnic disparities in health care*. National Academies Press.

Ivey, A.E. (1971). *Microcounseling: Innovations in interviewing training*. Charles C Thomas.

Landrine, H. & Klonoff, E.A. (1997). *Discrimination against women: Prevalence, consequences, remedies*. Sage Publications.

Linehan, M. (2014). *DBT skills training manual*. The Guilford Press.

Meyer, I.H.(2003). Prejudice, social stress, and mental health in lesbian, gay and bisexual populations: Conceptual issues and research evidence. *Psychological Bulletin*, 129, 674–697. doi:10.1037/0033-2909.129.5.674.

Maina, I.W., Belton, T.D., Ginzberg, S., Singh, A., & Johnson, T.J. (2018). A decade of studying implicit racial/ethnic bias in healthcare providers using the implicit association test. *Social Science & Medicine*, 199, 219–229. doi:10.1016/j.socscimed.2017.05.009.

Matoba, N. & Collins, J.W., (2017). Racial disparity in infant mortality. *Seminars in Perinatology*, 41(6), 354–359. doi:10.1053/j.semperi.2017.07.003.

Nelson, A. (2002). Unequal treatment: Confronting racial and ethnic disparities in health care. *Journal of the National Medical Association*, 94(8), 666–668.

Norcross, J.C. (2010). The therapeutic relationship. In B.L. Duncan, S.D. Miller, B.E. Wampold, & M.A. Hubble (Eds), *The heart and soul of change: Delivering what works in therapy*, 2nd ed. (pp. 113–141). American Psychological Association. doi:10.1037/12075-004.

Office of Disease Prevention and Health Promotion. (2022, January 10). Lesbian, gay, bisexual, and transgender health. www.healthypeople.gov/2020/topics-objectives/topic/lesbian-gay-bisexual-and-transgender-health.

Oliveira, V.C., Ferreira, M.L., Pinto, R.Z., Filho, R.F., Refshauge, K., & Ferreira, P.H. (2015). Effectiveness of training clinicians' communication skills on patients' clinical outcomes: A systematic review. *Journal of Manipulative and Physiological Therapeutics*, 38(8), 601–616. doi:10.1016/j.jmpt.2015.08.002.

Penner, L.A., Hagiwara, N., Eggly, S., Gaertner, S.L., Albrecht, T.L., & Dovidio, J.F.(2013). Racial healthcare disparities: A social psychological analysis. *European Review of Social Psychology*, 24, 77–112. doi:10.1080/10463283.2013.840973.

Poteat, T., German, D., & Kerrigan, D. (2013). Managing uncertainty: A grounded theory of stigma in transgender health care encounters. *Social Science & Medicine*, 84, 22–29. doi:10.1016/j.socscimed.2013.02.019.

Spencer, M.B., Dupree, D., & Hartmann, T. (1997). A phenomenological variant of ecological systems theory (PVEST): A self-organization perspective in context. *Development and Psychopathology*, 9(4), 817–833. doi:10.1017/S0954579497001454.

Spencer, M.B. (2006). Phenomenology and Ecological Systems Theory: Development of Diverse Groups. In R.M. Lerner & W. Damon (Eds), *Handbook of child psychology: Theoretical models of human development*, Vol. 1, 6th ed. (pp. 829–893). John Wiley & Sons Inc.

Sue, D.W. (2010). *Microaggressions in Everyday Life: Race, gender, and sexual orientation*. John Wiley & Sons.

Sue, D.W., Capodilupo, C.M., Torino, G.C., Bucceri, J.M., Holder, A.M.B., Nadal, K.L., & Esquilin, M. (2007). Racial microaggressions in everyday life: Implications for clinical practice. *American Psychologist*, 62(4), 271–286. doi:10.1037/0003-066X.62.4.271.

Swim, J.K., Aikin, K.J., Hall, W.S., & Hunter, B.A. (1995). Sexism and racism: Old- fashioned and modern prejudices. *Journal of Personality and Social Psychology*, 68(2), 199–214.

Thanasiu, P.L. & Pizza, N. (2019). Constructing culturally sensitive creative interventions for use with grieving children and adolescents. *Journal of Creativity in Mental Health*, 14(3), 270–279. doi:10.1080/15401383.2019.1589402.

Truax, C.B. & Carkhuff, R.R. (1967). *Toward effective counseling and psychotherapy: Training and practice*. Aldine.

Chapter 2

Ethical Helping Relationships

Many readers of this book are likely early in their preparation to become a licensed professional in a helping discipline. In this chapter, we will look at ethics and how a profession identifies and articulates a set of expectations established by a national organization of people in that discipline, and collectively agreed upon by scholars and practitioners in the field. You may not be fully aware of the difference between licensure law for professional practice, program accreditation, and your professional code of ethics, so our first focus of discussion will be identifying the points of difference between these related, but separate, concepts.

Licensure

There are many occupations that require an individual to hold a license to practice within the profession. From a very broad perspective, professions typically require a license to practice because there is some potential for harm to the people who would be served by that professional. Licensure law makes it legally necessary for a person practicing a given profession to possess a certain minimum standard of training, and after a license is granted, to document ongoing continuing education. Some licensure laws require that a licensed person graduate from an accredited training program.

As you might imagine, multiple problems can potentially arise from someone not being competent to provide a service. Such problems could include:

- a patient's condition being exacerbated;
- missing a critical window of time for treatment of a condition, such as a worsening nutrition problem or suicidality;
- perpetuation of suffering;
- alienating a patient from returning for services from a more qualified provider, which could have other long-term sequelae; and
- federal or state monies being wasted on programs that are ineffective.

DOI: 10.4324/9781003217589-3

Licensure laws are typically very explicit about the "scope of practice," what a person holding that license can and cannot do. In each profession, there are differences in scope of practice and license eligibility across states for licensure.

Program Accreditation

Professions typically have identified standards for training in that profession. Those standards are established by a corresponding professional organization. Professional organizations are administered and run by people in the field, often practitioners as well as academicians, and the accreditation standards represent the collective views and standards as established by the majority of those identifying with that professional group. In counseling, for example, the accrediting body of the Council for the Accreditation of Counseling and Related Educational Programs came into being in the late 1960s and early 1970s as a collaboration between two professional organizations, the Association of Counselor Educators and Supervisors and the American Personnel and Guidance Association. Representatives from each of those groups collaboratively developed a set of educational standards, that have continued to evolve in keeping with other movement and growth in the profession, since that time. These training standards cover a broad range of program aspects, including the qualifications and credentials of program faculty, the inclusion of particularly essential courses, specific content in those courses, specific amounts of time doing field-based training, and other program features, too (Council for the Accreditation of Counseling and Related Educational Programs, 2022).

Some state laws may actually require that an applicant graduate from an accredited program in order for a person to be eligible to hold the license. Other state laws may not require program accreditation, but instead could require applicants to produce a transcript that reflects coursework consistent with current program accreditation standards. Regardless of the specifics for each profession and each jurisdiction, there are mutually beneficial agreements between professions and license-granting boards that ensure standards for licensure and practice must be in place to protect the public.

Professional Codes of Ethics

Other sets of expectations for practitioners, separate from licensure law, are professional codes of ethics. Each professional organization corresponding to a discipline has established and made public a Code of Ethics. The Code of Ethics spells out what is considered to be moral, ethical behavior in that profession – what is generally considered "right" and "wrong" by learned people in the field.

Different professional codes of ethics use somewhat different language and formats, but there are several common factors across all of them. One common factor is that the ethics are predicated on core values that have been accepted by the majority of individuals in that profession. Another common factor is that each of them describe particular actions that are expected for individuals who practice in that discipline. Finally, all of them include components related to how to act toward individuals who are seeking our services, how to act in the places where we work, and our responsibility to the profession and/or the general community of people in the world.

When we are granted a license by the state board of our profession, we are thus expected to behave legally and ethically. When someone violates those ethical standards, they run the risk of having sanctions placed on their license and also may be liable for a lawsuit in which damages could possibly be awarded to someone who sustained physical or psychological injury as the result of the practitioner's unethical behavior. Ethical codes protect the public and provide an established set of parameters that can be used to evaluate potential quandaries and questions that occur in practice.

It is possible that some readers will encounter ethical principles with which they disagree. If this happens, it is critically important for that person to decide whether they will be capable of meeting the expectation they will act in ways that are consistent with professional values, even if they do not reflect that individual's own pre-existing personal values. We could go a step further to suggest that if our values are somehow opposed to the values of our chosen profession, this is a matter for serious reflection and possibly moving to a different profession. Engaging in behaviors that are not consistent with our values is a form of incongruence, which can likely be managed, but incongruence brings with it other cognitive and emotional challenges. Moreover, in the field of counseling, many authors have emphasized the importance of counselor congruence for relationship development as well as for modeling healthy congruence; positioning ourselves in a place of incongruence could lead to reduced effectiveness of our efforts as well as burn out.

Common Factors in Professional Codes of Ethics

Professional practice across diverse health professions looks different, and yet, their professional codes of ethics share many commonalities. Across diverse disciplines (e.g., Counseling, School Counseling, Social Work, Speech and Language Pathologists, Nutrition and Dietetics Professionals, Occupational Therapy, Physical Therapy), there is some variability in language for the essential ethical concepts; some use the term "Principles of Ethics," "Principles and Standards," and/or "Core Values" of the profession. The values and standards can broadly be categorized as considerations of patient treatment, considerations of the professional's orientation toward others in the profession, currency of skills through on-going training, and responsibility to the general public. Students in these professional training programs may take an entire course devoted to the ethical code and learning the process of applying the ethical code to various patient situations that often arise in that practice. There are five principles that are consistent across the aforementioned healthcare disciplines: autonomy, beneficence, non-maleficence, veracity, and justice. We will take a look at each of them and consider a practical example of how each principle might be reflected in a provider's behavior.

Autonomy

The basic idea here is that people being helped have the right to control their own lives and make choices regarding how they live their lives. Within the bounds of acceptable standards and safe provision of care, individuals are entitled to their choices without personal judgement or coercion from the provider. There may be occasions in your work with someone for whom to you, the healthy path for growth and positive change seems completely obvious. A counseling example could be a person who is continuing to choose friendships with others who are unkind to them, despite seeking counseling with you, owing to low self-esteem and social anxiety. Honoring that person's autonomy means holding an internal awareness of the boundaries of your relationship with them and recognizing that perhaps the counseling work lies not in her making other friend choices immediately, but instead gently exploring the possible connection between her socializing and friend choices and social anxiety and low self-esteem. Patients have the right to make choices, even if they are not the choices we would want them to make, or that we would make ourselves.

THE SPECIAL CASE OF MINORS' AUTONOMY

Working with people under the age of 18 brings an additional variable into the discussion of autonomy. Below the age of 18, a person is legally a minor, and as such, their parent(s) or legal guardian(s) are legally responsible for them. A minor must have a consenting adult grant permission for treatment that must be signed before receiving professional health care services. Legally, minors have limited autonomy. However, ethically, a minor still does have some level of ability to agree or disagree, a process referred to as minor assent. In research studies, researchers may be required to obtain a signed assent from the child participating in the study. Seeking a child's assent to participate is technically not necessary from a legal perspective; however, from an ethical perspective, giving a child the option to not participate is the right thing to do.

Personal Reflection

Can you recall a time when you were directed by a person in authority to do something that didn't align with what you wanted to do? What internal feelings were generated by being given those directives? What was the outcome of that interaction?

Case example of not honoring autonomy

Maribel is an 18-year-old senior in high school and is working with her school counselor on career plans after high school. Her stated occupational choice of becoming a travel agent sounds like a terrible choice to the school counselor working with her, because of the counselor's misperception that travel agent jobs are rapidly disappearing, even though data from the U.S. Bureau of Labor Statistics (2022) suggest otherwise. Even though the data is not aligned with the school counselor's perspectives, she also has a bias against the idea because she feels that Maribel should pursue a STEM field occupation to have a higher prestige career. The school counselor has several conversations with Maribel, telling her she's making a huge mistake and insisting that she identify alternate career goals.

Personal Reflection

What might be a better way for the counselor to discuss Maribel's career options, while also being respectful of Maribel's autonomy?

Beneficence

The principle of beneficence is that the service provider intends to do the best possible for the patient. Consider the following case example: Sandra began counseling with a client with whom she immediately felt a strong sense of connection and concern. After three sessions, the client made a disclosure about being the ex-in-law of one of Sandra's closest friends, a fact about which Sandra had been previously unaware. Despite Sandra's perceived connection and belief that she could be of help, she chose to refer the client to a colleague because Sandra recognized a potential dual relationship with the client that could hinder their work together.

Non-maleficence

This related term means that a service provider has no intent to do harm to the other person. An example of non-maleficence being violated would be if a service provider became highly frustrated with a person and then intentionally gave them misinformation or withheld information out of spite.

Consider this example of maleficence. Robert is a physical therapist who has been assigned to work with a young man who is experiencing spinal problems as the result of being in a widely publicized car accident in their community. This young man was texting and driving, causing a car accident in which a young mother and her child were killed. The young man was exonerated of the crime on a technicality. Robert is furious about several aspects of this patient's case. Besides the young man's lackadaisical attitude about the accident, he is also complaining about having to come to physical therapy, as well as complaining about the doctor not prescribing more opiates for pain relief. Given the patient's attitude along with the obvious lack of empathy or justice for the victims, Robert is seriously considering giving him exercises that will worsen the back pain.

Veracity

This principle pertains to being honest, communicating truthfully in interactions with others, including patients, as well as colleagues and other professionals. There is a broad variety of ways a provider might not be honest with a patient or colleague. Here is one example of how that might manifest. Imagine that a counselor has a new client whose brother is dating someone the counselor is friends with. It would be appropriate and important to honestly acknowledge the potential dual relationship and decide how to proceed, rather than attempting to ignore or compartmentalize what could become complicated and tricky in the future.

Justice

Justice is simply about making sure what's being done is fair and equitable for everyone. An example of injustice could be offering a free service to people but offering it at a location not easily accessible by public transportation, or inaccessible for people with mobility considerations. Another example would be tolerating a high number of unkept appointments with one client we like, while terminating another client with whom we don't enjoy working after two unkept appointments.

The Intersection of Ethical Considerations and Trauma-Informed Care in Helping Professions

In the past several decades, because of the findings of the Adverse Childhood Experiences (ACEs) study from the mid-1990s, more attention has been given to experiences of trauma and its impact on functioning. These experiences include but are not limited to: experiencing sexual, physical, or emotional abuse, witnessing the death or near death of someone else, living with a parent with severe mental illness, traumatic loss of a loved one, parental incarceration, parental divorce, parental substance abuse, and domestic violence. When practitioners are working with patients, ethical considerations must intersect with trauma-informed care practices to ensure that practitioners are not retraumatizing vulnerable patients. Keep in mind, many patients have experienced at least one adverse childhood experience. According to the Substance Abuse and Mental Health Services Administration (2020), by the age of 16 years old, more than 67% of young people will have experienced at least one traumatic event in their lives. According to the National Center for Post-Traumatic Stress Disorder, approximately 6% of the population in the United States will have Post-Traumatic Stress Disorder (PTSD) at some point in their lives (National Center for PTSD, 2022). The National Center for Post-Traumatic Stress Disorder found that about 12 million adults will have PTSD during a given year in the United States; 8% of women develop PTSD sometime in their lives compared with about 4% of men (National Center for PTSD, 2022).

These statistics are alarming. Considering the high likelihood that patients you will see will have experienced trauma, and in the spirit of non-maleficence, it is advisable to adopt a trauma-informed approach with everyone. The particulars of what a trauma-informed approach looks like will obviously vary across professions, and yet there are some common principles that are pertinent regardless of the specialty. The Substance Abuse and Mental Health Services Administration (2014) identifies the "four R's" when working with patients: Recognize, Realization, Respond, and Resist Retraumatization. The first component is to recognize the signs and symptoms of trauma. This may not happen automatically. So, as a provder, it is imperative to pursue additional professional development and training in the areas of trauma and trauma-informed approaches, if this is an area of growth. Regarding the second R, practitioners must have a realization about trauma and how trauma may impact the people they serve. The third consideration is that practitioners must respond by applying trauma-informed principles and approaches to all patients, as practitioners often do not know patients' past experiences with trauma. It is also important to note that sometimes our organizations may have policies and procedures in place that can be traumatic or retraumatizing for patients. As practitioners we may have to advocate on behalf of the patients for policies and procedures to be changed. It is also crucial to resist traumatization. Therefore, it is imperative to be aware of the environments where we serve patients to identify items that may be traumatizing to patients, and if they are traumatizing that we advocate for change within our systems and organizations.

Personal Reflection

Are you able to readily identify key events in your own development that were traumatic? How did those events influence the trajectory of your growth? What is the relationship, if any, between those events and how you interact with other people?

The Detrimental Impact of Ethnocentric Care

In the following chapter about serving people in a pluralistic society such as the United States, we will talk about majority and minority status, the power balance in society, intersectionality, and other topics related to multiculturalism and cultural competence in your profession. These are all topics connected to ethics and our responsibility for cultural competence. We will look too at differential health statuses across groups of people and how health care disparities are evident in our society. Ethical care is culturally competent care. Ensuring that healthcare services meet the social, cultural, and linguistic needs of patients is a foundational requirement for ensuring autonomy, beneficence, non-maleficence, veracity, and most notably, justice.

Despite this upcoming broad discussion of culturally competent care, we would be remiss in this chapter about ethics does not discuss the ethical dimensions of cultural competence and its opposing force, ethnocentrism. Ethnocentrism is defined as using one's own cultural background, values, role definitions, etc., as the basis for care and interpretation of patient behavior. The insidious and detrimental nature of ethnocentrism makes it critical that we identify it as a danger in multiple places throughout the book. Taking into consideration the various ethical principles reviewed and discussed previously, we want to propose that maintaining an ethnocentric perspective in serving people is highly unethical. The principles of justice, autonomy, non-maleficence, veracity, and especially beneficence, make it essential for a provider to have the cognitive flexibility to at least attempt to hold another person's worldview and values, as they work to establish rapport and a productive working relationship. Regardless of our own cultural identities and background, it is common to use our own experiences to come to the assumption that others have had similar experiences and that our own experiences are the basis for our determining what is desirable and acceptable.

Consider a counselor whose religious views are aligned with some specific traditions, rituals, and behavior expectations for the followers of that religion. If that counselor is working with a client who does not share those religious views, it is easy to see how the counselor might experience some internal pressure to maintain their own perspective about the patient's behaviors and choices. If these judgements are apparent to the client, the process of disclosing and seeking guidance from that counselor could feel unsafe, eliciting responses from the counselor that seem critical or judgmental. The provider must recognize that they themselves have the autonomy to believe and practice religion in the manner they desire, but they cannot apply those personal beliefs toward their patients nor shape their care and treatment based on those views.

Ethical Behavior

Up to this point in the chapter, we have primarily been examining ethical principles, with the focus on the negative impact of ethnocentrism and the need for trauma-informed care. What we have not yet explored is what ethical behavior actually looks like on the ground, among people who are licensed and successfully providing professional services. Thus, our discussion turns now to general guidelines about how ethical principles translate into broadly applied behavior in our professional roles.

1. Always maintain confidentiality: There are times that it is appropriate to discuss patients with others, such as during individual clinical supervision or in a supervision group. There may be occasions in which you would like to consult with a professional peer about your work with someone, and it is permissible for you to discuss a patient case without a release of information as long as you do not share the person's name or personally identifying information in your consultation with your colleague. In addition, clients always have the right to sign a release of information permitting a service provider to communicate with some other third party (e.g., another professional, an insurance company, a service agency such as Medicaid). Beyond these circumscribed situations, it is critically important to refrain from sharing information about patients unless you have a release of information. Many clients and patients will be sharing private information with you, be it health information or other content related to their past and present experiences. In order for the therapeutic relationship to feel safe, they need to believe, and feel, that you will honor their privacy.
2. Multicultural competence. Recognize that the person with whom you are speaking has the right to work with a professional who will honor and respect all the facets of their social and cultural identities.
3. Use a trauma-informed lens. Adopt trauma-informed strategies for all your clinical work. Work to actively maintain awareness that your patient's maladaptive behaviors may have arisen as a coping mechanism for stressors. It is not unusual for a child who has experienced trauma to exhibit behaviors in school that are negatively labelled, and for the child to be blamed for their "bad behavior," while that child may very well have had a trauma history. Advocate for trauma-informed practices at your place of employment.
4. Support patient autonomy. Maintain continual awareness of the power imbalance between you and your patient. Actively work to not be coercive in the process, and involve the patient in the goal setting and treatment planning.

5   Work within one's scope of practice. Recognize the limits of your competence and don't work with people whose concerns lie beyond what you have been trained to treat.
6   Maintain unconditional positive regard. Strive to find unconditional positive regard for your patients and clients. One strategy I (K.M.) use for finding compassion is to remind myself that this patient is someone's child. I think about how I would want a provider to act toward my own child, and then use that imagined interaction to access compassion, kindness, and tolerance.

Conclusion

Ethical practice requires commitment to fulfilling the overarching ethical principles and values within one's professional ethics code. Providing ethical care for patients is not an outcome that is achieved but rather is a never-ending process that requires continual self-evaluation and reflection. The foundational helping skills discussed in this text may appear benign and difficult to use in an unethical manner; however, they can be manipulated in ways that intentionally and unintentionally hurt patients. Commitment to ethical practice is the foundation for multiculturally competent helping relationships.

Questions for Small Group Discussion

1   What might be an example in which your profession's code of ethics are in conflict with what the law says? How would you handle finding a resolution?
2   How do the common values across ethical codes align or misalign with your own values?
3   Referring back to the case example about Robert the physical therapist, what might have been an advisable course of action for Robert to address his thoughts and feelings?

References

Academy of Nutrition and Dietetics. (2018). *Code of ethics for the nutrition and dietetics profession*. eatrightPRO – Academy of Nutrition and Diatetics. www.eatrightpro.org/-/media/eatrightpro-files/career/code-of-ethics/codeofethicshandout.pdf.
American Counseling Association. (2014). *2014 ACA code of ethics*. www.counseling.org/resources/aca-code-of-ethics.pdf.
American Dental Hygienists' Association. (2019). *ADHA code of ethics*. www.adha.org/resources-docs/ADHA_Code_of_Ethics.pdf.
American Occupational Therapy Association. (2020, November 1). *AOTA 2020 occupational therapy code of ethics*. https://research.aota.org/ajot/article/74/Supplement_3/7413410005p1/6691/AOTA-2020-Occupational-Therapy-Code-of-Ethics.

American Physical Therapy Association. (2020). *Code of ethics for the physical therapist.* www.apta.org/siteassets/pdfs/policies/codeofethicshods06-20-28-25.pdf.

American School Counselor Association. (2022). *ASCA ethical standards for school counselors.* www.schoolcounselor.org/About-School-Counseling/Ethical-Legal-Responsibilities/ASCA-Ethical-Standards-for-School-Counselors-(1)

American Speech-Language-Hearing Association. (2016). *ASHA code of ethics.* https://inte.asha.org/siteassets/publications/et2016-00342.pdf.

Council for the Accreditation of Counseling and Related Educational Programs. (2022, October 11). *About CACREP.* www.cacrep.org/about-cacrep.

Substance Abuse and Mental Health Services Administration. (2014). *Trauma-Informed Care in Behavioral Health Services: A Treatment Improvement Protocol.* U.S. Department of Health and Human Services, Substance Abuse and Mental Health Services Administration, Center for Substance Abuse Treatment.

U.S. Bureau of Labor Statistics. (2022, November 18). *Travel agents: Job outlook.* www.bls.gov/ooh/sales/travel-agents.htm#tab-6.

Chapter 3

Helping in a Pluralistic Society

We introduce this chapter with a reader advisory: the tone and content of this chapter may be disconcerting to you. Some readers may have anticipated that this chapter would be the written equivalent of a picture of diverse people, holding hands and smiling while encircling a globe. Unfortunately, though, the lived reality for many people is not that. Indeed, it can be painful to recognize that those who pursue careers in healthcare sometimes unintentionally inflict harm on their patients because of cultural incompetency. Those of us in the healthcare fields may view ourselves as beneficent people, with the highest intentions to do good in the world. It can be distressing to recognize that we might inadvertently hurt our patients because of our conscious or unconscious biases. However, it is a universal truth that none of us are free of bias, no matter how hard we try to be completely impartial. The best we can do is to become as aware as possible of what our own biases are, and to actively challenge and change ourselves so that those biases do not influence our behavior. We would go so far as to say that a provider who has not worked internally on this will at best diminish their potential effectiveness. At worst, their myopic view of helping could potentially help to perpetuate a legacy of systemic and individual oppression of the same people they are attempting to serve.

As a brief preview of the content you're about to read, one of our hopes for you is that you become aware, if you weren't before, of the ways a patient's barriers to participation or treatment compliance could be the result of something other than resistance or lack of motivation. Some barriers are legitimately external and are completely out of the patient's control, and if fact, need support from healthcare professionals to manage effectively.

An example of a specific incident was experienced by one of the authors (K.M.). Mr. T. was a 46-year-old cisgender man in counseling, receiving Social Security Disability Insurance because he had a diagnosis of schizophrenia and could not maintain employment. He lived alone and rented an efficiency apartment in a large apartment building. The landlord was in

DOI: 10.4324/9781003217589-4

Mr. T.'s apartment completing minor repairs and noticed some letters from Social Security Administration lying on the table. When the landlord questioned Mr. T. and discovered Mr. T.'s diagnosis, he informed Mr. T. that he would need to move out of the building. Mr. T. willingly agreed, although he had nowhere else to go. Mr. T. did not know that he was being discriminated against until he shared the information with his counselor during a counseling session. In the therapist's role, it becomes necessary to take steps that require the building management to comply with the Americans with Disabilities Act.

Our ultimate goal for this chapter is to boost your multicultural competence and thus your credibility and effectiveness with as many of your patients as possible. You will gain competence for working with diverse populations when you understand the impact of culture and social determinants of health on one's health and quality of life. Social determinants of health are the conditions of the environments where people live, work, learn, play, and worship. Although you won't often be able to "fix" some of the large-scale issues impacting your patient's circumstance, you will address them in a way that is compassionate and understanding of the whole picture of their life. Our other hope for you is that you become deeply aware of how privilege can afford a provider the ability to disconnect from awareness of inequality and oppression, which distances them from their patient as a whole person.

Establishing Trust

The process of seeking help for any problem requires vulnerability and trust in a provider. The Substance Abuse and Mental Health Services Administration identifies trustworthiness, transparency, and safety as key principles in creating trauma-informed approaches when serving patients. What does "trustworthy" even mean? Patients are asked to sharing information about themselves, such as emotional or physical concerns, equates to making themselves vulnerable; in sharing they open themselves to someone's scrutiny and possible judgement. The ability of a provider to assist in the healing process requires that the patient share as openly and truthfully as possible about the problem at hand. Sharing in this manner is predicated on an assumption that the provider is trustworthy, that is, honest and truthful, and that they are behaving in ways that are consistent with their professed "helping" role. In order for this process to function as intended, the patient must determine for themself that the benefit of vulnerability outweighs the potential cost. When we see ourselves as sincerely desiring to help another person, it can be difficult to recognize and accept that for someone whose trust has been violated by others (perhaps others who *should* have been trustworthy), we will not be experienced as "safe." When trust does develop, it generally happens gradually over many interactions in which we exhibit trustworthy behavior verbally and nonverbally. Consider for a moment how you decide that one person is trustworthy, whereas another person is not. Do you rely on an awareness of someone's past behavior to make predictions about their trustworthiness? This is a common perspective and aligns with the maxim in the field of psychology that 'past behavior is the best predictor of future behavior.'

It is with this understanding about the challenge of establishing trust that we embark upon exploring how the history of healthcare in western countries, such as the United States, has formed a fractured foundation with regard to the ways patients experience and view the trustworthiness of providers and the systems within which they work. The United States is a pluralistic country, yet the healthcare system often operates from an ethnocentric standpoint. An ethnocentric perspective assumes that all patients need the same type of care and experiences, regardless of their cultural background and identities. In addition to the ethnocentric nature of healthcare, providers themselves may operate in ways that are biased toward patients with minority cultural identities. It is important to emphasize that a 'minority' cultural group is a term that denotes a group's subordinate status within power hierarchy, not necessarily that it is a numerically smaller group in the larger population. Minority cultural groups have been, and continue to be, oppressed at the individual and systemic level in multiple realms of their lives including, but not limited to, healthcare. The result of these parallel realities is that minority communities experience disproportionately higher healthcare needs than majority communities, yet they receive care from systems that often are not designed to assist them. Later in this chapter we will be looking at the Minority Stress Model as a lens through which to understand how the stress of minority membership amplifies complex healthcare needs among people who have minority identities.

The modest aim of this chapter is to increase your self-awareness of your own cultural identities and the cultural identities of others, as well as improve your skill in thinking about, and providing, culturally competent care to a diverse array of patients. In pursuit of this aim, we will first provide a foundational understanding of key terminology and concepts related to diverse cultural identities, intersectionality, power (e.g., privilege and oppression). Second, we will discuss the model of nested systems that enables a culturally responsive view of human interactions and development, as well as provides a framework for understanding a multilevel conceptualization of institutional disparity. Through that lens, we will discuss the ethnocentric history of healthcare and how it has led to disempowerment and abuse of minority communities. This foundational understanding will also include a brief introduction to theories that allow providers to think in generalizable ways about how people with minority identities often experience increased stress in their lives. Lastly, we will look at trauma and present a model for understanding the impact of trauma, both historical and individual, on our patients and how providers can operate through a trauma-informed lens when serving patients. The trauma-informed care aspect of multicultural competence will be a foundational theme through the rest of this text, as we move into the chapters about specific types and forms of helping skills.

Foundational Concepts of Culture and Intersectionality

Our discussion of these topics begins by providing definitions of commonly used terminology, beginning with the ubiquitous 'culture.' The United Nations Educational, Scientific and Cultural Organization (2001) defined culture in their Universal Declaration on Cultural Diversity. They stated that:

> Culture should be regarded as the set of distinctive spiritual, material, intellectual and emotional features of a society or a social group, and that it encompasses, in addition to art and literature, lifestyles, ways of living together, value systems, traditions and beliefs.
>
> (p. 2)

An older, and relevant definition of culture by Geertz's (1973), denotes culture as a:

> ... historically transmitted pattern of meanings embodied in symbols, a system of inherited conceptions expressed in symbolic forms by means of which [people] communicate, perpetuate, and develop their knowledge about and attitudes towards life.
>
> (p. 89)

Taken together, these definitions convey that the cultures of social groups are nuanced, historically transmitted, and expressed and held across almost all of life's special and mundane practices. It is also critical to note that social groups contain just as much cultural variation and diversity *within* the group as is seen *between* groups.

Take a moment to reflect on cultural features of your own life and identities. You may recall memories of special foods, holiday celebrations, unstated practices in times of grief and celebration, or common dynamics within families. What you might also recognize is that cultural practices are not only features of racial and ethnic identities, but rather they also reflect other aspects of identity, such as religion and social class.

A broad understanding of the various categories of cultural identity groups can help practitioners understand both themselves and their patients with greater nuance. The ADDRESSING framework (Hays,

2008) is a helpful acronym for expanding one's understanding of overlapping cultural identity groups to which we all belong. The ADDRESSING framework stands for Age, Developmental and acquired Disabilities, Religion, Ethnicity, Socioeconomic status, Sexual orientation, Indigenous heritage, National origin, and Gender. All people can examine themselves and identify which groups they are a part of by using the ADDRESSING framework. Each of us holds an identity in each cultural group category, and our identity can afford us privilege or result in some diminished access to power and resources. At any given point in history, there are sociopolitical factors that heavily influence how particular characteristics are perceived in society. The ADDRESSING framework is specific to a time period and location, and within this book, this ADDRESSING framework is specific to the current time within western countries. See Table 3.1 for a review of categories.

A key feature of the ADDRESSING framework is the examination of privilege associated with various cultural identities. Before we begin

Table 3.1 ADDRESSING Framework

Cultural Group Category	Marginalized	Privileged
Age	Children, adolescents, elders	Adults
Disability (developmental)	People with disabilities	People who are temporarily able-bodied
Disability (acquired)	People with disabilities	People who are temporarily able-bodied
Religion	People who are Jewish, Muslim, and other non-Christian religions	Christians
Ethnicity	People of color and/or those with Hispanic ethnicity	White, non-Hispanic people
Socioeconomic Status	People living in poverty, working-class	Upper, middle, and owning-class
Sexual Orientation	People who are gay, lesbian and bisexual	People who are straight
Indigenous Heritage	Native and indigenous people	People who are non-native
National Origin	Immigrants and refugees	People who are U.S. born
Gender	Cisgender women, transgender and non-binary people, and intersex people	Cisgender men

examining privileged cultural identities, we must first define what is meant by privilege. Privilege entails the "...entitlements, advantages, and dominance conferred upon..." certain social groups from a society (Black & Stone, 2005, p. 243). The opposite of privilege is marginalization, meaning that groups which are not socially privileged experience barriers, disadvantages, and oppression. Being a part of a socially privileged group doesn't mean that a person doesn't experience difficulties, hardships, pain, and tragedy in their life. Everyone experiences challenges and the existential givens of life (i.e., death, isolation, searching for meaning) (Yalom, 1980), but those with greater privilege encounter fewer (or no) *systemic* barriers and disadvantages as they make their way through life. The ADDRESSING framework contains ten different groups of cultural identities; therefore, most people have a combination of identities, some of which are privileged and some that are marginalized. Some of the ADDRESSING framework groups are immutable aspects of the self, that is, a person cannot change this quality about themselves and have little to no control over how others interpret this aspect of themselves (i.e., age, ethnicity, national origin, indigenous heritage). Some of the groups can be fluid, changing, and/or self-defined (i.e., religion, socioeconomic status). Some of the groups are 'visible' in that they cannot be hidden (i.e., ethnicity, 'visible' disabilities), whereas others are internal and require disclosure to inform others of one's identity (i.e., sexual orientation, 'invisible' disabilities).

The result of this complexity is that people experience shifts over their lifetime regarding their level of privilege, depending on changes in their identities and expression of identities. Because of the systemic nature of privilege and marginalization, most people aren't likely to move from privilege to marginalization (or vice versa) if they remain in the same identity category throughout their life. It is possible, though, for some groups to see a slight lessening of marginalization during their lifetime when a society confers rights and protection upon a group. For example, although gender and sexual minorities still remain a marginalized group within society, there have been incremental gains in social acceptance and legal rights (Pew Research Center, 2020).

The next foundational concept is that of intersectionality of cultural identities. The term intersectionality was coined by Crenshaw (1989) to describe a framework to understand how overlapping cultural identities can lead to unique experiences of privilege and marginalization. Crenshaw's (1989) seminal work described how Black women experienced a distinctive form of oppression arising from a combination of racism and sexism together, identifiably different from the racism faced by Black men and the sexism White women face. Intersectionality allows us to understand how a Black man who identifies as gay experiences a different type of marginalization compared with a Black man who identifies as straight.

A common racist microaggression against Black men is a presumption of danger and criminality (Sue et al., 2008). A common microaggression against gay men is that of de-masculinization (Nadal et al., 2016). The intersection of these two forms of oppression is that a gay, Black man might be less likely to be perceived as "dangerous" if his sexual orientation is known or presumed by others. Ultimately however, although the presumption that one is "not dangerous" may be welcomed, it comes at the cost of being restrictively stereotyped as gay man.

Intersectionality can explain why people who hold mostly privileged identities (i.e., race, sexual orientation, gender) and who also hold a marginalized identity, such as being in a lower socioeconomic status, may not have the same access to power that could otherwise be afforded by their prevailing privileged identities. Socioeconomic level and social class are powerful factors in daily life; they often dictate access to housing, healthcare, education, and job opportunities. When a White person is living in poverty and struggles to afford adequate housing, find fulfilling and well-paying work, and access quality healthcare, they may struggle to recognize that while they *do* face socioeconomic marginalization, they *do not* experience the additional layer of racism, homoprejudice, or ableism.

Privilege is unearned and provides advantages in society. Privilege is often "invisible" to those who hold it and yet very apparent to those who do not. An example of White privilege is having a name that "sounds" White, compared with being a person who is Black and has a name that "sounds" Black in its origins. Bertrand & Mullainathan (2004) found that identical resumes with so-called White sounding names received fifty percent more callbacks compared with those with so-called Black sounding names. Evidence shows that this trend persists across employers of diverse sizes and industries.

Consciousness Raising

Gaining consciousness of the social implications of one's own and other's identities can be an uncomfortable process. Gaining awareness of privilege can evoke uncomfortable emotions like guilt and anger because privilege arises from a system that a person did not themself choose. DiAngelo (2018) articulated the process of White fragility, aptly identifying a process by which White individuals react defensively when Black individuals articulate their experiences of oppression and racism. Cook noted that the group of people with the highest degree of White fragility are educated White individuals with liberal political beliefs; people who perceive themselves as sympathetic to the cause of equality. For some people, it can be extremely difficult to accept that throughout their lives, they have benefitted from access to things simply because of their skin color, whether they wanted to benefit or not. When confronted with such information, many people have an initial internal reaction of defensive denial.

However, recognition of the systemic nature of privilege and marginalization can help everyone examine how to increase equity for those with minority identities by having an accurate perception and understanding of how a system benefits them for reasons that they did not seek or earn. The most pertinent component of understanding the complex nature of privilege and marginalization is to recognize that patients will arrive to our care with a history of experiences that has been shaped by their own privilege and oppression. If a provider does not understand the way that privilege and marginalization manifest in daily life, they are prone to respond to their patients in invalidating and insensitive ways. A provider who is unaware of the systemic nature of privilege and oppression might ascribe a patient's difficulties to personal failure or laziness as opposed to systems which the client has little impact to change. Consider the exchange between a provider and patient below.

Scenario 1: A nurse begins an appointment with a patient who was recently diagnosed with type two diabetes

PROVIDER: I see that you still haven't lost any weight since your last appointment.
PATIENT: Yeah, I know. I don't have a scale at home so I wasn't sure what it would say today.
PROVIDER: Well, like we talked about last time, losing weight it going to be an important part of managing your health, so you're going to want to make that a priority.
PATIENT: I know, I know...
PROVIDER: I suggest starting off with walking regularly or following along with some fitness videos on YouTube, just like I talked about last time. You're just going to have to make time for it since it probably hasn't been a priority for you until now. It's tough to get started but if you can build up your willpower then you'll be able to keep your momentum up! You're going to feel great once you get into a routine.
PATIENT: Sure, yeah, thank you for that advice.

Scenario 2: A nurse begins an appointment with a patient who was recently diagnosed with type two diabetes

PROVIDER: I see that you still haven't lost any weight since your last appointment. Can you tell me about how the weight loss process has been going?
PATIENT: It's been hard because I don't have a scale at home, so I don't really know if I'm losing weight. My clothes still fit the same, so I figured not much had changed.

PROVIDER: Tell me about some of the things you have been doing differently since we talked at your last appointment.
PATIENT: I did try to start getting more active, like you talked about, but one thing after another keeps coming up and making it hard.
PROVIDER: Oh okay, tell me about those things.
PATIENT: I can't remember if I told you but there's no sidewalks where I live, so if I want to go for a walk I have to walk on the road. That would be fine if it was just me, but I have my baby and I only have one of those little strollers that's not very sturdy, and there's no one to watch her so I have to take her with me. It doesn't feel really safe with all the traffic whirring by at like 55 miles per hour.
PROVIDER: Definitely, that would be scary.
PATIENT: I looked up some little exercise videos on YouTube that I could do, and I did one, but then my downstairs neighbor complained that I was stomping around too loudly, and I didn't want to make him mad. It seems like my only option is to do jumping jacks outside the apartment or something but that feels so embarrassing because there's no privacy and I'm self-conscious about my weight.
PROVIDER: It sounds like you've been trying out or thinking through different options but there's some barriers with where you live that it that are making this harder than anticipated.
PATIENT: Yes, that's what happening. I feel like I've run out of ideas for how to get more active.

The provider took two different approaches in the two scenarios above. In the first scenario, the provider was presumptive about the barriers to the patients' efforts to become more physically active. The first provider assumed that that patient was lacking in willpower and prioritization and therefore responded in a way that internalized the difficulty to the patient. The possibility that the patient didn't live in an area where it's safe to walk was never considered. Not only is this assumption inaccurate, but it also results in the patient's experience being minimized and the patient subsequently feeling devalued or maybe even unseen.

In the second scenario, the provider remained *curious* and *open* to what the possible barriers were for the patient. When asked, the patient was able to share more about the factors related to where she lives and her life circumstances (i.e., lack of sidewalks, lack of childcare, living in a second-floor apartment unit, insecurity over lack of private places to work out). Multiple of the barriers at play for this patient are linked to her socioeconomic status in that the only affordable and safe housing she can afford is an apartment in a rural area without sidewalks or privacy. When asked about barriers, the patient was able to share the external issues at hand and then hopefully she and the provider could explore possible workarounds, if the patient wanted such guidance.

In the first scenario, the provider appears to have unexamined socioeconomic privilege which led her to assume that her barriers (i.e., lack of willpower and prioritization) are the same barriers that her patient experiences. Increased awareness of her own socioeconomic privilege would allow her to recognize that she has access to sidewalks, a private indoor space without adjoining neighbors, and regular childcare *and* that people living in poverty face external barriers, and potentially the same internal barriers as well (i.e., lack of willpower, prioritization).

Bronfenbrenner's Ecological Model

Authors from a variety of disciplines have noted models of nested systems and the interconnectedness of levels of those systems. One example of understanding societal nested systems is to consider the human body. At the microscopic level of systems are individual cells. Cells are organized in a particular way to comprise organs. An organ is often part of a larger system, for example the heart, the lungs, and the circulatory system. A change in one or two cells can potentially involve the entire organ system, such as when cancer cells begin to multiply and populate an area of tissue. A change in one organ of the circulatory system, such as a fungal infection in a lung, can similarly result in profound changes at every level of those nested systems, from related organs such as the heart, the whole way down to individual cells within organs of the system.

This same conceptualization of nested systems can be applied to understanding organization of human society. The model we will look at more closely is Bronfenbrenner's Ecological Model (see Figure 3.1). Bronfenbrenner's work in child development resulted in the ecological model of human development. Bronfenbrenner (1979) defined human existence as a social experience. Our existence is internal in terms of how we define ourselves, and external in terms of how we perceive and define other people. All social definitions, experiences, and perceptions occur in nested groups. Many, many theorists over the years have focused on the primacy of the relationship between a child and those in closest physical proximity in the development of self-perception (e.g., Freud, Adler, Rogers, Bandura, Bronfenbrenner). The development of our internal self-definitions arises largely from the behavior of other people toward us and the meaning we attach to those behaviors.

The smallest social groups and units begin with a dyad of people and expand to the family of origin and progressively broader circles of human social organization, moving out as far as government and social policy and the passage of time. This represents a holarchy (Wilber, 2001), in which each set of interactions exists on its own and simultaneously represents a part of a larger whole. This holarchic progression can be visualized as a series of concentric circles, with the smallest unit at the center being the individual.

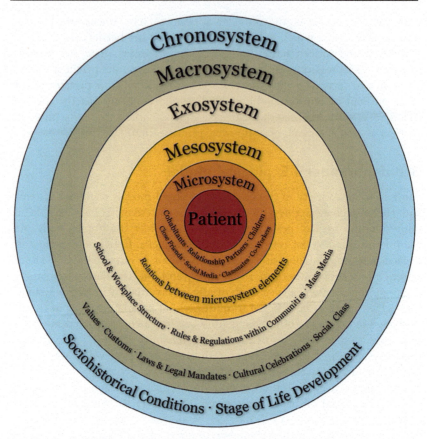

Figure 3.1 Bronfenbrenner's Ecological Model

Relationships between the individual and others in the environment move progressively outward. These systems are referred to as the microsystem level, mesosystem level, exosystem level, and macrosystem level. Bronfenbrenner posited that human development must be understood contextually, taking into account the influences exerted upon an individual at every level of group of which a person is a member.

Terry (2005) noted that in a later refinement of his model, Bronfenbrenner emphasized that each individual is at the center of their microsystem, and that the expectations and demands on behavior in a dyadic interaction is where the cultural roles and cultural values are most intensely expressed. The nature of those interpersonal interactions comprises a significant component of how a person sees themselves. Teny clarified that, "It is this interchange among internal and external systems that determines which environmental affordances will be perceived and activated ... in accordance with the role 'expectations, evaluations, and obligations' ...

that define one's conceptual self" (p. 20). In other words, the force of cultural values that are exerted from the macrosystem, which is most distal to the individual, the whole way down the hierarchy to the proximal microsystem, all influence an individual's self-perception.

Personal Reflection

Take a moment to diagram the circles of social connection and influence in which you find yourself right now, beginning with your most intimate relationship and moving outward. Consider how the relationship you have in each of those realms contributes to how you think about and define yourself.

Multicultural Competency

You might find yourself yearning to increase your competency in the realm of multicultural topics because you want to change systems that perpetuate inequality as well as provide your own patients with high quality care. The topic of increasing multicultural competency spans a range of healthcare fields (Hyter & Salas-Provance, 2018; Jeffreys, 2015; Leavitt, 2010; Sue et al., 2016), but there is common framework, the tripartite definition of multicultural competency, that is often used to help people evaluate their areas of weakness and strength. Multicultural competency encompasses the *awareness, knowledge,* and *skills* that a person holds related to a variety of cultural groups (Sue et al., 2019).

- *Awareness* is one's understanding of their own worldview, which can include their own values and the assumptions they make about other people and groups (which can include biases).
- *Knowledge* is understanding the worldview and experiences of others, including the values, practices, and norms of a variety of cultural groups. This type of knowledge also requires understanding the sociohistorical context of the lives of diverse people.
- *Skills* entail the application of one's knowledge of diverse groups, that is, the practice of engaging and intervening in the lives of diverse people in appropriate, helpful, and considerate ways (Sue et al., 2019).

Personal Reflection

Do you agree with Sue and Sue's statement (2003) that lacking multicultural competence is a form of cultural oppression? Why or why not? What relationship exists between this level of agreement and the personal experiences you have had related to your own race and ethnicity?

Developing one's multicultural competency is a process that begins with learning factual information about cultural groups apart from one's own but extends far beyond knowledge about a particular culture. This is a process that requires deep introspection, to look unflinchingly and with deep honesty at our own perceptions and beliefs, to be curious about the experiences of others, and to develop a heightened sense of awareness of the internal framework from which you serve culturally diverse individuals. The process of developing multicultural competency can be an emotionally intense process because most people become aware of biases they hold against cultural groups – that is, perceptions that were previously outside of their conscious awareness, and they also better understand the sociohistorical context of systemic oppression. For those of who hold many privileged identities, it can come as a shock that practices that have caused and reinforced inequities still exist today. It might be disturbing to recognize the unconscious biases that you hold against other cultural groups because this aspect of yourself is likely incongruent with how you see yourself, probably as a benevolent and caring person. Likewise, learning about systemic injustices that remain in place may evoke anger, hopelessness, and horror in the recognition that your own current behavior may be complicit with these systems. These emotional reactions are normal and a positive sign that you are allowing yourself to be emotionally connected to the experiences of others and that you value social justice and equity.

You now understand what is meant by terms such as culture, cultural identity groups, intersectionality, privilege, and marginalization. You also likely have a better understanding of your own intersecting identities and the ways in which those impact your experience of the world around you. Our hope is that this increased knowledge and self-awareness will provide the foundation for better communication skills with patients.

Healthcare Systems

Healthcare systems and providers are a routine context for interactions and support. Most babies experience their first moments of life outside the womb within a healthcare setting, given that 98 percent of US babies are born within hospitals (MacDorman & Declercq, 2019). Some go on to then have regular interactions with medical doctors, dentists, optometrists, and school nurses during their childhoods. As people grow and develop, their individual needs may require seeing specialist medical providers and mental health care professionals. Even mundane healthcare tasks involve interaction with healthcare systems, such as donating blood, receiving vaccinations, and picking up prescriptions. The later years of life can involve increased healthcare needs and end-of-life healthcare systems may involve family and friends of the person who is dying. Take a moment to consider all the healthcare providers you have met with in the previous year and how, for any given situation, you likely interacted with multiple types of healthcare providers. Healthcare providers are trained to provide services across the lifespan and are often integral for us to live a healthy and functional life.

The origins of the modern healthcare system in the United States are complex and reflect the combined impacts of scientific advances, wars, the industrial revolution, political power, and governmental policy. In brief, the modernization and advancement of healthcare services has paralleled the expansion of access to healthcare through increased availability of health insurance, both private and public options (e.g., Medicare, Medicaid). Many people in the U.S. do remain uninsured, though. The United States is unique among similar countries in that the U.S. spends more on healthcare costs in relation to Gross Domestic Product, and that the government funds a far smaller amount of healthcare costs (Fuchs, 2013).

Healthcare access has historically been dictated by two factors: those who could afford it, and those who could access it based on where they live. The United States has never had a compulsory or universal healthcare system. This means that Americans have relied on private insurance; employee-subsidized insurance; special programs for those living in poverty, older adults, or people with disabilities; have paid out-of-pocket; accrued medical debt, or simply went without care (Public Broadcasting Service, n.d.). Healthcare access is tied to socioeconomic status, one of the ADDRESSING variables discussed previously.

A critical component of the advancement of healthcare in the United States has been the efforts of healthcare professionals, scientists, and willing volunteers, which have led to new and better treatments for commonplace and rare health concerns. The history of this process though once again reflects the systemic abuse of minority populations.

Medical Mistrust and the History of Healthcare Abuse

Dehumanization occurs when a person or society denies a person (or groups of people) their full humanity. This might take form in various ways, and can include ignoring the pain, both emotional and physical, of obviously hurting people. History is replete with examples of the dehumanization of cultural groups in which their pain and concerns were ignored or denied, or powerful people took advantage of the group's dehumanized status to advance their own pursuits. Gamble (1997) highlights several examples of how African Americans have been abused by healthcare providers, including being tortured while being used as test subjects for medical inquiries and being denied healthcare. One of the most egregious abuses in medical research is the infamous Tuskegee study, "Untreated Syphilis in the Negro Male." Beginning in 1932, a total of 600 Black men were recruited to participate and told they were being treated for "bad blood," without being informed that this study was targeting syphilis. Their compensation for participation was free medical examinations, meals, and burial insurance. Eleven years later, penicillin had been identified as the preferred medication to cure syphilis, but the study subjects were not informed that there was a medication that could cure them. This withholding of treatment results in death, the spreading of syphilis to others, including babies and partners. The Tuskegee experiment is sometimes referred to in professional literature as being the basis of medical mistrust, although some authors have noted that Tuskegee alone is not the origin but rather exists as one example of a broader, more historically based, narrative that government officials and health officials are not trustworthy (Brandon, Isaac, & LaVeist, 2005). These powerful examples of healthcare abuse exist for other cultural groups as well, including people with disabilities. For example, women with intellectual disabilities experienced forced sterilization (Roy et al., 2012) in the 1900s. This history of abuse from supposedly trustworthy institutions and people can instill a functional paranoia of healthcare providers and systems.

In an editorial letter published in *The Lancet*, Dr. Kimberly Manning, who is a self-described 50-year-old Black American woman who descended from people who were enslaved, said the following:

> There are trust issues when it comes to African Americans and the US health-care system. There is also a justified fear that our human lives might be dispensable in exchange for scientific discovery benefiting those with privilege and who are white. The historical basis for this, which began long before the untreated syphilis study in Macon County, underscores a larger, ongoing issue—the value of Black lives. In the Antebellum period, it was the millions tortured through chattel slavery as property. Post Reconstruction, there was state-sanctioned convict leasing followed by Jim Crow laws and domestic terrorism. The uncovering of the disturbing events in the Tuskegee study was no more than another chapter over centuries in US history. It is a story that continues with the deaths of unarmed Black Americans, mass incarceration, the achievement gap, and the astounding health disparities seen every day and now amplified by COVID-19. All of it is intertwined.

We hope one of the biggest takeaways from this chapter is a deeper understanding of the fact that just because we see ourselves as worthy of someone's trust, it is not valid or even respectful to assume that our patient will share that view. It is essential that we recognize, understand, and especially respect, the presence of medical mistrust, particularly among our patients who regularly experience disempowerment in our society.

Improved communication with patients is vital in the effort to reduce the levels of medical mistrust within minority communities. Medical mistrust is a lack of trust with healthcare providers and their organizations regarding their capacity to provide honest, competent, and benevolent care (The Commonwealth Fund, 2021). Medical mistrust is anticipated given the history of healthcare with minority communities in the United States. Medical mistrust can be understood as a specific type of cultural mistrust. Cultural mistrust is the mistrust of White people, and primarily White institutions (PWI) (e.g., educational, criminal justice, and healthcare), by people of color because of negative experiences, both historical and contemporary (Brooks & Hopkins, 2017; Terrell & Terrell, 1981). Medical mistrust is emerging in the professional literature across health disciplines as a significant contributor to poor health outcomes (Benkert et al., 2019; Jaiswal, 2019; Powell et al., 2019). Efforts are being made across healthcare settings, at the individual and systems level, to decrease the levels of medical mistrust that exist for certain minority communities. Increasing validating, open, and empathic communication is viewed as a key point of intervention for decreasing medical mistrust (The Commonwealth Fund, 2021). Some providers might assume that because they hold a visible minority identity themselves that they will be automatically trusted within the healthcare setting by minority patients. However, minority patients may question the credibility and trustworthiness of a provider of minority identity/ies because of the provider's affiliation with a PWI and therefore may be seen as a "sellout" (Sue et al., 2019, p. 64). Ultimately, providers will need to strive to develop empathic, validating, and competent helping relationships with those they serve.

Although you will soon be joining a helping field to provide your profession's unique knowledge and care, the landscape of the healthcare world and its triumphs and failures will pre-date your entrance. Providers must understand the ways in which the healthcare field in general, and one's own specific profession, have served (or have failed to serve) the needs of diverse clients. This knowledge is the first step in ameliorating the mistakes of the past while also building equitable systems for the future. We also encourage you to understand that the systems that produced inequities and atrocities may still be in place today.

The Minority Stress Model

Access to high-quality and appropriate healthcare for minority populations, and the legacy of medical abuse, are only part of the challenges that minority populations face in relation to seeking and receiving healthcare. Another co-occurring negative influence that minority populations face is the additive stressors linked to their membership in a socially oppressed group, and that these stressors are above and beyond those faced by most non-minority individuals in daily life. The stressors faced by minority individuals result from social influences, such as discrimination, harassment, and prejudice, and account for unique additive stress and negative mental health outcomes (Meyer, 2003). This theory is called the Minority Stress Model (MSM) (Meyer, 2003) and has been applied to gender and sexual minority populations, religious minorities, people with disabilities, and international students (Botha & Frost, 2020; Every & Perry, 2014; Rogers et al., 2021; Wei et al., 2008). The MSM is a useful framework for understanding how factors beyond one's control (i.e., discrimination, harassment, prejudice) can negatively impact the well-being of minority populations.

It is important to distinguish, however, that holding values, practices, and norms that are different from a majority population is not cause of higher rates of negative mental health outcomes in minority populations, but rather the experiences of discrimination and harassment are responsible for such stress. Being a culturally competent provider requires understanding the experiences of people with a broad array of cultural identities, beyond those that have been oppressive and unjust. To understand the values, practices, and norms of a variety of cultural groups is beyond the scope of this textbook, and many academic training programs for healthcare specialties require coursework that provide students with a foundation for learning about a variety of cultural groups.

Historical and Individual Level Trauma

There is one other essential area of focus in our exploration of variables of diversity in the patients you will be serving and with whom you will be striving to establish rapport. The concept of trauma-informed care has been a recent emergence in mental health literature. One of the first places that trauma-informed care was visible was with the Veterans Administration in their efforts to treat "shell-shock syndrome" in World War I, which eventually became known as Post-Traumatic Stress Disorder. In the many years since that time, it has become evident that people who have experienced exposure to acute and/or chronic traumas are at higher risk for developing problematic trauma-based symptoms and behaviors. Moreover, many people who were exposed to trauma have not recognized themselves as having a traumatic history and so have not actually made the connection between their life experiences and their current concerns. Many practitioners have not been trained to inquire about, or to respond to, disclosures a patient may make regarding traumatic experiences.

There is compelling data regarding the frequency of traumatic experiences from large scale studies by the federal government. Kessler et al. (1999) identified that 61 percent of men and 51 percent of women had experienced at least one trauma in their lives. Adverse Childhood Experiences (ACE) frequently plays a role in the development of negative outcomes that can been seen in childhood and moving forward into adulthood. The Centers for Disease Control and Prevention (2021a) define adverse childhood experiences as "potentially traumatic events that occur in childhood, for example experiencing violence, abuse, or neglect; witnessing violence in the home or community, or having a family member attempt or die by suicide." There are additional components of a child's living environment that can result in a child feeling unsafe, without a sense of predictability and safety, or an experience of being nurtured. The outcome of these conditions on a child's development has been strongly correlated to chronic health problems, challenges with mental health, and problematic substance usage. Secondarily then, a person's ability to lead a stable, functional, satisfying life is diminished.

In this categorization of trauma, are the terms "big T" and "little t" trauma. These terms are often used in counseling contexts that are not necessarily reflected in professional literature, but are recognized, nonetheless. "Big T" traumas are precisely what is implied; highly significant, highly disruptive, and impactful life events that are often readily identifiable as precipitants when someone develops Post Traumatic Stress Disorder. These types of events could include life threatening events, serious physical injury, and sexual violence. On the other hand, "little t" traumas are those which are also painful but perhaps don't involve near death, devastating physical injury, or sexually based violence. "Little t" traumas might seem less likely to be disruptive, but an accumulation of them can strain a person's coping ability. A high number of smaller traumas happening at a time when a person's coping ability is already compromised for any reason can result in a response that is consistent with trauma exposure.

Referring back to the Bronfenbrenner ecological systems model, trauma can occur at any level of system. While we might generally think about trauma occurring on an individual level, perhaps in the form of events such as a devastating car accident, a hurricane, or a sexual assault, there also exist generational traumas that affect large numbers of people simultaneously. Examples include internment camps for Japanese Americans following World War II, or the 9/11 attacks in the U.S. Finally, also on a broad level are the even more broadly based racial traumas that have occurred for many non-majority people over recorded history. A historical example is the genocide experienced by Native American tribes at the hands of European explorers.

The value of trauma-informed care is that the patient's care can be adjusted to account for their trauma history, because symptoms and concerns can be understood as reactions to trauma and thus treated appropriately. In addition, a trauma-informed approach will resist retraumatizing a patient and thus your relationship development with them can be enhanced and strengthened. Acknowledging a person's feelings and perceptions results in them experiencing validation, which is a meaningful way of communicating to them that we care about them and for them. Rather than saying to someone, "Come on, tell me, you can trust me," we instead instill trust by acknowledging responding in a gentle and curious manner that avoid judgement and assumptions.

Summary

Becoming a culturally competent provider requires raising your consciousness of your identities, values, and biases as well as the experiences of other cultural groups you are not a member of, and then combining those together to act in skillful ways with an array of patients. This learning process requires that providers recognize that historical healthcare abuses result in medical mistrust for some communities, and that you will not automatically be assumed to be a trustworthy or helpful provider by some patients. If you hold a curious and non-judgmental stance you can demonstrate to a new patient that you are ready to learn about their experiences and background based on what they share with you, not based on preconceived notions. You will learn how to use microskills in this text that can use to convey back to the patient that you hear and understand them.

Questions for Class Discussion

1   What is the relationship between your cultural and social identities and your thoughts about the multicultural competence standards?
2   How have your own family's cultural values affected your choice to become a professional counselor?
3   To what extent do you believe it is a counselor's responsibility to offer counseling in a manner consistent with a client's worldview?
4   What are examples of clients and worldviews with whom you absolutely could not work? Why would you be unable?

References

Benkert, R., Cuevas, A., Thompson, H.S., Dove-Medows, E., & Knuckles, D. (2019). Ubiquitous yet unclear: A systematic review of medical mistrust. *Behavioral Medicine*, 45(2), 86–101. doi:10.1080/08964289.2019.1588220.
Bertrand, M. & Mullainathan, S. (2018). Are Emily and Greg more employable than Lakisha and Jamal?: A field experiment on labor market discrimination. *Research Papers in Economics*, 304–308. doi:10.4324/9780429499821-53.
Black, L.L. & Stone, D. (2005). Expanding the definition of privilege: The concept of social privilege. *Journal of Multicultural Counseling and Development*, 33, 243–255. https://doi.org/10.1002/j.2161-1912.2005.tb00020.x.
Botha, M. & Frost, D.M. (2020). Extending the minority stress model to understand mental health problems experienced by the autistic population. *Society and Mental Health*, 10(1), 20–34. doi:10.1177/2156869318804297.

Brandon, D.T., Isaac, L.A., & LaVeist, T.A. (2005). The legacy of Tuskegee and trust in medical care: Is Tuskegee responsible for race differences in mistrust of medical care? *Journal of the National Medical Association*, 97(7), 951. https://pubmed.ncbi.nlm.nih.gov/16080664.

Bronfenbrenner, U. (1979). *The ecology of human development: Experiments by nature and design*. Harvard University Press.

Brooks, R.T. & Hopkins, R. (2017). Cultural mistrust and health care utilization: The effects of a culturally responsive cognitive intervention. *Journal of Black Studies*, 48(8), 816–834. https://doi.org/10.1177/0021934717728454.

Centers for Disease Control and Prevention. (2021a, April 6). Fast facts: Preventing adverse childhood experiences |violence prevention|injury center|CDC. www.cdc.gov/violenceprevention/aces/fastfact.html?CDC_AA_refVal=https://www.cdc.gov/violenceprevention/acestudy/fastfact.html.

Centers for Disease Control and Prevention. (2021b, April 20). *Tuskegee study - Timeline - CDC - NCHHSTP*. www.cdc.gov/tuskegee/timeline.htm.

Crenshaw, K. (1989). Demarginalizing the intersection of race and sex: A Black feminist critique of antidiscrimination doctrine, feminist theory, and antiracist politics. *University of Chicago Legal Forum*, 139–167.

DiAngelo, R. (2018). *White fragility: Why it's so hard for white people to talk about racism*. Beacon Press.

Every, D. & Perry, R. (2014). The relationship between perceived religious discrimination and self-esteem for Muslim Australians. *Australian Journal of Psychology*, 66(4), 241–248. doi:10.1111/ajpy.12067.

Fuchs, V.R. (2013). How and Why US Health Care Differs from that in Other OECD Countries. *JAMA*, 309(1), 33–34. doi:10.1001/jama.2012.125458.

Gamble, V.N. (1997). Under the shadow of Tuskegee: African Americans and health care. *American Journal of Public Health*, 87(11), 1773–1778. https://doi.org/10.2105/AJPH.87.11.1773.

Geertz, C. (1973). *Interpretation of cultures* (5th ed.). Basic Books.

Hays, P.A. (2008). *Addressing cultural complexities in practice: Assessment, diagnosis, and therapy* (2nd ed.). American Psychological Association. https://doi.org/10.1037/11650-000.

Hyter, Y.D. & Salas-Provance, M.B. (2021). *Culturally responsive practices in speech, language, and hearing sciences, second edition* (2nd ed.). Plural Publishing, Inc.

Jaiswal, J. (2019). Whose responsibility is it to dismantle medical mistrust? Future directions for researchers and health care providers. *Behavioral Medicine*, 45(2), 188–196. doi:10.1080/08964289.2019.1630357.

Jeffreys, M.R. (2015). *Teaching cultural competence in nursing and health care: Inquiry, action, and innovation* (3rd ed.). Springer Publishing Company.

Kessler, R.C., Sonnega, A., Bromet, E., Hughes, M., Nelson, C.B., & Breslau, N. (1999). Epidemiological risk factors for trauma and PTSD. In R. Yehuda (Ed.), *Risk factors for posttraumatic stress disorder* (pp. 23–59). American Psychiatric Association.

Leavitt, R.L. (2010). *Cultural competence: A lifelong journey to cultural proficiency* (1st ed.). Slack Incorporated.

MacDorman, M.F., & Declercq, E. (2019). Trends and state variations in out-of-hospital births in the United States, 2004-2017. *Birth-Issues in Perinatal Care*, 46(2), 279–288. doi:10.1111/birt.12411.

Meyer, I.H. (2003). Prejudice, social stress, and mental health in lesbian, gay and bisexual populations: Conceptual issues and research evidence. *Psychological Bulletin*, 129, 674–697. https://doi.org/10.1037/0033-2909.129.5.674.

Nadal, K.L., Whitman, C.N., Davis, L.S., Erazo, T., & Davidoff, K.C. (2016). Microaggressions toward lesbian, gay, bisexual, transgender, queer, and genderqueer people: A review of the literature. *Journal of Sex Research*, 53(4–5), 488–508. doi:10.1080/00224499.2016.1142495.

Pew Research Center. (2020). *The Global Divide on Homosexuality Persists*. www.pewresearch.org/global/2020/06/25/global-divide-on-homosexuality-persists.

Poushter, J. & Kent, N. (2020, October 27). The global divide on homosexuality persists. Pew Research Center's Global Attitudes Project. www.pewresearch.org/global/2020/06/25/global-divide-on-homosexuality-persists.

Powell, W., Richmond, J., Mohottige, D., Yen, I., Joslyn, A., & Corbie-Smith, G. (2019). Medical mistrust, racism, and delays in preventive health screening among African-American men. *Behavioral Medicine*, 45(2), 102–117. doi:10.1080/08964289.2019.1585327.

Public Broadcasting Service. (n.d.). Healthcare crisis: Healthcare timeline. Retrieved November 10, 2022. www.pbs.org/healthcarecrisis/history.htm.

Rogers, M.L., Horn, M.A., Janakiraman, R., & Joiner, T.E. (2021). Examination of minority stress pathways to suicidal ideation among sexual minority adults: The moderating role of LGBT community connectedness. *Psychology of Sexual Orientation and Gender Diversity*, 8(1), 38–47. doi:10.1037/sgd0000409.

Roy, A., Roy, A, & Roy, M. (2012). The human rights of women with intellectual disability. *Journal of the Royal Society of Medicine*, 105(9), 384–389. doi:10.1258/jrsm.2012.110303.

Sue, D.W. & Sue, D. (2003). *Counseling the culturally diverse: Theory and practice* (4th ed.). Wiley.

Sue, D.W. (2016). *Multicultural social work practice: A Competency-Based approach to diversity and social justice* (2nd ed.). Wiley.

Sue, D.W., Nadal, K.L., Capodilupo, C.M., Lin, A.I., Torino, G.C., & Rivera, D.P. (2008). Racial microaggressions against Black Americans: Implications for counseling. *Journal of Counseling and Development*, 86(3), 330–338. https://doi.org/10.1002/j.1556-6678.2008.tb00517.x.

Sue, D.W., Sue, D., Neville, H.A., & Smith, L. (2019). *Counseling the culturally diverse* (8th ed.). Wiley.

Terrell, S.L. & Terrell, F. (1980). An inventory to measure cultural mistrust among Blacks. *The Western Journal of Black Studies*, 5(3), 180.

Terry, M. (2006). The ecological paradigm. Retrieved April 19, 2008. https://scholar.google.com/scholar?hl=en&as_sdt=0%2C36&q=Terry%2C+Marion+The+Ecological+paradigm&btnG=.

The Commonwealth Fund. (2021, January 14). Understanding and ameliorating medical mistrust among Black Americans. www.commonwealthfund.org/publications/newsletter-article/2021/jan/medical-mistrust-among-black-americans.

United Nations Educational, Scientific and Cultural Organization. (2001). Universal declaration on cultural diversity. www.ohchr.org/sites/default/files/diversity.pdf.

Wei, M., Ku, T.Y., Russell, D.W., Mallinckrodt, B., & Liao, K.Y.H. (2008). Moderating effects of three coping strategies and self-esteem on perceived discrimination and depressive symptoms: A minority stress model for Asian international students. *Journal of Counseling Psychology*, 55(4), 451–462. doi:10.1037/a0012511.

Wilber, K. (2001). *The eye of Spirit: An integral vision for a world gone slightly mad*. Shambala.

Yalom, I.D. (1980). *Existential psychotherapy*. Basic Books.

Chapter 4

Human Development and the Helping Process

In this chapter, we will look at the process of development from a couple different angles. First, we will review some models of human development and consider universal processes as well as other aspects that vary depending on the cultural context in which the development is occurring. Then our developmental focus will shift from individual development to an exploration of how helping relationships grow and develop. The ultimate goal of this chapter is for you to have a broad understanding of the nuanced connection between your patient's stage of development, your and their social and cultural identities, and how all those factors may potentially influence the way the helping relationship unfolds between the two of you. This level of knowledge and self-awareness will allow a provider to use helping skills in a nuanced way to align with the patient's needs, based on their development.

Lifespan Development

Many professional education programs across the helping professions require a course in human development. One common assumption about development that transcends aspects, models, and cultures, is the assumption that development is mostly linear and occurs in predictable stages, as well as the assumption that particular developmental milestones must be observed and achieved in order for the next stage of development to be attainable. There are similar models of development pertaining to numerous aspects of human growth: cognitive functioning, social and emotional functioning, behavioral functioning, identity, and so on.

Perhaps not surprisingly, many of the expectations for particular behaviors or skills emerging at a given chronological age are culture bound. Thus, when we talk about early stages of motor development in the U.S., for example, the assumption is made that a child must have mastered head control and neck strength before they are able to sit upright without support. Sitting upright without support must precede the ability to pull oneself to a standing position, which must occur prior to walking.

DOI: 10.4324/9781003217589-5

Interestingly, even stages of motor development are culturally influenced and vary from group to group as a result of the physical environment in which a child is growing, the cultural expectations about a child's behavior, and members/features of the family. For example, Super and Harkness (2009) observed rural Kenyan infants to have a different sequence of gross motor development milestones. Kenyan infants appeared to bypass creeping and crawling in their progression from mastery of trunk and neck control to walking.

Regardless of the specific cultural differences, it is advisable for a provider to have a general sense of their patient's stage of development and level of functioning, and then to adjust their techniques for conversing and helping them, accordingly. A child who is five will likely not be having the same conversation as a child who is fifteen about their feelings of sadness. The active listening skills demonstrated by the provider must be offered at the same level as the child's development in order to avoid a mismatch. Mismatch could take the form of speaking in language too complicated or abstract to be understood by a child, as well as speaking in a concrete, simplistic style could be off-putting to an adolescent.

Before we move on with exploring the models of human development in this chapter, it is critically important to recognize the inherent limitations that have historically been embedded in the developmental research and literature. Those limitations involve the lens through which development has been seen, up until very recently when the impact of trauma—and the notion of race-based trauma—became increasingly recognized as a crucial contextual factor in studying and understanding development, especially for people who have not been represented in the normative samples of research studies. The following quote by Spencer, Dupree, and Hartmann (1997) articulates this concept in more detail:

> Across the life course, experiences in different cultural contexts (e.g., home, school, peer group, community) influence how one perceives oneself. This statement could simply mean that there is a relationship between life experiences and self-esteem. However, this assertion goes further than that. We assert that the processing of phenomena and experiences not only influences how much one feels valued or valuable (e.g., self-esteem), but it also influences how one gives meaning and significance to different aspects of oneself (e.g., abilities, physical attributes, behaviors, and activities). More specifically, it is not merely the experience but one's perception of experiences in different cultural contexts that influences how one perceives oneself.
>
> (p. 817)

This assertion forms the basis for the proposed revision to Bronfenbrenner's ecological systems theory (Spencer, 2007; Spencer, Dupree, & Hartmann,

1997). Bronfenbrenner described the nested systems of influence upon development of self-concept in children, ranging from the microsystem of dyadic interaction with a caregiver, up through the broad, diffuse influence exerted by exosystemic societal factors such as governmental policy, religious doctrine, etc. Spencer (2007) argued that to be truly valid and generalizable, ecosystems theory (EST) must be modified through incorporation of the phenomenological variants (PVEST). Essentially, this consists of retaining the same levels of system influence, but also incorporates variables of race, gender, ethnicity, socioeconomic status, immigration status, faith, skin color, and nativity. Thus, PVEST offers a more accurate, trauma-informed, responsive model for developmentally assessing a patient.

Developmental norms serve as a basis for assessing a child's behavior; they provide a sense of whether a child is further ahead, further behind, or similar to most of their age peers with regard to some aspect of their presentation. For example, there may be significant differences across cultures in how long it is considered socially acceptable for a child to suck their thumb. In the U.S., we might not be surprised to see a child of 18 months sucking their thumb as a way of self-soothing. If we saw a person of 18 years sucking their thumb to self-soothe, we would very likely notice them doing something unusual for a person of that age. Similarly, consider the concern of bedwetting (i.e., nocturnal enuresis). In the U.S., most children are no longer wetting the bed by about the age of five. However, bedwetting is not considered to be clinically significant until the child is over the age of seven, with incidents of bedwetting at least twice a week for a minimum of three months. By defining the behavior with such specific rules for age and frequency of occurrence, the diagnostic criteria create a relatively small proportion of children whose development is not following the "typical" age curve in comparison to their age peers (Cleveland Clinic, 2019). Some of the individuals and families seeking counseling and other healthcare services will be having challenges, problems, and symptoms that may be developmentally atypical or even related specifically to developmental struggles. There are many aspects of development and many ways a person might present as either developmentally advanced or developmentally behind their age peers, but we just don't have the space and time review all of them here. Know that whatever your helping specialty is, it will be important for you to have a sense of two things: 1) an understanding of the cultural context in which the concern is occurring; and 2) what "typical" development suggests in that realm of functioning in their culture, so that you have a sense of where the person you're helping might need support in order to improve and maintain optimal functioning.

One of the authors (K.M.) was assessing a 4th grade child for a learning disability at a small public school in a very rural area. One of the test questions was, "Name the four seasons of the year," to which the student replied, "Rabbit, duck, turkey, and deer." While he earned 0 points on the standardized scoring for that test question, which would suggest he lacks knowledge, is family in fact had a subsistence lifestyle, and his answers were relevant to his life and family. This is a concrete example of how important it is to consider the realm of necessary daily functioning in that person's specific culture.

As mentioned at various times throughout this text, it's completely expected that as we read new information, we compare it to our own lived experiences as a way to gauge the accuracy of what we're reading and learning. All of us have the tendency to use our own life experiences as a source of information about what's "normal" and "abnormal." This is a great starting point, but it should never be our ending point! Our training as professional helpers requires that we recognize the limitations of only using our own experiences, and that we strive to understand and value ways other people and cultures view child rearing and human development. Even among others who have similar cultural backgrounds to our own, there will be differences across family units in what behavior is expected from members at various ages and stages of development.

Trauma-Informed Human Development

Earlier in the text, we discussed some traumatic events our patients may experience. The impact of adverse childhood experiences and other traumatic events can have a lasting impact on patients whom we serve. Adverse childhood experiences could be but are not limited to living with a parent with mental illness or suicidality, divorce, emotional abuse, physical abuse, sexual abuse, parental incarceration, substance abuse of parent/caregiver and domestic violence (Felitti et al., 1998). Some of the areas that researchers have found that are impacted by traumatic experiences are brain development, attachment and relationships, the body, emotional responses, behavioral concerns, cognition, and long-term health outcomes. When working with patients it is imperative for us to consider human development and potential traumatic events that patients have been exposed to that have had an impact on the various areas addressed above. Traumatic experiences can disrupt typical developmental processes and may mimic other physical or behavioral issues, but are ultimately the result of trauma.

Realms of Lifespan Development

Humans develop and change in different domains of functioning; physically, cognitively, emotionally, socially, and in respect to identities and career. These are just some of the common domains of human development that a provider can take into consideration as they get to know their patient.

Understanding a patient's status in various developmental realms does not always impact the use of helping skills. However, it should be taken into conscious consideration to examine relevance for your work with a patient.

Physical development across the lifespan encompasses changes in bodily functioning and capacity. These developments begin prenatally and are ever evolving until we die. Some of these areas of development include body growth, brain development, motor development, and perceptual development. Changes in brain development underlie many of the cognitive and emotional development processes that have direct implications for how we use our helping skills with patients. Cognitive development theories abound and capture a variety of areas of change including language, information processing (e.g., working memory, attention, executive functioning), intelligence, and moral development. Some of the relevant theorists in this realm are likely familiar names such as Piaget, Vygotsky, and Kohlberg. Changes in cognitive functioning also underlie the development in emotional development, which include emotional understanding, emotion regulation, and emotional expression. Combined together, changes in physical, cognitive, and emotional development statuses reciprocally interact with other people in one's environment and give way to development in the social realms of one's life.

Social development models capture the changes in relationships with groups such as family, peers, and romantic partners. Milestones across social development can be linked to cultural expectations such as typical age of leaving home, pursuing first romantic relationships, and the degree of expected intimacy with others. Coinciding with these developmental areas (i.e., physical, cognitive, emotional, social) include the processes of internal development such as those linked to identities and career. For example, people develop in their understanding of their racial and ethnic identity, their gender identity, and their sexual orientation. Some relevant theories for further reading of racial and ethnic identity development include Asian American racial identity development (Kim, 2012), Black racial identity development (Worrell et al., 2001), Latine American racial identity development (Ferdman & Gallegos, 2012), multiracial identity development (Renn, 2008), Native American racial identity development (Horse, 2012), and White racial identity development (Helm, 1995). Other relevant models include those related to sexual orientation identity development (D'Augelli, 1994), transgender identity development, (Brill & Kenney, 2016), and ability status identity development (Forber-Pratt et al., 2017). Lastly, many individuals undergo a process of career development throughout their lifetime, and these are captured in theories such as Social Cognitive Career Theory (Lent et al., 1994) and Super and Savickas' work (Savickas, 1994). All these models reflect the diversity of development within a single person based on the cultural and social identities that they hold.

A helpful take-home message regarding each of these theories is that people are dynamic. The patient you meet with is likely in the midst of a larger process of development regarding their identities, capacities, and milestone accomplishments. Taking note of where they are at on salient development models can help you fine-tune your use of the microskills to meet them where they are at, most relevantly, to their cognitive and emotional level of development.

Implications for Helping Skill Usage

To effectively develop rapport with our patients, we need to consider their cognitive level of understanding (e.g., ability to think abstractly and meaning making, ability to answer a question), and then be able to adjust our approach to their developmental stage. Essentially, consider what would be typical of a person of that age/stage and respond and ask accordingly. Children and adolescents are generally more focused on the here and now than they are on long-term implications or consequences. Similarly, an adolescent, by virtue of life experience and overall maturity level, might be more inclined to make meanings that are concrete and short-term. Although some adults also tend to think in the short term and more about themselves than others, in general, as people mature, their concerns and worldviews expand to consider long-term implications of actions or values. The dialogue comparison in Table 4.1 gives a statement and counselor response with an adolescent of 17 years at various psychosocial stages of development ranging from below average to average to above average maturity.

Commonalities in Development Across Cultures

One commonality in human development across cultures is that there are particular roles and behaviors that correspond to stages of the biological life cycle from birth to death. This means that different groups and cultures will certainly have different names and definitions for social expectations of roles. To use an obvious example, the age at which an adolescent transitions to young adulthood and exhibits the typically expected behavior of young adults varies from group to group. For example, the stage of *emerging adulthood*, refers to the stage at which young adults assume increased responsibility and become functional in adult roles and behaviors. A number of studies in the U.S. have observed an increasingly prolonged period of transitional time from dependence on the family of origin toward establishing one's own autonomous life (Li, 2018; Nelson & Padilla-Walker, 2013). Those elongated years of transition are seen in both developed countries (Arnett, 2016) as well as in countries where hardships like high unemployment are common (Scabini et al., 2006; Vleioras & Mantziou, 2018).

Table 4.1 Dialogue and Patient Maturity Level

17-year-old girl in 11th grade, Emily: First I found out that Joe has been calling and texting Mariah behind my back, and before when I asked him about it, he lied and said he barely even knew her and why would he be texting her. Then my friend Molly saw Joe and Mariah at the coffee shop sharing a caramel latte, with two straws in one glass! Lattes were my favorite drink I used to like to share with him. I can't believe he's out doing that behind my back with Mariah! What a jerk! I'm so glad I found out now.

Advanced Maturity Level
Counselor: I get the sense that you see this as a reflection of him being a jerk. Sounds like you are thankful that you got information that Joe is not trustworthy, before spending a lot more time and energy on your relationship with him. Trust is one of the most important things to you in a friendship, and if you don't trust the other person, it sounds like it might not be worth having them as a friend.
Emily: Even if I did accept his apology, I'd still always wonder if he was telling the truth.
Counselor: In your experience, history repeats itself in relationships. So if it happened once, that's a good indication that it's probably going to happen again.

Average Maturity Level
Counselor: Joe went behind your back and is doing some of the things that you thought were special between you and him. Joe and Mariah both betrayed your trust.
Emily: Right! How am I supposed to show my face at school? I'm never going into that coffee shop again.
Counselor: Being lied to by two good friends was extremely embarrassing for you. You expect that other kids at school will look down on you because two of your friends lied to you.

Below Average Maturity Level
Counselor: You're really mad that they both went behind your back and Joe lied to you about it. Then they shared the drink you've always shared with him.
Emily: Exactly. And now I want to figure out what to do to get back at them.
Counselor: You think you'd feel better if you could get some revenge for your hurt feelings.

And yet, the *process* of transition remains a constant. From a cross-cultural perspective, it is of critical importance to have a solid understanding of the group-specific norms for various stages of human development. Gardiner (2001) stated:

> If asked to select just one word to describe the present status of cross-cultural development and the direction it might be headed at this time, that word would be *contextualization*, or the view that behavior cannot be meaningfully studied or fully understood independent of the (cultural) context in which it takes place.
>
> (p. 187)

Context is an essential aspect of understanding another person's past development and current state.

It is also of obvious importance to recognize that those developmental shifts from stage to stage are likely going to be characterized by certain process variables. By this we mean that each time a person moves from one developmental stage to the next, the other individuals in that family system also need to shift and move in their expectations and responses in order for the system to contain those transitions.

If you think about a family system with whom you are familiar, you might be able to imagine what it looks like when a family system resists changing to accommodate the changing developmental needs of a member. One example might be a family member who has historically been the primary person bringing income to the household. It would cause problems for the individual, as well as for the family system, if the other family members refused to recognize that at 78 years old, this person who has been the financial anchor is no longer physically and emotionally capable of carrying that level of responsibility within the family system. At the other end of the spectrum are families who are resistant to young members acquiring increasing levels of independence and responsibility. This can result in what is sometimes referred to as "helicopter parenting," in which the parents intervene when challenges present themselves, rather than giving the young adult an opportunity to learn problem-solving. One outcome of not encouraging independent problem-solving could be lack of confidence and lack of ability to effectively manage challenges as they arise.

Helping Relationship Development

If you stop and think about how *any* relationship develops, regardless of whether it's family, a new friend, a co-worker, or a therapist, the very first thing that must occur is a period of meeting and familiarizing. Professional helping relationships are a very particular type of relationship because in those cases, the socially expected behavior for each participant has already been clearly defined. As you know from your reading and learning ethics, with your professional license to practice, you will have a very specific scope of practice as determined by the license law in your state or jurisdiction. Beyond the specific scope of practice at the place where you provide services, there may be some expectations for the patient's behavior too. This could include actions such as keeping scheduled appointments and following through on providing insurance or billing information. Beyond those basic business-oriented aspects of roles, and perhaps more important, is the social and emotional connection made between you and your patients. We are referring here to the difference between process and outcome. "Outcome" refers to the extent to which the person's concerns are satisfactorily and appropriately resolved, while "process" refers to the unfolding sequence by which that help is offered and received. A discussion like this one, about how you can maximize the chances from which the client will benefit, must focus on the process, as in what specific considerations and behaviors will be conducive to that goal.

As mentioned earlier in this text, there is an inherent power imbalance between a service provider and the person seeking services. The service provider (e.g., counselor, nutritionist, physical therapist) is being sought out for their skill in some activity by a patient in a state of need. The particulars of that helping relationship, and the rules by which someone can offer and receive that help, of course vary across helping professions. What does not vary, however, is the importance of establishing ourselves as wanting to help and being clear in our own minds about our role and our scope of helping (i.e., professional boundaries). Many students reading this text will have had occasions on which they have sought professional advice of some type. Furthermore, some readers will have themselves experienced varying types of trauma. Based on your own experiences with traumatic events, you have some awareness that withholding trust and being wary of others can be a long-term outcome, and that being willing and able to again trust others can be a slow process that occurs over a prolong period.

Know that depending on the nature of the trauma and a host of other sociocultural variables, a patient may not be readily willing to fully trust you. The necessary precursor to therapeutic trust is a perceived sense of safety. We don't recommend that you say to your patients, "It's really okay – you can trust me!" Some people may be even less inclined to trust you than they would if you'd said nothing; they might wonder why those words had to be stated at all. A far better approach is to demonstrate our trustworthiness through your behavior.

How might we communicate trustworthiness? We show up! "Showing up" extends way beyond keeping scheduled appointments. It means following through on things we say we will do. It means listening with all our attention to what they are expressing, and that we share with them our understanding of their communication, without judgement. Even if your profession is one that is highly circumscribed, such as physical therapy, your clients will be more inclined toward keeping appointments, trusting you, and trying to comply with directions, if they feel that you value them, are striving to truly understand them, and are trustworthy. Treatment outcomes may be positively affected if they perceive a sincere connection with you.

Patient Readiness to Change

A major influence on the helping relationship is a patient's readiness to change their own behavior, where needed. As many readers might agree, some people are inclined to persist in unhealthy behaviors despite their acknowledgement of significant health care risks. Unhealthy behaviors can take the form of lifestyle habits related to nutrition, sleep, stress, etc., and many of those habits can be very difficult for people to change. Since the late 1970s James Prochaska has been a prolific author and contributor to the body of knowledge regarding how to implement empirically based health care strategies. The Transtheoretical Treatment Model (TTM) was first presented in 1979 (Prochaska, 1979), followed by two manuscripts that presented compellingly positive results from a smoking cessation research study implementing TTM strategies (Prochaska & DiClemente, 1982, 1983).

TTM represents a model for guiding positively oriented behavior change based on meta-analyses of treatment outcome research. This framework identifies observable stages of change through which people progress as they strive to make healthier choices. It further provides a structure for providers to use as they develop intervention strategies for the patient. This TTM has been established as an effective approach in numerous additional aspects of health care. Examples include eating healthily and controlling sun exposure as cancer prevention (Prochaska et al., 2004; Prochaska et al., 2005). Most recently, Prochaska and colleagues (Prochaska, Norcross, & Saul, 2020) have proposed application of the TTM in mental health care. Indeed, there are already community mental health centers that use the TTM as the basis for programming among their clients.

Briefly, according to the TTM, the stages of Readiness for Change are as follow:

> **Precontemplation:** People in this stage see no need for change; from their perspective, things in their life are working just fine. Other times, they may non-committally make the self-observation that they "should" change their behavior, yet there is no evidence of any true intent to change their behavior in the foreseeable future. At this stage, there are specific emotional and/or social benefits that are gained by maintaining the problem behavior. For example in smoking cessation, the cigarettes might be offering stress relief as well as social opportunities by gathering outside for conversations and fun with other smokers.
>
> **Contemplation:** In this stage of change, people begin to become more fully aware of the cost or undesirable outcome associated with maintaining the problem behavior. For example, a person who is having discomfort (e.g. chronic painful cough from smoking) might begin to be more inclined to consider behavior change that could eliminate the discomfort.
>
> **Preparation:** In the preparation stage, the patient begins focusing on developing concrete plans for making behavioral changes. Inherent in this process is the client is fully invested in the belief that change

is possible, and has moved to a place of hopefulness that they will accomplish the goal no matter what. The agency (i.e., capability) and pathway (i.e., concrete steps) both become clearer and more tangible to the client during this stage.

Action: Here is the stage where visible behavior change begins to emerge. The counseling techniques at this stage correspondingly should become much more behaviorally focused. Clients also become highly aware of the environments and situations that make a return to old problem behaviors more likely. A plan for how to avoid those situations, and specific steps to take once a person actually finds themselves in a high-risk situation, is imperative. This is referred to as creating a *relapse prevention plan.*

Maintenance: In some ways, maintenance might be the hardest stage of all. The excitement and frequency with which one receives praise/positive reactions from others begins to taper off. The reality of losing the payoffs of the problem behavior might become more apparent, and there may be times when people pine and mourn for the "good times," "back in the day." Successfully remaining at the maintenance stage requires continued commitment and refusal to return to the problem behavior, not giving in to the self-talk of "Oh, it will be okay just this once."

Early in her career, one author (K.M.) worked as a therapist in a community mental health center. Her early training in counseling was cognitive-behavioral in orientation, which is a directive treatment approach. Clients routinely were given homework assignments to collect baseline data related to their targeted problem. Many would return to their second or third appointment with their homework not completed. Some therapists might perceive clients' lack of follow-through to reflect lack of their commitment to counseling. An alternative perspective, though, is that some of the clients who did not follow through were not at a stage of readiness to begin taking action, even if that action was only in the form of recording information about their problem. Patients in earlier stages of change often benefit from Motivational Interviewing (MI), which aims to resolve ambivalence between values and behaviors and increase self-efficacy and potential for change (Miller & Rollnick, 2012).

Typical Stages of the Counseling Process

In addition the client's readiness for change, there are several ways that the stages of the counseling process can be conceptualized. The term *process* can refer either to the interaction and how the relationship unfolds within one particular session, or to the overall progression of counseling throughout the counselor/client involvement. The process in a single session parallels the process that occurs over the long-term working relationship. In both cases, the most simplistic conceptualization would be a three-stage process: warm-up, working, and termination/closing down. We will look first at a single session.

Stages Within a Single Session

Warming-Up

The warm-up is a stage in which both individuals make "small talk" or otherwise ease into the process of communication. "Small talk" refers to a brief and casual conversation. This informal interchange can happen on the walk to the provider's office, either from the waiting room or another space. Examples of small talk might include a comment about the weather, asking your patient if they had any trouble finding your office, or some other benign and impersonal comment or inquiry. The purpose of initiating a brief amount of small talk is to begin the process of connection with low stakes, inconsequential topics that enable them to learn about your communication style and for you to learn a bit about theirs.

We discussed confidentiality in the ethics chapter, and now we touch upon it again. Since the topics and concerns with which people present are so often deeply personal, a perceived sense of safety when making disclosures is critical. Therefore, it is advisable in a first meeting to explain to your patients about your limits of confidentiality, if deemed appropriate given your discipline. People need to know before they begin speaking that you are bound by law to report certain information. Knowledge of the reporting requirements in your state is very important; there is some variability as to the conditions under which you will be required by law to break confidentiality.

Depending on a provider's approach to relationship development, the patient might be solely responsible for determining the process and direction of each session. A completely nondirective counselor might not say anything whatsoever and wait for the patient to initiate a conversation about whatever is on their mind. A slightly more directive yet still person-centered opening question might be, "So what would you like to talk about today?" A provider whose orientation is more directive might jump right into the reported concern and begin inquiry and discussion of the concern. Regardless of their orientation, some providers may work with their patient to come to some agreement about what will be accomplished in the meeting that day. The provider's orientation of directiveness and collaboration influences the emphasis for the session. This practice is referred to in Gestalt counseling as "contracting for a piece of work," meaning that there is explicit discussion about what the patient's goals and hopes are for the session. An example of the benefits of setting an agenda together follows.

Case Example

> A mock "client" in a counseling skills class was role playing a practice counseling session with another student. The "client" said he was seeing the counselor to discuss a problem with his future mother-in-law. He further explained that his fiancée's mother was overly involving herself in the couple's wedding planning. The counseling student spent the entire 20-minute practice session trying to convince the client to solve his problem by telling his fiancée's mother how he felt about her behavior. The "client" finally exclaimed, exasperatedly, that all he really wanted from counseling was to get his feelings off his chest, not to do anything about the problem.

Mismatched expectations can lead to frustration and disengagement that ultimately result in the person not being helped. You may clarify expectations by asking your patient some questions, such as:

- What do you want to work on today?
- What do you think would be the best use of our time?
- What shall we start with?
- What is the most pressing part of this problem for you right now? Would you like to work on that?

The length of time that a provider has with a patient varies greatly by discipline. Providers in some health disciplines may have a brief amount of time, say 20 or 30 minutes at maximum, and will need to have an abbreviated warm up process. In mental health disciplines, a standard session time may be 50 to 60 minutes. Given a 50-minute block of time, about five minutes at the beginning may be spent on small talk, then about 35 to 40 minutes working on the goals that have been set, and then the last five to ten minutes reviewing what was accomplished in the meeting and discussing any directives ("homework"), or outside activities the patient might do before the next counseling session. School counselors may have much briefer periods of time to connect with their students and will likely jump more quickly into the working stage in order to maximize their time together.

Through mindful use of your patient observation skills to be discussed in Chapter 5, during the initial warm-up interchange, you can be assessing the patient's demeanor and their readiness to move toward discussion of the concerns. Observe the nonverbal and paraverbal behavior, and mentally compare that to how the patient appeared on previous occasions as part of your data collection. When patients appear hesitant, reserved, or guarded, then the provider can utilize their helping skills to inquire about how the patient is feeling about discussing the concerns at hand. This attention to the process allows a patient to feel fully seen and acknowledges that discussion of their concerns may be difficult for them.

Working Stage

A variety of things could happen in the working stage. If the contact is the first one or two meetings with the patient, the provider may be mostly actively listening, gathering information, or trying to help the patient articulate and define what their overall goals are going to be. Throughout the working part of the session, your discipline, orientation, and values will influence what you define as "helpful" intervention. Regardless of the nature or style of intervention, the use of basic helping skills will serve as the backbone of the provider's interactions with the patient. Regarding the counseling field, a complete discussion of specific counseling techniques is beyond the scope of our present discussion. For the sake of example, though, the "work" might be focused on gaining insight into unhelpful cognitive and behavioral patterns (i.e., cognitive behavioral therapy), or the focus might be on gaining insight into why someone is having some emotional reactions about a circumstance in their life (i.e. person-centered or existential therapy), or on what the client would need to express or do to gain closure on some unfinished business (i.e., Gestalt therapy).

Termination

There are a variety of ways that providers choose to end a session with a patient. As the allotted time with your patient is drawing near the end, make sure to allow time for you and the patient to review what occurred in the session, if needed. This provides a means of closure and consolidation and also gives you the opportunity to ensure that the patient is sufficiently composed emotionally to go on with their day, if the content of the session was emotionally evocative. One gentle way to initiate the closing process is to make the statement, "Well, (*patient's name*), we have about five minutes left together, so we need to begin winding down." The gradual closing of a meeting with a patient models healthy time boundary setting skills on the part of the provider and allows the provider to maintain their established schedule.

Personal Reflection

What are your feelings about closing a session when a patient is in obvious emotional pain? On a scale of 1 to 10, with 10 being impossible, what rating would you assign to your comfort level with regard to keeping a session to the set time? How does this relate to your definition of what your role is with your patient?

Keep in mind that if your patient is in acute distress or for some other reason is clearly not able to leave yet, you must carefully work with them to gain some composure and emotional control. Some patients will have an event or circumstances that legitimately constitutes an acute state of distress. Other patients, though, may be chronically in crisis or consistently push the time boundary. Differentiating between "state" and "trait" is a skill that you will hone through work experience and good supervision. And, assuming that your patient is not in an acute crisis, consider the following comments. Although it may feel as though you are cutting your patient off, it is important for you to observe the time boundary. The patient may be relieved that you are watching the time, so they don't have to worry about keeping track of the clock. Sometimes people are emotionally capable of focusing on difficult, painful issues only for brief periods of time and will welcome your move toward closure of the session. It also provides a model for your patient of how to set appropriate boundaries with another person.

Another completely pragmatic reason to carefully observe the time is to manage your own work day and stress level. You may be on a tight schedule; if one session extends past the scheduled time by just ten minutes, and you continue to exceed the scheduled time for each session by ten minutes, by the end of the day you could be working at least one extra hour! This will happen occasionally, but it is not advisable on a regular basis; your self-care is also important.

Following your initial statement that time is growing short, it can be quite informative to then ask, "As you think back over our meeting today, what stands out the most?" You may discover that *your* perception of what you said or what had the most impact and your *patient's* perception of those things could be worlds apart. This can be enlightening to you as you discover more about how your patient perceives you and the nature of your interaction with them. The information gained can provide an opportunity for you to clarify or correct any misperceptions your patient may have.

Process Across the Course of Counseling

If we look at the process of counseling over the whole course of treatment, there is a parallel progression of the process that occurs in an individual meeting. The initial stage is the intake and assessment phase during which time a working alliance also needs to be developed, the middle stage is the working phase, and termination occurs when the provider and patient agree that the goals have been achieved and the patient is satisfied with the outcome. Hill (2004) describes these stages as *exploration, insight*, and *action*. Before we look at the important tasks accomplished in each stage of counseling, we need to consider broadly some situational factors that will impact how the working relationship develops.

Referral Source

When a person is self-referred to counseling, we can surmise that they are in some noticeable degree of discomfort with their circumstances. This level of discomfort can sometimes motivate people to make some changes that they otherwise might not. They are seeking your services because they need to do something different, and they may be more open to engaging with you than someone who has been sent to counseling. When a person has been sent to counseling by the court, or family services, or by an unhappy relationship partner who has given an ultimatum to change or else end the relationship, they may be defensive or unwilling to be vulnerable. It is important to acknowledge their reluctance, and to validate that being referred for counseling might be annoying, insulting, or intrusive.

In Crisis or Regularly Scheduled

When a patient is in crisis, the goals, methods and strategies for the session look somewhat different than when someone has a regularly scheduled appointment. Crisis counseling generally occurs when a person's struggles, symptoms, or external situation have resulted in destabilization and inability to use any of their previous coping skills to manage themselves. Initial sessions might vary a lot depending on the provider's theoretical orientation and the setting in which they are seeing the patient. In contrast, regardless of the particular setting or theoretical orientation of the provider, a crisis counseling session with someone needing an emergency appointment may be highly structured with the provider working to quickly establish rapport and lines of communication to gather specific information in a short period of time and establish a short-term plan for stabilization.

Warming Up: Intake, Assessment, and Relationship Development

Each professional specialty and setting will have some standard procedures for conducting an initial meeting with a patient. We will touch upon initial contact here only from the standpoint of process. Concomitantly with gathering objective intake information and information that will help inform an accurate diagnostic impression, establishing a solid working alliance needs to occur in this stage. The following is a case example of what *not* to do.

Case Example

Adara and Cal were a married couple, both in their mid-30s who went to a counselor to get assistance with parenting their adolescent child. Both spouses were second-generation Greek Americans, who strongly identified with their cultural heritage, values, and beliefs. When Adara and Cal went for their first counseling session, the counselor informed Adara that she was excessively focused on taking care of everyone else in the house. The counselor adamantly advised that Adara needed to quit doing that and start worrying more about herself.

The counselor's comments caused extreme discomfort for both Adara and Cal; so much discomfort, in fact, that on the ride home in the car, Cal apologized to Adara for the counselor's behavior, which both Adara and Cal had experienced as an attack. Adara went on to disclose to her friends that she felt completely unheard by the counselor. The couple never returned for help to this or any other counselor, stating that they would handle their problems within the Greek community at their church. Unfortunately, Adara and Cal's counselor never got the feedback that her counseling behavior was inappropriate because Adara and Cal never returned for a second appointment. People don't return for a variety of reasons; sometimes they aren't ready, can't afford it, have transportation problems, or as in the case of Adara and Cal, feel misunderstood by their counselor.

The example of Adara and Cal illustrates how lack of cultural competence and poor timing can undermine the counseling process. The counselor offered advice at the outset of the counseling relationship when the counselor did not know the couple adequately enough to offer guidance. As will be discussed throughout this text, counselors rarely offer such direct guidance, particularly not at the beginning of a counseling relationship. In addition, the counselor failed to consider the cultural context for what typical and healthy parenting behaviors look like within the client's community.

One of the overriding process goals in a first session is to adequately engage the patient so they will want to return to meet with the provider again. Beyond the cultural and contextual factors that influence medical mistrust and reluctance to seek treatment, there are other general factors that have been identified as being barriers to counseling. Vogel, Larsen, & Wester (2007) explored psychological factors that inhibit people seeking help. Awareness of these factors will help a provider address potential resistance and reluctance they might be feeling. The factors identified by Vogel, Wester, and Larsen that inhibit people seeking counselling are:

- Social stigma and fear of negative evaluation by others in their social network
- Fears about what treatment involves
- Fear of having to discuss painful emotions that are more easily avoided or suppressed
- Low expectations as to how helpful it will be (i.e., a low cost-benefit ratio)
- Discomfort with self-disclosure and a preference for privacy

- Social norms regarding how socially acceptable it is to have a therapist
- Self-esteem impact of not being willing to admit one needs help

Be aware that even if your patient voluntarily scheduled an appointment with you, some of the above listed factors may contribute to ambivalent feelings about coming to counseling. It may ease the patient's ambivalence somewhat if you are attuned to these possible reasons for reluctance, and if you validate rather than minimize your patient's concerns about seeking treatment.

Homeostasis

One additional source of resistance or reluctance that is sometimes observed among patients, but not mentioned in the Vogel et al. (2007) study, is *systemic* resistance to counseling. As we learned in Bronfenbrenner's ecological model, patients are embedded in social systems; many of them will be embedded at varying degrees of emotional connection to systems. The concept of *homeostasis,* borrowed from physiology, refers to the process by which an organism regulates its internal environment to maintain a stable, constant condition. When one member of a system makes changes (or the larger systems change), other members of the system must flex to accommodate the new behavior patterns. If a member within a system makes changes that are too big or dramatically different from prior patterns of behavior, other system members may attempt to exert energy to reestablish the earlier balance of the system.

Personal Reflection

Think about the extent to which you have changed since your childhood. If you have changed substantially, do you still have family members or friends who think of you and see you the way you were when you were much younger? If so, how does this affect your interactions with them?

Consider the case example with Adara and Cal presented earlier. Besides the mistake the counselor made in ignoring potential cultural value differences, the counselor ignored the possible ripple effects in the system had they followed her advice. What might have happened in that family system if Adara had, in fact, gone "on strike" and simply stopped grocery shopping, doing the laundry, cleaning, and handling family members' appointments and arrangements? Perhaps the first results would have been family members trying to push Adara back into the role she had formerly been filling. Had that not worked, a family crisis might have ensued until a new, different level of homeostasis could be established by the group.

When you have an individual patient, they may be faced with some degree of systemic resistance to whatever changes they are trying to make.

It might not be to others' advantage, for example, for your patient to become more assertive and vocal about their needs. The patient may consequently experience some amount of negative reaction, or systemic backlash from others in their family or social network, in response to efforts to change. These changes to the functioning of the system might be worth the disruption, however, these should be explored preemptively.

So how can we make sure our new patients want to come back for the next session? First and foremost, knowing that you could potentially make a faux pas or clinical mistake that would impair your relationship with the patient may help you to remember the importance of proceeding respectfully and carefully. Don't mistakenly assume that because you are familiar with the diagnosis of the patient or the life circumstances that you already know how they feel, or what they need to do to address the problem. Look and listen for opportunities to sincerely validate their experiences and give them the sense of being heard by attending, paraphrasing, and reflecting their feelings.

It seems to make intuitive sense that patients who are similar to us on some key variables might feel more comfortable or connected with us. There has been research that supports this supposition (e.g., Towberman, 1992). However, more recent data suggest that there is not necessarily a clear pattern of patient preference regarding similarity to their counselor (Anderson, 2005). Perhaps what is more important than similarity on demographic variables is being a nonjudgmental listener, including giving the person room to talk about aspects of coming to counseling that are hard for them.

Another important consideration that we have been referencing consistently is being culturally responsive. If you have taken the time and responsibility to be culturally informed and intentional about being trauma-informed in your overall approach to the relationship as well as the conversational interactions, you will be demonstrating behaviorally that you are committed to cultivating a respectful and helpful relationship with them. Essentially, the first meetings with a client are an opportunity to set the stage regarding what can be expected from you as the provider, from them as the client, and from the process as a whole. Clients who are naïve (i.e., unfamiliar) with the therapy process, will benefit from brief psychoeducation on what to expect from your time together. Taken together, a new client will hopefully leave a first session with a sense of initial rapport and trust in you as the provider and some hope that their efforts will result in positive outcomes.

Working Phase

The working phase of a counseling relationship accounts for the majority of the time spent together as client and counselor. The working phase aligns with Hill's (2004) conceptualization of the work constituting the client coming to insights about their circumstances. These insights usually stem from the extension of the warming up/exploration phase in which the client shared information about themselves with the counselor. Although the primary intent of the client sharing about themselves during the warming up/exploration phase is to inform the counselor of their life circumstances, many clients begin coming to insights as they speak out loud about things they had never shared with a third party before. Accordingly, the client may begin piecing together insights across several areas of their life which allow for larger insights. A new way of understanding one's life and circumstances can have a host of beneficial outcomes such as feeling validated, making meaning of pain, and having clarity for how to move forward in their life.

The working phase also allows for the cathartic experience of talking about one's difficulties in a validating space. This process can encourage a client to come into emotional contact with thoughts and feelings that they might otherwise avoid, which can strengthen their ability to manage their emotions and provide space for processing them. This increasing clarity and strength can then lead the client to begin making changes in their life to support their well-being. This is the stage that Hill (2004) describes as the action stage. Essentially, a client with new insights is needs to decide how to manage about potential dissonance between their understanding of a problem and their current circumstances. If a client's circumstances (e.g., their behavior, their relationships, their living or work situation, etc.) will worsen or exacerbate, or is responsible for, their issues, then they must decide if they want to initiate a change process. Some change processes are harder than others, especially when a change does not result in immediate benefit. Therapy can be quite useful as a space to process the difficulties of change when the long-term benefits have yet to appear.

The length of time that a client and counselor are in the working stage is influenced by the client's diagnosis and level of functioning, the counselor's theoretical orientation, and the client's goals. The working stage could be as brief as a couple sessions or as long as several years. The achievement of therapy goals and relief of symptoms are indicators that the insight and actions phases are ending and that terminating the therapeutic relationship is the next goal.

Termination

When, and under what circumstances, does a counseling relationship end? Interestingly, despite all the research about counseling process and outcome, there has been very little work done in the area of termination after successful goal attainment, and how clients and counselors come to agreement in that regard. Ideally, counseling ends when the agreed-upon goals have been attained. Jakobsons, Brown, Gordon, & Joiner (2007) identified a small number of studies that have investigated reasons for termination. One notable finding (Todd, Deane, & Bragdon, 2003) arose from a study that used matched pairs of clients and counselors. The authors reported that although 28 percent of the counselors stated that termination was due to the clients' goal attainment, only 14 percent of the clients cited goal attainment as the reason for ending counseling. However, the number of clients reporting that they terminated counseling, owing to dissatisfaction with counseling was quite small (8 percent), whereas the most frequently endorsed reason had to do with external factors. The external factors included the client moving away, financial cost, and schedule conflicts. This is a finding consistent with some of the counseling outcome literature about the degree of influence of extra-therapeutic factors in treatment outcome.

A set of structured, identifiable criteria may be of assistance in deciding when the time has come to end counseling. Jakobsons et al. (2007) offered the following signals as indication that termination is appropriate:

- Decrease of the symptoms with which the person initially presented
- Stable symptoms decrease for at least eight weeks
- Decrease in functional impairment
- Evidence that the client is using new skills, resulting in less frequent or intense symptoms
- Ability to use new skills at times when the person formerly would have been vulnerable to symptom exacerbation
- A sense of pride about new skills (i.e., self-perception of increased self-efficacy)
- Ability to use new skills in areas other than those specifically targeted in therapy

Personal Reflection

What are your thoughts about sharing the credit with your patient when treatment is successful? What are some advantages of your taking credit for the work? What are your own internal needs in that regard?

Terminating with patients who have grown or successfully processed and integrated their pain or other difficulties, can be hugely rewarding. However, we must be humble when a patient attributes their growth to us as the provider. Providing good counseling has some similarity to being a good parent. Some theories of counseling actually do conceptualize counseling as a process of re-parenting, giving patients an opportunity to receive the unconditional regard and guidance they were not fortunate enough to receive in their family of origin. Regardless of whether you think of the counseling process in that way, one of the overriding goals is to teach your patients how to function and cope independently (i.e., without you), the same way parents may teach their children how to function as independent adults. The counselor's intent must be for the patient to develop and hone their skills to successfully navigate life's challenges in a healthy, adaptive way. This statement is made with the acknowledgement that we are not referring to affiliation in the filial sense; we are not trying to move people who are collectivistic toward individualism, only trying to provide them support that we will eventually remove when they are able to cultivate and maintain their own culturally relevant supports in their own systems.

The learning process requires both a teacher and a student. As the counselor, you may offer or guide the learning experiences to facilitate the growth process. Nevertheless, the decision about how to respond to what you have offered rests with your patient. Individual autonomy always guarantees everyone the latitude to make that choice, regardless of whether we have been forced into treatment or come voluntarily. Thus, success in counseling is most accurately seen as largely the result of the *patient* working, not the counselor. When a patient says, "You saved me" or "I couldn't have done it without you," it is more honest to respond with a statement that acknowledges the patient's contribution to the process. One example of a constructive response could be, "The way I see it, I asked you some tough questions and you trusted that your painful search for those answers would help you. *You* chose to rise to the occasion and do the hard part."

Research findings (Weinberger & Rasco, 2007) support the belief that gains made in therapy are most likely to be maintained over the long term if the patient completes counseling with a sense of mastery and self-efficacy. Otherwise, when the person encounters the next set of inevitable life challenges, they may believe themselves to be incapable of coping with those challenges without you, or some other professional helper.

Technology Developments

Bronfenbrenner's Ecological Systems Model denotes the passage of time as the outermost influence on an individual's experiences. This passage of time encapsulates the developmental processes discussed in this chapter thus far such as individual development but also captures sociohistorical context and change. Some of the most pertinent changes that influence an individual at all levels are those associated with technological developments in society. Technological developments have led to obviously positive impacts to the human species, such as medical technology advances that extend the human life and provide humane treatment for illness. Other technological advances have opened up contentious debates about the existential threats posed by algorithmically driven social media. Some of the technological advances are mundane on their face but have increased communication and speed in the health professions, such as the move to electronic health record systems. In addition, the Covid-19 pandemic accelerated some technological advances in healthcare, such as the proliferation of virtual appointments across many disciplines, and a general move toward virtual spaces for meeting and communicating for healthcare professional activities such as continuing education and supervision/consultation.

One set of technology developments in healthcare has been the move toward increasingly timely and comprehensive clinical documentation. Clinical documentation, that is, creating a record of what occurred during an interaction with a patient, is necessary for a variety of reasons (e.g., practical, insurance reimbursement, ethical obligations). Clinical documentation, sometimes referred to as writing notes, charting, or simply, documentation, is a necessary part of being a healthcare professional. Historically, taking notes would occur after the conclusion of a meeting with the patient, aside from some brief notes that may be taken in-session to jog one's memory later. However, because clinical documentation is usually an "unbillable" activity, that is, it won't be reimbursed by a third-party payer, there is a motivation to complete it as quickly as possible. This move has led many healthcare fields and agencies to move toward the practice of concurrent documentation. Concurrent documentation occurs when a healthcare provider completes the documentation during the meeting with the patient.

Concurrent documentation is a difficult task to balance with using basic helping skills as a novice provider. Concurrent document asks the provider to split their attention between a computer and the patient. As we will discuss in the forthcoming chapters, effectively attending to a patient requires focusing almost all of one's attentional capacities on the person in front of you. Developing the ability to provide focus and attention to the patient while also typing and attending to queries within a clinical document is an advanced skill. In one's early training as a healthcare provider, we encourage you to err on the side of focusing on the patient even if it means that some of the documentation may need to be edited or reviewed outside of the session. Although completing comprehensive and accurate documentation is imperative, so is ensuring that the patient feels you are listening and are tracking them. Some providers find ways to engage in concurrent documentation at the outset of the session (e.g., when setting the stage for what the session will focus on) and at the close of the session (e.g., reviewing what transpired in session). This pattern allows the working-phase of the session to be free from technology distractions. Regardless of the documentation practices in your discipline or place of practice, the goal is to ensure that your attention is not pulled in other directions, whether it be because of technology or simply other distracting circumstances (e.g., loud sounds, visual commotion).

Conclusion

Heraclitus, a Greek philosopher, is quoted as saying "Change is the only constant in life." As providers, we must be cognizant of where our patients are at in their larger developmental process, and thus, how it impacts our interactions with them. In addition, as providers we must recognize that our patients are evolving people and are likely to grow and develop during their time in our care, in ways related to our work with them and other realms as well. Lastly, we are undergoing our own development as people and as providers, and this influences the way that we work with our clients. The moment in time in which we interact with our clients is irreplicable; the next time we meet we will be slightly different and so will they, as will the stage of working relationship with them. Some of these changes will have implications for our work with them and others are simply to be observed.

Questions for Class Discussion

1   To what extent is establishing a relationship with a minor client's parents an essential aspect of a good counseling outcome? If you believe that it is important, what are some ideas about how to maintain a minor's trust if they perceive you as being aligned on the parents' side?
2   Can you identify particular ways that your birth order influenced your parents' (or caregivers') expectations for you? How has your perception of their expectations affected the adult you have become?

References

Anderson, J.D. (2005). *Client perception of counselor characteristics* [ProQuest Information & Learning]. In Dissertation Abstracts International Section A: Humanities and Social Sciences (Vol. 66, Issue 2–A, p. 484).
Arnett, J.J. (Ed.). (2016). *The Oxford handbook of emerging adulthood.* Oxford University Press.
Benkert, R., Cuevas, A., Thompson, H.S., Dove-Medows, E., & Knuckles, D. (2019). Ubiquitous yet unclear: A systematic review of medical mistrust. *Behavioral Medicine,* 45(2), 86–101. doi:10.1080/08964289.2019.1588220.
Brill, S. & Kenney, L. (2016). *The transgender teen: A handbook for parents and professionals supporting transgender and non-binary teens.* Jersey City, NJ: Cleis Press.
Bronfenbrenner, U. & Morris, P. A. (2007). The bioecological model of human development. *Handbook of Child Psychology,* 1. doi:10.1002/9780470147658.chpsy0114.
Cleveland Clinic. (2019). Bedwetting (nocturnal enuresis): Diagnosis, tests, management and treatment. https://my.clevelandclinic.org/health/diseases/15075-bedwetting.
D'Augelli, A.R. (1994). Identity development and sexual orientation: Toward a model of lesbian, gay, and bisexual development. In E. J. Trickett, R. J. Watts,

& D. Birman (Eds), *Human diversity: Perspectives on people in context* (pp. 312–333). San Francisco, CA: Jossey-Bass.

Elder Jr., G.H. & Shanahan, M. J. (2007). The life course and human development. *Handbook of Child Psychology*, 665–715. doi:10.1002/9780470147658.chpsy0112.

Felder, F., Davy, L., & Kayess, R. (2022). *Disability law and human rights: Theory and policy (Palgrave studies in disability and international development)* (1st ed.). Palgrave Macmillan.

Felitti, V.J., Anda, R.F., Nordenberg, D., Williamson, D.F., Spitz, A.M., Edwards, V., Koss, M.P., & Marks, J.S. (1998). Relationship of childhood abuse and household dysfunction to many of the leading causes of death in adults: The Adverse Childhood Experiences (ACE) Study. *American Journal of Preventive Medicine*, 14(4), 245–258. doi:10.1016/S0749-3797(98)00017-8.

Ferdman, B.M. & Gallegos, P.I. (2012). Latina and Latino ethnoracial identity orientations. In C. Wijeyesinghe & B.W. Jackson (Eds), *New perspectives on racial identity: A theoretical and practical anthology* (pp. 51–80). New York, NY: New York University Press.

Forber-Pratt, A.J., Lyew, D.A., Mueller, C., & Samples, L.B. (2017). Disability identity development: A systematic review of the literature. *Rehabilitation Psychology*, 62(2), 198–207. doi:10.1037/rep0000134.

Gardiner, H.W. (2001). Culture, context, and development. In *Handbook of Culture and Psychology*, pp. 101–117.

Greenfield, P.M., Keller, H., Fuligni, A., & Maynard, A. (2003). Cultural pathways through universal development. *Annual Review of Psychology*, 54(1), 461–490. https://doi.org/10.1146/annurev.psych.54.101601.145221.

Helms, J.E. (1995). An update of Helms's White and people of color racial identity models. In J.G. Ponterotto, J.M. Casas, L.A. Suzuki, & C.M. Alexander (Eds), *Handbook of multicultural counseling* (pp. 181–191). Thousand Oaks, CA: Sage Publications.

Hill, C.E. (2004). *Helping skills: Facilitating exploration, insight, and action.* American Psychological Association.

Horse, P.G. (2012). Twenty-first century Native American consciousness. In C. Wijeyesinghe & B.W. Jackson (Eds), *New perspectives on racial identity: Integrating emerging frameworks* (2nd ed.) (pp. 108–120). New York, NY: New York University Press.

Huang, C. (2018). How culture influences children's development. *The Conversation.* http://theconversation.com/how-culture-influences-childrensdevelopment-99791.

Jakobsons, L.J., Brown, J.S., Gordon, K.H., & Joiner, T.E. (2007). When are clients ready to terminate? *Cognitive and Behavioral Practice*, 14, 218–230. https://doi.org/10.1016/j.cbpra.2006.09.005.

Keller, H., Borke, J., Lohaus, A., & Dzeaye Yovsi, R. (2011). Developing patterns of parenting in two cultural communities. *International Journal of Behavioral Development*, 35(3), 233–245. doi:10.1177/0165025410380652.

Kim, J. (2012). Asian American identity development theory. In C. Wijeyesinghe & B.W. Jackson (Eds), *New perspectives on racial identity: A theoretical and practical anthology* (pp. 138–160). New York, NY: New York University Press.

Lent, R.W., Brown, S.D., & Hackett, G. (1994). Toward a unifying social cognitive theory of career and academic interest, choice, and performance. *Journal of vocational behavior*, 45(1), 79–122.

Li, J. (2018). The timing of marriage matching (Master's thesis). University of North Carolina. https://doi.org/10.17615/4ac4-e247.

Miller, W.R. & Rollnick, S. (2012). *Motivational interviewing: Helping people change.* The Guilford Press.

Nelson, L.J. & Padilla-Walker, L.M. (2013). Flourishing and floundering in emerging-adult college students. *Emerging Adulthood, 1(1),* 67–78. https://doi.org/10.1177/2167696812470938.

Prochaska, J.O. (1979). *Systems of psychotherapy: A transtheoretical analysis.* Dorsey Press.

Prochaska, J.O. & DiClemente, C.C. (1982). Transtheoretical therapy: Toward a more integrative model of change. *Psychotherapy,* 19(3), 276–288. doi:10.1037/H0088437.

Prochaska, J.O. & DiClemente, C.C. (1983). Stages and processes of self-change of smoking: Toward an integrative model of change. *Journal of Consulting and Clinical Psychology,* 51, 390–395. doi:10.1037/0022–0006X.51.3.390.

Prochaska, J.O., DiClemente, C.C., & Norcross, J.C. (1992). In search of how people change. Applications to addictive behaviors. *American Psychologist,* 47, 1102–1114. doi:10.1037/0003-066X.47.9.1102.

Prochaska, J.O., Norcross, J.C., & Saul, S.F. (2020). Generating Psychotherapy Breakthroughs: Transtheoretical Strategies From Population Health Psychology. *American Psychologist,* 75(7), 996–1010. doi:10.1037/AMP0000568.

Prochaska, J.O., Velicer, W.F., Redding, C., Rossi, J.S., Goldstein, M., DePue, J.,... Plummer, B.A. (2005). Stage-based expert systems to guide a population of primary care patients to quit smoking, eat healthier, prevent skin cancer, and receive regular mammograms. *Preventive Medicine: An International Journal Devoted to Practice and Theory,* 41, 406–416. doi:10.1016/j.ypmed.2004.09.050.

Prochaska, J.O., Velicer, W.F., Rossi, J.S., Redding, C.A., Greene, G.W., Rossi, S.R., Plummer, B.A. (2004). Multiple risk expert systems interventions: Impact of simultaneous stage-matched expert system interventions for smoking, high-fat diet, and sun exposure in a population of parents. *Health Psychology,* 23, 503–516. doi:10.1037/0278-6133.23.5.503.

Renn, K.A. (2008). Research on biracial and multiracial identity development: Overview and synthesis. *New directions for student services,* 2008(123), 13–21. doi:10.1002/ss.282.

Savickas, M.L. (1994). Measuring career development: Current status and future directions. *The Career Development Quarterly,* 43(1), 54–62.

Scabini, E., Marta, E., & Lanz, M. (2006). *Transition to adulthood and family relations: An intergenerational perspective.* Psychology Press.

Spencer, M.B. (2007). Phenomenology and ecological systems theory: Development of diverse groups. *Handbook of Child Psychology.* doi:10.1002/9780470147658.chpsy0115.

Spencer, M.B., Dupree, D., & Hartmann, T. (1997). A phenomenological variant of ecological systems theory (PVEST): A self-organization perspective in context. *Development and Psychopathology,* 9(4), 817–833. doi:10.1017/s0954579497001454.

Super, M.C. & Harkness, S. (2009). The developmental niche of the newborn in rural Kenya. In *The Newborn as a Person: Enabling Healthy Infant Development Worldwide,* pp. 85–97.

Todd, D.M., Deane, F., & Bragdon, R.A. (2003). Client and therapist reasons for termination: A conceptualization and preliminary validation. *Journal of Clinical Psychology, 59*(1), 133–147. https://doi.org/10.1002/jclp.10123.

Towberman, D. B. (1992). Client-counselor similarity and the client's perception of the treatment environment. *Journal of Offender Rehabilitation, 18*(1–2), 159–171. https://doi-org.proxy.ulib.csuohio.edu/10.1300/J076v18n01_07.

Vleioras, G. & Mantziou, A. (2018). Social role transitions and perceived adulthood status: Which ones matter for whom? *Emerging Adulthood, 6*(3), 200–205. https://doi.org/10.1177/2167696817722470.

Vogel, S., Larson, L, & Wester, S. (2007). Avoidance of counseling: Psychological factors that inhibit seeking help. *Journal of Counseling Psychology, 85*(4), 410–422. https://doi.org/10.1002/j.1556-6678.2007.tb00609.x.

Wang, Q. & Wang, Y. (2019). Culture and emotional development: Introduction to the special issue. *Culture and Brain, 7*(2), 95–98. doi:10.1007/s40167-019-00088-9.

Weinberger, J. & Rasco, C. (2007). Empirically supported common factors. In S.G. Stefan & J. Weinberger (Eds), *The art and science of psychotherapy* (pp. 103–129). Routledge.

Worrell, F.C., Cross Jr, W.E., & Vandiver, B.J. (2001). Nigrescence theory: Current status and challenges for the future. *Journal of multicultural counseling and development, 29*(3), 201–213.

Section II

Techniques for Helping

Chapter 5

Helping Behaviors: Nonverbal and Paraverbal Skills

Body language and the way someone speaks provide a great deal of information to supplement the words a person says. As a person in the world, you have probably noticed that the *way* something is said can be more important than *what* is said. Imagine that you see your colleague in the breakroom at work and ask how their day is going, but before responding they pause, take a deep breath, and state "Fine" while crossing their arms and furrowing their brow. You might interpret the nonverbal behavior as over-riding the content of the response and thus, respond to them differently than if they smiled gently, nodded, and said "Fine." Skilled communicators do not have magical mind-reading powers but rather use their observation of nonverbal and paraverbal behavior to guide their responses. Ivey and Ivey (2007) noted that 85 percent of conveyed meaning in a spoken communication is conveyed through non-verbal means, not the words themselves. Learning how to keenly observe the nonverbal and paraverbal behavior of your patients will assist you in responding in empathic ways that are more likely to get to the heart of what they're expressing.

Not only is it important to fully consider the nonverbal and paraverbal behavior of your patients, but it's also equally crucial to monitor and adjust one's own nonverbal and paraverbal behavior in response to the needs of the situation. Let us consider another example, but this time, imagine that you are the patient. Imagine that you are meeting with your primary care doctor for your annual physical exam. Your primary care doctor asks you how you've been feeling lately, and you respond. While you're speaking you notice that your doctor's eyes are partially closed, they glance down at their vibrating smartwatch from time to time, and they have no change in expression when you tell them that you recently fainted during a workout. How might you interpret this provider's behavior? How would this interpretation impact you for the remainder of the appointment? You may assume that the provider is tired, distracted, or disinterested. Although your doctor might respond in a way that is appropriate and logical in response to *what* you said (e.g., ask further

DOI: 10.4324/9781003217589-7

questions, suggest follow-up testing), you may find yourself disappointed with their response overall because of the perception that they were not emotionally present when you discussed your concerns. You might feel dismayed and invisible. You might describe their behavior to someone else as seeming like they "didn't care."

Given that you are learning these skills so that you can be a provider of helping services, then you might wonder how you would have responded if you were the provider in that circumstance. When you were reading the example in the previous paragraph, you may have had empathy for the provider themselves because you considered that they may have had a stressful circumstance in their life that led them to feel tired and distracted, yet they were doing their best to assist the patient despite the situation. Potentially you yourself have been distracted and tired after being up with a sick child for an entire night and still needed to "show up" and be "on" at work the next morning. You might wonder to yourself, what is the right balance of being authentic to your true experience (i.e., being exhausted and worried) and being emotionally attentive to the person in front of you?

We hope to answer that question in this chapter, but first, it is important to note that the goal of adjusting our own nonverbal and paraverbal behaviors is to demonstrate to our patients that we are present and ready to hear them, not to be an inauthentic version of ourselves. The circumstances of our lives can make it difficult to be emotionally present with our patients at times, and yet, there will likely be times that we need to "bracket" our own feelings and thoughts in order to be fully present with our patients. When we learn how to use our bodies and our language in skillful ways, we can both be true to our inner experiences while also being present for the people in front of us.

This chapter will discuss nonverbal and paraverbal behavior with the goal of helping you better observe the behaviors of yourself and others. Part of this process will be learning to self-observe and be curious about your own behavior. The other component of the learning process will be forming tentative hypotheses about the behavior of others and responding in a way that is aligned with the salient emotions the patient is expressing. Sometimes the skill of responding to patients is made more challenging when there is incongruence between *what* is being said and *how* it is being said – these will be times for a gentle balancing act of responses. Before discussing the basics of nonverbal and paraverbal behavior though, let's discuss what it means to "self-monitor."

Self-Monitoring

Self-monitoring refers to the degree to which a person is paying attention to their own behavior in the present moment as well as their ability to change their behavior given the opportunities, norms, and situational demands (American Psychological Association, 2021). Self-monitoring behavior occurs on a spectrum ranging from "high" to "low." High self-monitoring is a degree of self-observation in the present moment. In some cases, this might be described as being "self-conscious," hyper-aware of what we are saying and doing and how it is being received by others in our environment. This can be debilitating at times because it leads a person to be so preoccupied with their own behavior that they cannot pay adequate attention to other circumstances or people.

At the other end of the spectrum, low self-monitoring behavior can be similarly problematic. A low self-monitor is someone who becomes so engrossed in their own experience (feelings and perceptions) of circumstances or people that they fail to notice how their own distracting or unhelpful behavior is impacting their environment.

An ideal level of self-monitoring in professional settings is one that allows for a level of awareness in which one can attentively observe the other person's behaviors and quickly ascertain the needed adjustments to their own behavior while still being primarily focused on the person with whom they are interacting. This will likely prove to be a fairly easy process to master for people who are high self-monitors and might require more intentional perceptual adjustments for people who are low self-monitors.

What is your level of self-monitoring? Review the questions below to reflect and identify your level of self-monitoring.

1. Without looking, what facial expression are you making right now? What allowed you to be aware of your facial expression? What position is your body in and in what ways have you been moving your body while you've been reading? Were you already aware or did you need to direct your attention to how your muscles feel or actually look at yourself?
2. Videorecord yourself having a conversation with a friend or family member (with their permission) either in person or while on the phone. Watch the recording back and take note of your nonverbal behaviors. What patterns were you aware of and what ones were surprising to you and why?
3. Ask someone who knows you well to describe your common body language habits. How much did their observations fit with your self-perception?

Social Stimulus Value

The next concept we'll introduce you to is that of social stimulus value. Social stimulus value refers to observable characteristics about a person that elicit evaluative or stereotypic thoughts (Ford, Miura, & Masters,

1984). The evaluations that we make of another person based on their observable characteristics, such as their hairstyle, clothing, or height, may come from unconsciously held stereotypes. Sometimes these stereotypes work in our favor. For example, when a counselor is wearing a cardigan and naturally holds a soft smile on their face, they may be perceived as caring and compassionate. Other times, the stereotypes that inform someone's evaluations of a person are inaccurate, detrimental, and limiting. For example, when that same therapist is a person with grey hair and a slight stoop in their posture, their new patient may make the inaccurate assumption that this therapist is "too old" to understand their concerns. In the case of this second example, the counselor's stimulus value activated ageist stereotypes that the new patient held that may detrimentally impact the patient's behavior. For example, the new patient may not share the details of an upsetting social media fight they are involved in because the patient inaccurately assumes that the counselor is unfamiliar with social media and the way technology is affecting their life.

Providers cannot control the assumptions and biases that patients hold. However, it can be helpful to be aware of what your stimulus value is because it can help you predict how patients may respond to you when they don't yet have much other information about you or your skill in providing care. For example, if a provider is aware that their resting facial expression might be interpreted as disinterested or bored, they may make effort to put on a gentle smile when first meeting a patient or ensure that their verbal responses convey their interest and care to counteract their resting facial expression. Sometimes visible demographic factors about us can elicit responses from patients that we can proactively address. Consider the example of a masculine presenting, cisgender man who is a healthcare provider in a shelter for people, primarily women, who have experienced domestic violence. This provider may recognize that his gender may be unnerving for some of the women who have experienced domestic violence from a man. This provider may take special care to speak softly, sit in a 'non-provocative' manner (i.e., sitting with legs together, not spread), and avoid quick physical movements. This provider's behavior stems from his self-awareness of his social stimulus value and that simple nonverbal and paraverbal behavior can increase the likelihood that his patients feel at ease in his presence.

At times, the assumptions that a patient may make about a provider based on their stimulus value can actually undermine the competency and integrity of the provider. These are usually assumptions that are made based on stereotypes and biases that patients hold; these may be racist, homoprejudiced, ageist, or classist in nature. As a provider, it can be exhausting to combat these potential biases through monitoring and modifications in one's own behavior. In many cases, it is most appropriate to let your skills as a provider speak for themselves and recognize that you cannot control the initial assumptions that your patients make about you based on your stimulus value. The goal of being aware of one's stimulus value is to identify reasonable shifts that you can make in your nonverbal and paraverbal behavior that feel congruent with who you are and increase the likelihood that a new patient will feel at ease. During these initial interactions with patients, it is important to remember that the goals of the provider are to ensure that patients feel safe and to avoid traumatizing or retraumatizing patients that are often nervous about seeking treatment and seeing a provider.

Personal Reflection

Take a moment to reflect on your social stimulus value as a provider. What assumptions might future patients make about you based on your observable characteristics? How accurate are these assumptions? Do you feel any responsibility to counteract these assumptions with reasonable adjustments to your behavior? Why or why not?

Nonverbal Behavior

Nonverbal behavior is commonly called 'body language.' Body language refers to the ways that people position and move parts of their body, including their facial reactions. At times, our body language is outside of our conscious awareness. Awareness of our body language is usually linked to our degree of self-monitoring. Our body language sometimes conveys a more accurate expression of our emotional state than our words. Consider the interviewee who is smiling and providing thoughtful answers in a job interview while also twirling a pen and rapidly shaking their feet. It is a common emotional experience to feel nervous during a job interview, and while the interviewee likely wouldn't disclose their anxious emotions verbally, their body language may provide a window into their emotional state. When we are in the position of providing health services, it is important to recognize the emotional state of the patient. Intentional observation, and understanding the emotional state of a patient, provides us with valuable information about their functioning and may alter the actions we take with them.

Observing the Nonverbal Behavior of Others

You already arrive at this skill with a degree of pre-existing knowledge from your life experiences up to now. Like other types of language, understanding body language is learned in passive ways via continual exposure to the behavior of others. Nonverbal behavior is also complex and can vary from cultural community to cultural community. The primary goal of learning to observe the nonverbal behavior of others is to sharpen the acuity of our observation and to develop reasonable hypotheses based on the information that we have available to us. The secondary goal is to respond to patients in a way that acknowledges both what they're saying and how they might be feeling.

Facial Expression

The first aspect of nonverbal behavior that we'll discuss is facial expression. Humans often look at faces to make determinations about the motives and disposition of others, and human brains seem to have evolved to pay special attention to faces (Kamps et al. 2020). Facial expressions can vary in both the nature of expression and the intensity. Let's practice: take a moment to position your face as if you just learned of some disappointing information. How does your face look regarding the shape of your mouth, your eyes? Now position your face as if you just learned some mildly pleasant news. Notice the difference in your mouth, eyes, and other parts of your face and how these can signal a change in your emotions. Lastly, position your face as if you just learned of a big, long-awaited announcement of pleasant news. What changed in your face that signaled an increased intensity of emotion? Maybe your smile broadened, or your eyes were open wider, and your eyebrows were raised.

There are common patterns of emotion expression in the face that are considered universal across diverse cultural communities. Ekman and Friesen (1971) identified "universal" emotions that are quickly identifiable in a facial expression, even across diverse combinations of the person expressing the emotion and the person perceiving the emotion. The universal facial expressions are surprise, anger, disgust, fear, happiness, sadness, and contempt. See Figure 5.1 for a visual representation of these common facial expressions. The shape of the mouth, eyes, and forehead combine to create recognizable patterns (Paul Ekman Group, 2022).

Another component of facial behavior is eye contact. Eye contact patterns vary across cultures and as well as within cultures depending on the person and circumstance. Don't draw firm conclusions from someone's eye contact when you have minimal other information to corroborate your assumption. Similar to observing facial expression and body language, there are situational and cultural factors to integrate with observations regarding eye contact. For example, in some cultures, direct eye contact with authority figures is considered disrespectful, whereas other cultures interpret direct eye contact as a sign of confidence. Another example is the common eye contact pattern when the speaker looks elsewhere while speaking and upon finishing their speech, they will reconnect eye contact with the listener, sometimes as a subtle cue that they are finished speaking. Listeners often hold eye contact with the speaker while they are

Helping Behaviors: Nonverbal and Paraverbal Skills   95

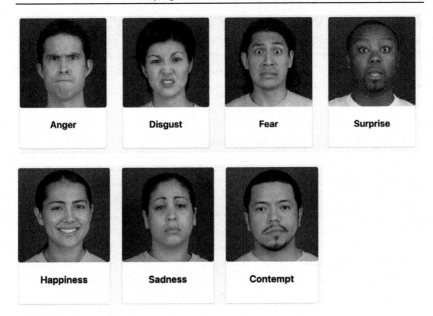

Figure 5.1 Universal Emotions

talking, even if the speaker is looking elsewhere. The goal is to objectively observe the behavior and generate hypotheses that support an explanation that takes into consideration the patient's culture and the circumstance.

Body Position & Movement

When observing body posture, consider the general open or closed nature of their body while sitting or standing. Some body postures are inward facing or closed off, such as hanging one's head, crossing arms, rounding the back, and keeping the body tight. Other body postures are outward facing and open, such as standing holding a straight back, upright head, and a relaxed openness of extremities. It's also important to observe the movements of the body, which can range from total stillness to a variety of gross and fine motor movements, such as wiggling one's feet, picking at one's fingernails, or touching one's hair. Once again, the goal is to objectively observe the body positions and movements and to generate likely hypotheses.

Another observable body movement that's linked to our verbal expression is gesticulation, more commonly called "talking with your hands." Like other nonverbal behaviors, gesturing may be linked to one's cultural upbringing and the norms for communication within one's family and community. Gesticulations can add another layer of information to one's spoken words and should be taken into consideration when listening and observing your patient. Take note when gesticulations provide emphasis, clarity, or express an emotional experience. Observing and acknowledging gesticulations and demonstrating curiosity when their meaning is unclear can demonstrate to your patients that you are fully taking in what they are expressing to you.

Engaging in Helpful Nonverbal Behavior

In addition to observing the nonverbal behavior of your patient, as the provider *you* will need to demonstrate nonverbal behavior that is welcoming and non-distracting. Provider nonverbal behavior should be *open* and *calm*. Open body postures are ones in which arms are at one's sides or gently in their lap, the back is straight, and the head is upright so that patient is easily in the line of sight. The body should be relaxed, not tense, and with minimal distracting movements (e.g., shaking feet, playing with hair, picking at skin, pulling at clothes). Avoid holding any objects that can serve as a distraction, such as pens, mugs, etc., unless they are actively needed in that moment. These open and calm nonverbal behaviors typically communicate to a patient that you are ready to listen and in a calm state.

There are also active behaviors that the provider can engage in that communicate their attention to the patient. Nodding the head and leaning forward are active ways to demonstrate that you are following along as you listen to the patient. Regarding their own facial expression, providers should aim for a neutral, relaxed face that subtly mirrors the expressed emotions of the patient. Mirroring a client's emotions via one's own facial expression should be done with caution though because patients may express conflicting emotions together and the provider must decide which emotion to reflect in their own face. The goal of most interactions between a provider and patient is to have a candid dialogue about the concern at hand, and this usually requires acknowledging emotions that the patient might find unpleasant or uncomfortable. For example, consider the example of a psychotherapy client who is laughing about her difficulties with low self-esteem. The client might be feeling disappointment, frustration, confusion, and rejection and yet she might be conveying a flippant and unaffected attitude with her laughter and smiling. The counselor may convey subtle sadness and disappointment in their own face as an invitation for the client to access those emotions as well, versus bypassing them through smiling and laughing along with the client. When a person's laughter is incongruent with the content of their disclosure, and we laugh with them, we are reinforcing their incongruence. For reasons that will be discussed later in the text, as counselors, it is important for us to model congruence of content and affect for our clients.

Paraverbal Behavior

Paraverbal behaviors, also known as paralinguistics, are the vocal behaviors beyond simply the words themselves. These vocal behaviors include the volume, speed, and pitch/intonation. Volume is in reference to the relative quietness or loudness of speech, which is a function of the forcefulness with which a person talks. Speed refers to the quickness or slowness of speech. Pitch is the highness or lowness of tone, while intonation is the use of changing pitch to convey meaning. In addition, the prosody of the patient's speech can provide information. Prosody refers to the combination of intonation, word stressing, and rhythm of speech. Providing examples of this impact of paraverbal behavior is difficult in this textbook, given the inherent auditory nature of paraverbal behavior. Take a moment to practice with someone by engaging in the following exercise:

1 Select a sentence that could express different meanings dependent on the paraverbal behavior such as, "I'm going to see my mom today for the first time in two years" or "I decided to leave the company."
2 Say the sentence out loud to a partner several times and attempt to convey different emotion meaning each time.
3 Ask your partner to identify what the possible meaning of the statement was and to explicitly identify what paraverbal behaviors supported this view. Then flip roles and do the same for them.
4 Now say the reflective phrase, "You decided to leave the company" as a question. What did you do with your voice that communicated it as a question rather than a statement?

Becoming aware of our own paraverbals as we learn how to counsel is of tremendous value. There are ways to use our voices that can actually deepen, or lighten, the tone of a question in a way that can influence the emotional intensity of an interaction. Then, by directing our focus to the patient, as was referenced at the outset of this chapter, we learn that the way a patient says something provides equally important information. In fact, in a counseling context, the patient's paraverbals convey more personally accurate information than the words they speak. Providers may also find it helpful to acknowledge and focus on the paraverbal behavior of the patient. For example, consider a psychotherapy client stating, "I'm over it. I'm not impacted by the situation anymore," and continuing in a loud, slowed pace, "I'M OVER IT! I'm... not... impacted... by... the... situation... AN-Y-MORE!" The counselor would likely hypothesize there is potential anger, exasperation, and an observed, apparent contradiction between what the client is saying (the content) and how they're saying it (the affect). In a moment like this, the therapist would be advised to acknowledge the emotional valence of the client's expression as a means of demonstrating that they hear the intensity and importance of what the client is conveying. The therapist may say "I hear the exasperation in your voice when you said that just now." Once again, acknowledging the emotional aspect of the client's expression provides permission for the client to further experience and acknowledge this emotion themselves.

Similar to nonverbal behavior, providers should be cautious about drawing firm conclusions about the meaning of patient paraverbal behavior until they have sufficient information about that person's context. Some commonly observed paraverbal patterns that have been seen by the authors include: lowering the volume of one's voice when discussing a topic that feels secretive, shameful, or embarrassing; speaking softly while disclosing a feeling of rage, talking at a fast pace when feeling anxious or avoidant; engaging in a prosody that conveys silliness or lightness when avoiding a serious or distressing topic; and raising voice volume when angry. It's also important to recognize that people have a range of paraverbal behaviors and may default to being quieter or louder, faster or slower, higher or lower pitched, and intensity or flatness in their intonation. Getting to know patients over time will assist a provider in understanding what is typical of a patient and what changes are noteworthy. Also, depending on the nature of your work as healthcare provider, the nonverbal and paraverbal behavior of the patient may be of varying importance to your work with them. There is almost always benefit in acknowledging nonverbal and paraverbal behavior, and in some healthcare professions, such as mental healthcare, deeper exploration of nonverbal and paraverbal behavior is warranted.

Cultural Considerations

You learned about medical mistrust in a previous chapter. As a reminder, medical mistrust is lack of trust for healthcare providers and their organizations regarding their capacity to provide honest, competent, and benevolent care (The Commonwealth Fund, 2021). Medical mistrust is experienced by many individuals; it is perhaps most often seen among groups of people with diverse identities, who have been deceived and violated in years past, and sometimes still today. People with certain cultural identities have experienced healthcare providers and systems as discriminatory, unhelpful, dangerous, and/or uninformed. Medical mistrust may manifest in a client's verbal and paraverbal behavior. Take a moment to consider what body language could convey distrust, apprehension, and/or fatigue. Maybe you picture this person with closed body language or a stern look on their face. They may convey minimal emotions in their face and paraverbals, also known as flat affect. Withholding the expression of some emotions and prioritizing the expression of distrust can convey to a provider that the patient is guarding their emotional vulnerability until they believe they can trust the provider. Acknowledging unspoken emotions, such as those conveyed via the body and how words are spoken, can strengthen rapport between patient and provider when other dynamics may be present, such as medical mistrust. When a person verbalizes distrust or anger outwardly, it will help the relationship if the provider can acknowledge those feelings without trying to convince them otherwise. By allowing space for their feelings and acknowledging their validity, the provider demonstrates trustworthiness, which facilitates building a foundation of credibility and trust. It is important to remember that a provider's individual behavior is unlikely to eliminate a patient's medical mistrust. The goal rather, is to develop the greatest degree of authenticity and rapport possible in this particular patient-provider relationship.

Consider the exchange below and how the provider uses observation, acknowledgement, and curiosity of patient nonverbal and paraverbal behavior to strengthen their rapport.

Scenario

An African American woman in her late-40s seeks mental health counseling for symptoms of depression for the first time. The provider is a White man in his mid-20s, and this exchange occurs about 30 minutes into their first session together.

PROVIDER: So... one topic we haven't discussed yet is suicidal ideation, I know you've been talking about feeling depressed and it's quite normal for people to have thoughts of suicide when they're feeling this way. Have you been having any thoughts of suicide?
PATIENT: Oh, no. Not at all. [*Patient affect is flat.*]
PROVIDER: Okay, no thoughts of suicide recently. What about in the past?
PATIENT: No, nope. [*Patient affect remains flat. Patient does not elaborate although they have elaborated on other all topics earlier in this session.*]
PROVIDER: Okay yeah, so it sounds like you haven't had any thoughts of suicide recently or in the past.
PATIENT: [*Patient nods, holds a neutral face and sits stiffly in her chair.*]

... 15 seconds pass...

PROVIDER: You know, sometimes people can feel apprehensive about talking about suicide because they're worried about how the therapist will react. Um, I wonder if that's something that might be happening for you. I say this because you've been pretty forthcoming in the session so far, but I noticed that you didn't elaborate much on what you just shared and that your body stiffened up a bit. I don't want you to feel like you're under the microscope here, but I wanted to acknowledge that this topic can be hard to discuss when you've just met someone and you're not too sure about them yet.

PATIENT: Hmph, yeah, I can see that. [*Smiles very slightly.*]

PROVIDER: I know we just met and you don't know me well yet, but I wonder if you're feeling any apprehension about any of the topics we've discussed so far today?

PATIENT: Well, this is my first experience in therapy and I've heard some nightmare stories from friends. And to be fully honest, I was hoping to have a therapist who was closer in age to me or similar in other ways.

PROVIDER: Thank you for sharing that with me. I really appreciate your honesty. That makes a lot of sense, it sounds like you're worried that this counseling session could go poorly and that maybe if I was more similar to you, maybe in race or age [*slight upspeak to indicate a question*], then maybe there would be less likelihood that I could misunderstand you?

PATIENT: Yeah, yeah, that's about right. [*Slight smile, shoulders relax.*]

PROVIDER: Could you tell me a little more about what you worry could happen if I were to misunderstand you?

PATIENT: I'm not sure exactly, I guess. Um, I mean, I just don't want to be locked up for being seen as *crazy*. I don't have any idea about what you're used to hearing from people or what you're familiar with.

In the exchange above, the patient and provider navigated a delicate acknowledgement of the patient's apprehension to elaborate on the topic of suicide. The provider observed some paraverbal and nonverbal cues (e.g., tense shoulders, flat affect, and no elaboration) and acknowledged his observation of these to the patient. He also posited a hypothesis for why this might be occurring that was sufficiently broad to capture a variety of reasons why a client might become less open. He attempted to demonstrate curiosity to understand what was happening for the patient in that moment instead of bypassing the observation altogether or by making overly confident assumptions about her behavior. The patient was willing to acknowledge her apprehension and disclose a bit more about the reason behind her apprehension in that moment. They will eventually circle back around to the topic at hand, with the patient providing more depth to her answer, but the meta-conversation, that is "talking about talking about it" provided some assurance for the patient that this provider is observant and curious.

There are other culturally based reasons why a patient may demonstrate nonverbal and paraverbal behavior that is noteworthy to you. Once again, the first step is to make a non-judgmental and unassuming observation in your mind (i.e., "The client is speaking in a loud volume and with a frown and narrowed eyes"). A foundational understanding of other cultures can help you generate possible explanations for patient nonverbal and paraverbal behavior that are culturally informed and non-pathologizing. Explanations for paraverbal and nonverbal behavior often reflect culturally appropriate behaviors when speaking with an authority figure, when talking about sensitive topics, or when in need of help.

Provider Paraverbal Behavior

Attunement to the patient's paraverbal behavior will provide you with valuable information about how they feel about the topic they are discussing. The patient will also be noticing, consciously or unconsciously, *your* paraverbal behavior as the provider. Once again, the general goal of the provider is to demonstrate warmth, empathy, and understanding via their behavior. We have discussed how nonverbal behavior, such as a calm and open body posture, can set a strong foundation for demonstrating your attention and attunement to the patient. Now we will discuss how providers can make effective use of their voice.

Providers will want to attend to all the aspects of paraverbal behavior that were just discussed in relation to the patient: volume, speed, pitch/intonation, and prosody. Once again, it's important to highlight, all providers will have their own unique voice that reflects their personality and upbringing. The goal is not for all providers to have a universal voice but rather to tweak and adjust their own voice to be most effective for the clinical circumstance at hand. The baseline expectations are for the providers voice to be loud enough to be heard, slow enough to be understood, and using prosody and intonation pattern that highlights what is most important. Take a moment to consider your own paraverbal patterns: are you a loud or quiet talker? Are you a rapid or slow talker? Do you have prosody patterns that could obscure your meaning or confuse the listener, such as trailing off quietly at the end of sentence or conveying incongruent emotions? If you observe that you might be at the extreme end of one of these spectrums, then you'll need to consistently attend to your paraverbal patterns so that you can modify your paraverbals in the moment (e.g., increasing your volume, slowing your pace).

Now that you've considered your default paraverbal behavior, you'll need to consider how to adapt your paraverbal behavior in response to what and how the patient is saying verbally and nonverbally. One guideline is to try to mirror the patient's paraverbal and nonverbal behavior to some extent as a means of demonstrating emotional tracking. This means that if the patient is smiling gently and speaking slowly and softly as they reminisce on happy memories of a deceased loved one, you as the provider would also smile gently and speak in a slow, soft tone. When a patient is talking about a frustrating work experience and is grimacing and speaking loudly, you as the provider may also convey some frustration on your face and use intonation that emphasizes words that convey your understanding of their frustration. These subtle behaviors as the provider may come naturally for you, and the best way to examine your ability to mirror a patient is to watch videorecorded interactions with real or mock patients and to observe the alignment and impact of your behavior. Observe times when you expressed an incongruent emotion compared to what the patient was expressing and take time to explore what your motivations were in that moment.

There are circumstances when mirroring the patient's paraverbal and nonverbal behavior is counter-indicated. One of our first recommendations is that when a patient is expressing incongruence between what they're saying and how they're saying it, you must consider what emotion you want to convey back to them and why. For example, the first author was once providing psychotherapy to a client and the client was laughing and using a light-hearted prosody as he discussed a tragic circumstance regarding his father. The first author observed the dichotomy in expressed emotions: verbal content that conveyed sadness and fear and nonverbal/paraverbal expression that expressed silliness and humor. Given that this was a psychotherapy session, and the goal was to assist the client in connecting to his authentic emotional experience, the first author held a somber look on her face with a slight smile that acknowledged the client's pain and attempts to laugh at the painful experience. When it was the first author's chance to speak, she did not laugh and instead used a quiet and slow tone and volume that matched the content of what the client was expressing. These nonverbal and paraverbal behaviors conveyed a message to the client that "I see you laughing at this circumstance and yet I hear that this is actually deeply upsetting." If the first author had chosen to "joke along" and mirror the incongruent emotions then there was potential for the deeper emotional experienced to be bypassed, thus, not meeting the goals of the psychotherapy session.

There will also be times in which the opposite circumstance plays out: the patient is expressing a lighthearted sentiment in their words whereas their nonverbal and paraverbal suggests an incongruent emotional experience. Consider the example at the beginning of this chapter in which a coworker curtly stated they were "fine" with furrowed brow and crossed arms. The incongruence in the verbal content with their paraverbal and nonverbal behavior suggests that they may not actually be "fine" and that they likely are having a different emotion experience than "doing fine" would suggest. In this moment, assuming you have the time and capacity, you might respond with a look of concern on your face and state the word "fine?" back but with so-called upspeak at the end, that is, when the pitch is raised to imply a question. The use of these nonverbal and paraverbal behaviors demonstrate that you understand that even though they said they're fine, that there is greater complexity that they haven't elaborated upon and that you are curious to better understand their circumstance.

In essence, you can see that the content of speech does not always align with the nonverbal and paraverbal behavior and this can obscure the person's authentic emotional experience. Most health professionals need to respond to the authentic emotional experience to be an effective helper. The home hospice nurse needs to respond to the confusion and apprehension in a caregiver's face after they claimed they understood the complex medical instructions given to them to care for their loved one. The medical sonographer needs to acknowledge the trembling and fear in the voice of their patient as they ask if they have any concerns or questions, and they respond "no." The physical therapist needs to acknowledge the sarcasm and dismay in the voice of their patient who said that their at-home physical therapy practice was going "just fine." Recognition, acknowledgement, and exploration of these in-congruences allows for a deeper level of interaction. Although the provider cannot always solve the problem at hand with the patient, they can join the patient in empathic understanding which allows the patient to feel less alone in their struggle. This can potentially result in a better response to treatment and thus, improved conditions for the patient.

Attending Behavior in the Real World

Nonverbal and paraverbal behaviors are often called attending behavior because they convey attention and active listening. Conveying strong attending behavior is easiest when we're in an environment that is free of distractions. However, the environments and circumstances of where we practice do not always afford us with calm, quiet, and the ability to focus only on the patient in front of us. In the real world, we might be in a noisy environment or one where people or circumstances are competing for our attention. Whenever possible, make the necessary modifications to ensure the ability for both you and the patient to focus on the task at hand. This might involve white noise machines, silencing all electronics, and creating a space that is private, warm, and welcoming.

Concurrent Documentation

Sometimes there are distractions that are unavoidable, such as the practice of "concurrent" or "collaborative" documentation. This is the practice in which the provider engages in clinical note writing on a computer while in the presence of the patient. The best practice is to inform the patient the first time you meet that this is a required part of your practice so that you can mitigate any misperception that you are using the computer for other reasons. As much as is possible, the provider should maintain eye contact with the patient and orient their body toward the patient. This is especially important in the first minutes of an initial meeting with a patient. Patients are "sizing up" providers based on *what* they say and *how* they respond to the patient, and it is important to make a good first impression that conveys your capacity to attend to them. Using strong attending behaviors such as nodding, eye contact, and mirroring client emotions in one's face can counteract the inherent distraction of typing while the patient is speaking. Be aware that there are circumstances when you should stop typing and give one hundred percent of your attention to the patient, such as when a patient is emotionally upset or is disclosing sensitive information. The most important thing is that the patient feels seen and understood; the documentation can get done later.

Concurrent documentation can potentially be especially obstructive in a counseling relationship if the therapist is using a laptop that obscures their upper body or part of their face. If at all possible, we recommend situating the technology such that the direct space between the patient and provider contains no physical barriers. Some medical offices have chairs that spin and the helper can turn toward the patient to speak, then turn back to their screen and keyboard to enter information.

Some providers enlist their patients to be engaged with them in the final moments of their time together to complete the documentation together. A provider might use their summarization skills, discussed in a future chapter, and say something like, "How about we summarize what we discussed together and see if we're on the same page so I can put that into my notes here." Briefly enlisting the patient's help in the documentation process can provide greater amounts of time where the provider is not using the computer at all.

Provider Emotional State

Another "real world" factor that impacts provider attending behavior is the provider's emotional state. The example at the beginning of the chapter highlighted the difficulty of a provider who was physically tired and emotionally distracted while also attempting to attend to their patient's needs. The role of a health care provider can require the so-called "bracketing" of emotions so the provider can focus on the needs of the patient. Regulating one's own emotional state takes practice and will serve you well in your career as a healthcare provider. Readers who perceive that their ability to regulate their emotions is lacking may appreciate further reading on Marsha Linehan's work from Dialectical Behavior Therapy, specifically on the topic of emotion regulation. Learning simple and accessible behaviors to regulate one's emotion can prepare providers to the fast-paced world of healthcare that involves alternating between various patients' needs and one's own life circumstances. As a reminder, the goal is not to be entirely disingenuous to ourselves, but it is to find a window of helpful attending behavior that overlaps with one's true emotional experience. Occasionally there will be a time in which our own emotion state is so intense that we cannot function effectively in our role as a provider. These are times when we must understand our limits and step away from our work, whether it be for a day or longer, to serve our patient's needs.

One other observation related to provider emotional state is that our ability to bracket is directly related to our own overall ability to maintain our self-care. When we allow ourselves to become sleep-deprived, overly hungry, or in some other highly distracted state, it becomes more difficult to bracket our own feelings. The inability to bracket can result in reactions to clients, some of which may be completely visible to them, and thus impact the relationship in a negative way.

Conclusion

Provider nonverbal and paraverbal behaviors have a profound ability to amplify our empathic words or undermine our efforts. Learning how to balance self-monitoring with focus on the patient will allow you to make necessary adjustments so that the patient feels understood and cared for. Monitoring and adjusting our own behavior will be "autopilot" behavior on our good days and may take a fair amount of effort on difficult days or in difficult circumstances. As providers, we will also be observing the paraverbal and nonverbal behavior of our patients so that we can fully understand their circumstances and act accordingly. Once again, the goal is to make objective observations in our mind and withhold making any definitive conclusions about the meaning of our observations until we have sufficient evidence. Withholding immediate firm conclusions allows us to consider a variety of explanations and interrogate our own thinking for potential bias or assumptions. In addition, as we get to know our patient's history, their salient cultural identities, and their current circumstances, then we can formulate a holistic understanding of their nonverbal and paraverbal behavior.

References

American Psychological Association. (2021, December 27). Self-monitoring. https://dictionary.apa.org/self-monitoring.

Ekman, P. & Friesen, W.V. (1971). Constants across cultures in the face and emotion. *Journal of Personality and Social Psychology*, 17, 124–129.

Ford, M., Mirua, I., & Masters, J. (1984). Effect of social stimulus value on academic achievement and social competence: A reconsideration of children's first-name characteristics. *Journal of Educational Psychology*, 76(6), 1149–1158. https://doi.org/10.1037/0022-0663.76.6.1149.

Ivey, A.E. & Ivey, M.B. (2007). *Intentional inter- viewing and counseling: Facilitating client development in a multicultural society* (6th ed.). Belmont, CA: Thomson Higher Education.

Kamps, F.S., Hendrix, C.L., Brennan, P.A., & Dilks, D.D. (2020). Connectivity at the origins of domain specificity in the cortical face and place networks. *Proceedings of the National Academy of Sciences*, 117(11), 6163–6169. doi:10.1073/pnas.1911359117.

Paul Ekman Group. (2022). Universal Emotions. www.paulekman.com/universal-emotions.

The Commonwealth Fund. (2021, January 14). Understanding and ameliorating medical mistrust among black Americans. The Commonwealth Fund. www.commonwealthfund.org/publications/newsletter-article/2021/jan/medical-mistrust-among-black-americans.

Chapter 6

Helping Behaviors: Verbal Skills to Encourage

This next set of microskills are grouped together because of their common impact: the ability to encourage a patient to speak more. There might be several so-called "sources of data" that help you understand your patient (e. g., test results, forms they have completed, clinical documents from other providers), but you will likely rely heavily on patient self-disclosure, that is, listening to the patient speak. For some of the providers reading this text, say those working as counselors and social workers, they may almost fully rely on patient self-disclosure (or self-report) to understand their patients. And although a superficial coincidence, *listen* and *silent* contain the same letters. Therefore, the skills you will learn in this chapter will help you yield space and time for your patient to express themselves and for you to convey your understanding of what they have said.

Influences on Patient Self-Disclosure: Lifespan, Context, and Culture

A first element to consider is the incredibly wide variation you will see regarding the depth and breadth of self-disclosure across patients. Patient self-disclosure is influenced by a multitude of factors; we will highlight those related to lifespan, context, and culture. The stage of a person's *lifespan* can greatly influence how much and what they will, or can, share with a provider. For most children, progression through the childhood years increases their capacity to communicate with others; therefore it is entirely expected that younger children usually need accompaniment from an adult caregiver to facilitate and support their communication with a provider. On one end of the lifespan spectrum, infants, toddlers, and those in early childhood either cannot yet verbally communicate or are "unreliable historians" – clinical jargon for acknowledging that a patient may have low credibility in their self-report. Children in the middle stages of childhood and adolescence have improved capacity to communicate and self-report accurately; however, they may still be unfamiliar with the depth of sharing that is necessary for different healthcare contexts, so they

DOI: 10.4324/9781003217589-8

may need some provider guidance on what and how much to share. Adults, across the lifespan, have wide variability in their patterns of self-disclosure — other factors such as context and culture are likely to influence how and what they share with their providers. At the other end of the lifespan spectrum, among elders, there will be a great deal of variability between individuals in how accurately and articulately they are able to recount health information or other case-related information with a health care provider.

Personal Reflection

What messages were you given in your family of origin about being forthcoming with information to people both within, and outside of, your immediate family? Were those messages or rules overtly communicated to you, or were they implied through other behaviors from the adults in the house?

The *context* of the helping relationship sets the stage for the purpose of the interaction and therefore what is expected from each person involved. For example, some helping relationships may feel transactional in nature to one or both parties, and therefore the provider may expect minimal self-disclosure from the patient. However, the patient still may seek connection and rapport with their provider if they perceive that it is welcomed. For example, a medical sonographer might see some patients in their day who remain mostly silent during an appointment and do not elaborate beyond what is asked of them. These reserved patients may perceive that the most important information to the sonographer comes from diagnostic imaging technology that they use during the appointment. Other patients, however, may share a great deal more and will expect empathy from the provider. Consider a woman with a high-risk pregnancy and has frequent appointments with the medical sonographer. She might freely share her thoughts, questions, and emotions with the sonographer if she perceives that the provider is empathic, understanding, and welcomes the opportunity to connect. Other contexts implicitly require extensive self-disclosure from a patient, such as mental health counseling. Most patients who arrive for a first therapy session will assume (accurately) that they will be talking much, if not most, of the time. As providers, we might have our own expectations for the degree of sharing needed from the patient; however, it is important to remember that patients will vary in their desire to share openly and their view of the necessity of sharing. Occasionally, the provider needs to encourage more sharing from the patient, either implicitly via the skills in this chapter or by explicitly making them aware that their thoughts and feelings are important to their care.

Regarding *culture*, in previous chapters we have discussed how one's cultural and social identities may shape their values and perspectives related to communication. A variety of communication behaviors are impacted by culture, such as the pace/direction and the overtness of verbal communication. The balancing of the implicit and nonverbal versus the explicit in communication is known as the high/low-context continuum. High-context (HC) communication prioritizes implicit and nonverbal communication, whereas low-context (LC) places primary emphasis on direct, unambiguous verbal communication. LC communication values explicit and detailed communication that is relevant and accurate. LC communication will be lengthier than HC communication because everything that is important must be shared verbally. In contrast, HC communication may include intentional ambiguity that relies on the listener to infer the speaker's true meaning. HC communication may be briefer because other important information is being conveyed simultaneously via nonverbal behavior. This HC communication pattern allows for maintaining harmony within a group by giving the speaker the opportunity to convey information while also subtly sharing their true emotions, without overtly stating this in their verbal communication (McKay-Semmler, 2017). One style of communication is not inherently "better" than the other but rather, the two polarities of style reflect expected variation across cultures and people. As healthcare providers it is usually helpful to adapt to our patient's style of communication, which may require under- or over-emphasizing nonverbal and implicit communication, depending on our own existing communication style.

Cultures also vary in their perspective on time and the influence of time on communication. Trompenaars and Hampden-Turner (1997) proposed that some cultures are *sequential* and others are *synchronic* in their understanding of time. Sequential cultures may view time as a commodity and time as linear. Communication in sequential cultures may value punctuality, efficiency, and speed in communication. Synchronic cultures may view time as subjective, interchangeable, and interconnected to the past and future. Communication in synchronic cultures may value loose time limits for conversation, focus on multiple topics at once, and simultaneous focus on past, present, and future (Macduff, 2006). These cultural differences in time conception, and therefore communication, will influence the amount, style, and nature of patient disclosure. Providers, often working within Eurocentric frameworks of time that are sequential in nature, need to recognize that free-flowing communication styles emanating from synchronic cultures is not a "waste of provider time" but rather the patient expressing themselves in alignment with their understanding and valuing of time. In order to be culturally responsive, a provider must be able to recognize and join with their patient in these varying styles of information sharing.

The Impact of Being Understood

Using the skills in this chapter will have varying effects on your patients. At a foundational level, these skills intend to give patients the space and time to discuss what is important to them. Patients will feel valued and recognized as experts on themselves and their experiences. Providers can use these skills to show that they are "tracking" a patient, that is, they are comprehending the unfolding narrative the patient is providing. The impact of this tracking is that the patient will continue their sharing. Another impact of these skills is the opportunity to closely understand what a patient is expressing, which allows for feelings of validation. When patients feel valued and validated, they are more likely to continue sharing because the provider is implicitly communicating, "I understand what you're saying and want to know more."

Take a moment to consider the behaviors that detract from your own sharing when in conversation with others. At a basic level, if someone's non-verbal behaviors indicate distraction, then you might reduce or lessen your sharing because you perceive they are not paying attention. If someone isn't allowing you to speak because they are dominating the conversation and not allowing for silence, then it might be nearly impossible to share yourself even if you hoped to. When they do leave space for you to speak, however, you may not want to share because you perceive that they are simply awaiting their turn to talk again and are not interested in what you have to say. Other detractors could include someone who is unable to understand or follow along with your sharing. Consider the extreme example of trying to communicate with someone who is intoxicated: they simply cannot "track" the conversation and you may therefore stop sharing altogether as you recognize they cannot understand you adequately.

The skills in this chapter are simple in nature and yet have a powerful impact. Let's explore the first skill: silence.

Silence

Labeling silence as a skill might seem counterintuitive, you might wonder how can "not talking" possibly be a skill? Let's reconceptualize silence from "not talking" to "listening and waiting." Simply put, patients cannot speak if they are not given silence. Patients, indeed, everyone, have a personal preference for the degree of silence they desire in conversation. As the providers, however, we need to provide a baseline level of silence that allows for patients to speak, even if we prefer less silence in our lives outside of professional communication.

Personal Reflection

What are your feelings about silence when you're alone? When you're with just one other person? When you're in a group setting? When do you find the silence most comfortable and the least comfortable? How might these personal preferences impact your behavior as a provider?

Preferences for the amount of silence in conversation can also be culturally influenced. Hofstede (2001) identified that cultures vary in their tolerance of *uncertainty avoidance*. Cultures high in uncertainty avoidance may prefer less silence because silence can produce ambiguity (e.g., "Should I say something?" "What do they want me to do right now?"). Cultures low in uncertainty avoidance may feel more comfort with silence because they can tolerate, and indeed welcome, the ambiguity that silence can provide. Once again, you likely have your own preferences for silence that may or may not be culturally linked; we are not asking you to become a different person but rather to expand your awareness of preference and possibly to increase your level of comfort with silence, so you can allow for an acceptable minimum level of silence when interacting with patients. This is very likely to have a positive impact on your level of professional effectiveness.

Types of and Times for Silence

Times for Silence

Silence occurs at predictable times within the interactions between patients and their providers. The two main types of silence occur: 1) after a provider speaks/before the patient speaks; and 2) after a patient speaks/before the provider speaks. Let's discuss the first opportunity for silence: when the provider is done speaking. Providers may have asked their patient a question or prompted them to speak on a topic. Although it may seem obvious that the provider should then remain in silence and yield space, it is not uncommon for novice providers to interrupt their own silence. Sometimes the provider thinks their question was confusing and begins to rephrase the question. Other times the provider begins to offer thoughts on how the patient might respond to the question. This inclination to fill the silence with additional queries or conversation could occur if the provider is feeling time pressure to gather information and move on. Nevertheless, filling silence immediately, rather than allowing conversational space, is usually unhelpful because it takes away valuable time for the patient to think and respond themselves. It can help to carefully observe the client's non-verbal behavior during their silence; there may be some behavioral indicators that the person is deeply engaged in self-reflection, or perhaps that they are struggling to put their feelings or thoughts into words. Some people require more time than others to readily self-identify their emotional experience, or to decide how they wish to respond to what was just said to them. If the question a provider asks is truly incomprehensible, then the provider can wait for the patient to seek clarification.

The second opportunity for silence is when a patient appears to be done speaking. We say "appear" because oftentimes if the provider allows for a bit more silence after the patient has concluded, the patient will begin talking again. This doesn't mean that providers need to leave an uncomfortable amount of silence before they speak but rather, allow for enough silence that the speaker can say more if they wish and keep the conversation at a non-hurried pace. Some providers believe that they must respond immediately after a patient finishes speaking as a means of showing their attentiveness. In social conversations, recent research has suggested that rapid responding to one another increases the perceived sense of connection to the other person (Templeton, Chang, Reynolds, Cone LeBeaumont, & Wheatley, 2022). However, in a professional helping context, a provider's rapid response to the patient may contribute to a rushed pace to the conversation. A common non-verbal behavior is that people break eye contact when speaking (sometimes looking at something else in the room or out a window) and reconnect eye contact with the listener when they have finished speaking. This reconnection of eye contact from the speaker is a subtle signal that the speaker is done and is giving the listener permission to speak. Once you're aware of this common pattern, you can better gauge when the patient is "done" speaking. The provider can still allow for a bit more (i.e., a few seconds) of silence before responding, once again, as an opportunity to slow the pace of conversation and allow the patient to say more if they wish.

An additional reason to allow space after your client is done talking is to give yourself a moment to carefully choose your next words. In a professional counseling interaction, we generally want our client to have more "airtime" than we are taking, and so deciding how to communicate our thoughts before we begin speaking can also increase our effectiveness. When we "think out loud," meaning we talk before we have fully gathered our thoughts about our response, we may take a lengthy amount of time speaking to express something we could have said in one sentence if we had given ourselves a moment to decide what we wish to communicate. One option is to disclose that you want a moment to reflect so the other person realizes you are pondering what they expressed.

Types of Silence

As you can see, we want to encourage you to use silence more liberally than you might currently utilize it. This does not mean though that all protracted silences are helpful in communication with patients though. Consider thinking about silences as "productive" or "unproductive." Productive silences allow for either person to think more deeply and therefore share more accurately and thoughtfully. Productive silences can allow for someone to come to insights or make sense of complex information. Productive silences can allow for a patient to feel and acknowledge emotions.

Unproductive silences are unneeded silences. There is no purpose in their use because there isn't a deeper thought to consider, or emotions to acknowledge. A provider may not know what to say in response to a patient, so they don't say anything at all. This can lead to an awkward moment in which the patient is literally looking at the provider, awaiting their response, and the provider is silent. Essentially, these silences occur when there is a misperception, usually on the behalf of the provider, about the amount of silence that a patient needs. So how can we know when it is, or is not, useful to break a silence? The best information will be carefully observing their nonverbal behavior. Besides having re-established eye contact as they finish speaking, other indications that a patient is done speaking and are looking at the provider expecting them to break the silence can include fidgeting, shifting their seating position, and subtle smiling and eye contact. Sometimes a silence may be *unwanted* by the patient, but productive nonetheless. An example of this could be having been asked a question that is difficult to answer, or because they are intentionally withholding some information. As you can see, the decision about when and how to break the silence in a counseling session is highly nuanced. In some cases, specifically in a counseling context, silence is important for cognitive and emotional processing, even if uncomfortable.

Novice providers can struggle with allowing for silence in their patient interactions. This may arise from a sense of responsibility to fulfill their role as "helper." New counselors might wonder, "How can I be helping someone if I'm not saying anything?" As mentioned before, cultural values may be a relevant factor and the goal is to find a minimum level of silence that is culturally congruent. Other factors might be more amenable to change, such as anxiety-driven talking or faulty beliefs about how to be helpful. Providers may experience anxiety in interpersonal interactions and may speak as a way of avoiding silence that allows for ambiguity. Speaking over possible silences can be an anxiety-driven method for control. The other factor leading to inadequate silence might be a provider holding a faulty belief that to be helpful to the patient they must speak at every possible moment during their time with the patient. Providers do have a wellspring of information and wisdom to share with their patients; however, it's not possible or necessary to speak non-stop to be helpful to patients. Once again, the power of silence cannot be underestimated, and sometimes the gift that providers can give their patients is unhurried silence in the presence of a warm and caring provider.

Minimal Encouragers

Minimal encouragers are the nonverbal behaviors and verbal utterances that motivate a patient to continue speaking. Nonverbal behaviors include nodding one's head, maintaining a facial response that shows engagement, and slightly leaning forward. Verbal utterances include "uh huh," "yes," "okay," "hmm," and "sure" among others. A combination of behavioral and verbal minimal encouragers gives the patient a subtle signal that the provider is listening and engaged. The use of minimal encouragers can range from apathetic to animated; both ends of this spectrum likely have negative consequences for building rapport with a patient. A stoic and unaffected pattern of behavior (e.g., neutral face, no body movements, complete silence) can suggest to a patient that the provider isn't listening or isn't impacted by what the patient is saying. This lack of minimal encourager use is likely to lead patients to share less and feel unheard. The opposite end of the spectrum is a degree of minimal encourager use that is distracting to patients. Excessive nodding, dramatic facial reactions, and constant verbal utterances take the attention from the patient and put it on the provider.

Take time to observe yourself in the coming days to assess for your existing use of minimal encouragers. What minimal encouragers are you naturally utilizing already? The best way to assess your degree of minimal encourager use is to observe yourself in video recordings of interactions with mock patients. Novice clinicians tend to be overly critical of their minimal encourager use when they are asked to pay attention to it. It's important to remember that a wide range of minimal encourager use is functional, and this behavior only needs modifying when it falls on the ends of the spectrum. Questions you can use to self-assess the functionality of your minimal encourager use would be: *1) Is it apparent that I'm listening? 2) Do I look like I care about the person in front of me? and 3) Are my reactions distracting?*

A question that novice providers consider is the appropriateness of mirroring the patient's emotions when the patient is expressing emotions that are incongruent with the topic at hand. Consider when a patient might be laughing while talking about a serious topic: *what are the benefits and drawbacks to smiling along with them?* A benefit might be that you are tracking the patient's emotional reaction and "meeting them where they're at;" however, an obvious drawback is that you minimize the seriousness of the conversation, possibly foreclosing a deeper and emotionally meaningful discussion of the topic. We recommend subtle mirroring of patient emotion when emotions are *congruent* with the discussed topic. When patient emotion is *incongruent*, it is usually helpful to subtly mirror the content-congruent emotion but acknowledge the lack of congruence with the patient to explore the discrepancy. Knowing how to comment upon what you see and hear your patient saying will encompass the next set of skills in the chapter.

Restatements, Paraphrasing, and Summarizing

The next set of skills entail verbally demonstrating to your patient that you understand what they are expressing to you. Restatements, paraphrasing, and summarizing require that the provider listen and then share back with the patient the *essential content* of what the patient said. Essential content is the important core message and relevant details that the patient shares. These three skills require the provider to be non-interpretive, that is, to "stick closely" to what the patient is stating. The provider needs to avoid putting their own interpretation on what the patient has stated so what the patient is communicating can be jointly understood. These three skills (i.e., restatements, paraphrasing, and summarizing) are similar to one another but have slight differences.

Restating and paraphrasing greatly increases the likelihood of clear, effective communication between two people. In our context, communication refers to information exchange between two individuals and is the responsibility of the helping professional to ensure that communication is indeed accurate. In common social conversations, we may be less likely to seek such precision, but in fact a similar strategy of paraphrasing can support relationship enhancement. When Person A expresses a thought, they assume their intended message has been understood in the way they intended it. When Person B receives Person A's message, they assume that their perception of the message is precisely what was intended. Sometimes, these assumptions are accurate; other times, particularly with a person we don't know very well, miscommunications can be happening without either person being fully aware there are inaccuracies in how they are understanding the other. For reasons that are self-apparent, as a professional helper it is our responsibility to ensure explicitly clear communication with the people we are serving; anything less is doing them a disservice.

Restatements

Restatements are verbatim statements of what the patient has said. They can be one or two words or an entire sentence. The restated words or phrases should be ones that reflect something of importance or of something you want to know more about. Using upspeak (i.e., raising the pitch of voice at the end of a word or sentence) when restating a single word implies that you are curious about that word and what to know more.

One other valuable type of restatement is key word repetition. As our client is speaking and we are listening as well as observing, there may be particular words that they emphasize with their paraverbals. Notice any shift in volume, force, pitch, or physical movement that accompanies particular words or phrases. These shifts may suggest a heightened emotional activation around those words. By repeating a key word in upspeak, they may be able to more deeply experience and express the associated feelings. Observe the impact of just using minimal encouragers and restatements in the following exchange.

Scenario

A client is telling their mental health therapist about a situation that occurred in their life recently.

PATIENT: I don't think I told you about what happened with my coworker the other week at work. Okay, well, you already know that she's been trying to get close to me and has been taking her lunch breaks when I take mine. I usually just want to scroll on social media while I eat my lunch but she sits in the break room and looks at me while I'm eating.

PROVIDER: Mmhmm. [*Gentle head nod*]

PATIENT: Well, I thought that behavior was kind of weird, but I just ignored it in the past. But last week I finally got sick of it and decided to go eat my lunch outside on the back loading dock. Guess what? She followed me outside to eat her lunch there too!

PROVIDER: Oh! [*Widens eyes*]

PATIENT: I know, right? So then I told her what she was doing was creepy and weird.

PROVIDER: Creepy?

PATIENT: Yeah, like, it felt like she was stalking me and being invasive but not like, explaining herself. So, she just frowned and looked sad when I said that, but it worked because she stopped staring at me and following me during my lunch breaks. I also think she stopped because I told my boss what was happening, and I think he talked to her about it. But here's the part that I feel bad about, my boss told me that this woman had a head injury a few years ago and apparently that sometimes she acts like this but doesn't realize it's socially unusual behavior. I didn't know that. Now that I know that I feel like I overreacted to her and was kind of mean.

PROVIDER: Kind of mean?

PATIENT: Yeah, like, I automatically assumed she had weird intentions and was harsh with my tone. I feel guilty for treating her that way now.

The therapist is only using minimal encouragers and key word repetition in this brief clinical exchange. These brief verbal utterances and statements conveyed that the therapist was tracking what the client was saying while also gently guiding the conversation toward a deeper understanding of the client's perceptions of the situation and himself. A word of caution though: do not overuse restatements. Using restatements too much can give the impression that you don't have original thoughts and are only able to parrot back what you hear the patient say. In addition, some patients find restatements to be frustrating, and may respond in an aggravated tone by saying something like, "Yes, I know. I just told you that." This emotional reaction usually signals that they have some underlying frustration about something else but that they also find restatements to be unhelpful because they assume that you are following along without having to make it explicit. If this occurs, it can be helpful to calmly state, "Of course, I wanted to make sure I was hearing you correctly," and then reduce your use of restatements moving forward with that patient.

Paraphrasing

Paraphrasing is the next skill in this category and is the workhorse of patient-provider communication. Paraphrasing is putting the patient's words into your own words. This skill truly allows for mutual understanding between patient and provider because it requires understanding what the patient has said to a degree that the provider can put it into their own language. An important caveat about this skill: just because you paraphrase what the patient is saying doesn't mean that *you* also think that, believe that, or endorse what they're saying. Paraphrasing simply communicates that you understand what the patient is saying. For example, a patient might communicate that they are "so angry with [their] partner at times that [they] want to hit them!" A provider might respond with the following paraphrase: "I hear that your emotions lead you to want to act out physically against her." The provider is not suggesting to the patient that hitting their partner is a good idea but simply that the provider hears what they are expressing and is following along. A particularly effective paraphrase is one that uses some of the counselor's own words while incorporating client key words or phrases. The goal of paraphrases is to ensure that you are understanding what the patient is sharing.

There is potential for misinterpretation when providers use a paraphrase, so it can be helpful to use qualifiers and accuracy checks in conjunction with the paraphrase itself. Qualifiers are statements at the beginning of the sentence that acknowledge the counselor's ownership of the perception and denote the potential for misunderstanding such as, "If I'm hearing you correctly…" and "It sounds like you're saying…" Accuracy checks are used at the beginning or end of the paraphrase and add a query about the correctness of the provider's paraphrase. Accuracy checks can include, "…does that sound right?" and, "Tell me if I'm not following you here, you're saying that…" There is great value in using the accuracy check because it gives the client the opportunity to correct misperceptions. By affording them the space to clarify what they are expressing, we are giving them space to be fully heard. In addition, it reduces the power imbalance between the client and counsellor, because the client is in control of the content. Finally, when a counselor takes the time to correct a misperception, the meta-message communicated is that understanding the client fully is of utmost importance. This has obvious positive implications for the relationship.

Review these examples for how paraphrasing looks when used with a variety of levels of qualifiers and accuracy checks.

PATIENT: I don't know how much longer I can manage. The burden is too much but I can't afford the financial cost of having a live-in nurse. His care is becoming more than I can handle on my own, especially at night. Every day I just feel like I'm going to break, physically and mentally.

PROVIDER: I hear that you're feeling like you're out of alternatives and that this current set-up of caretaking isn't sustainable for you.

*

PATIENT: I'm finally in a good spot with my job and relationships. It just feels like everything is going the way I hoped it would. It almost doesn't feel real. The other shoe seems like it's going to drop, or at least that's what it feels like. I can't seem to trust that it could be this good for long.

PROVIDER: It's hard for you to feel secure in this new phase of your life, like it is almost too good to be true, right?

*

PATIENT: From now on, I'm afraid that she's always going to be this way. She is self-absorbed and doesn't care about her granddaughter's life anymore. It breaks my heart because I want her to give my daughter time and attention, the way my grandmother did for me, but it just doesn't seem possible. After the divorce she's become this entirely new person and it seems like she wants to be a teenager again. I have empathy for her but at the same time I miss my mom and the grandmother she used to be.

PROVIDER: You're saying that you see your mother as regressing in her age in a way and it feels like a loss to you?

As discussed above, sometimes a provider will misunderstand what the patient is expressing, and the paraphrase won't be accurate. Although the novice provider might feel like they "failed" in this moment, this is an opportunity for increased clarity for the patient and the provider. If the patient is willing to let the provider know that the paraphrase was inaccurate, the patient will hopefully reshare in a way that provides greater understanding for both parties. See this example for an exchange that had a positive result of enhanced, shared understanding:

PATIENT: The friendship is dying off from both ends. I don't think either of us had a good time the last time we hung out. I know I didn't have fun and I don't think she did either, but neither of us said that. It's almost like it's too painful to acknowledge out loud that the friendship is coming to an end. I don't ever find myself wanting to talk to her and she doesn't call me much either.

PROVIDER: I hear that you are ready for the friendship to come to an end, does that sound right?

PATIENT: Not really, it's not that I want it to come to an end but that I can feel it coming to an end and I don't want to acknowledge it.

PROVIDER: Ah, I hear you. You don't wish this was how it was, and it also feels even worse to jointly recognize it.

PATIENT: Yes, that's it. It's like two bad things: we've grown apart and since we never thought that would happen, it's like we don't want to acknowledge it because it makes it real.

The challenge of paraphrasing is determining what is the essential content of the patient's sharing, and what is ancillary detail. Paraphrases need to be concise so that the provider is not taking up too much of the talking time. Paraphrasing is the process of distilling the core message of the patient into one's own language. An accurate paraphrase will convey to the patient that you understand what they are expressing, which usually encourages the patient to continue speaking (all while feeling understood). Providers need to look past minor details so as to focus on the most important sentiments. Providers also need to recognize that they may not acknowledge something that the patient is saying because of their own discomfort with the topic or because they perceive that it isn't important. Provider paraphrases are often compared to "holding up a mirror" to the patient so that the patient can examine what they are saying with increased scrutiny. If the provider fails to "hold up the mirror" on certain topics (by ignoring or excessive focus on other topics) then they risk steering the conversation away from what is essential and important. Provider self-awareness is critical for rich communication that follows the lead of the patient.

Personal Reflection

What topics of conversation do you tend to avoid? What rules (implicit and explicit) do you hold regarding what is acceptable to discuss? To what extent do you avoid discomfort in your life?

Summarizing

The final skill in this category is summarizing. Summarizing involves condensing a large amount of what a patient has stated into one's own words in a concise manner. Summaries are usually longer than paraphrases given the amount of content to be condensed. Even more than a paraphrase, a summary needs to highlight the most important information and move beyond the minor details. Summaries allow the provider to demonstrate to a patient that they've been carefully listening for an extended period and can identify the most salient details and themes. This skill may be used after the patient has been sharing for an extended period without interruption, or they can be used to integrate what the patient has shared across a conversation or even multiple meetings. In addition to ensuring that the provider understands the connections between the topics brought up by the patient, summaries also provide opportunities for patients to gain insight themselves on the connection between discussed topics. Sometimes, as a patient hears their counselor offer a summary, they become more aware of themes in their content of which they were previously unaware.

Effective Use of Paraphrases and Summaries

An important component of paraphrasing and summarizing is ensuring that the paraphrase/summary itself is developmentally appropriate for the patient's level of cognitive capacity. As previously discussed, the patient's stage in their lifespan will influence what and how they share their thoughts with the provider. In general, a person's capacity for complex verbal communication will increase during their childhood and adolescent years. Other factors that impact complexity in communication include familiarity with the spoken language, intelligence, and life experiences. The goal is to match your paraphrasing/summarizing (as well as subsequent skills) to the patient's language and vocabulary. This is not the time to show off advanced vocabulary if that is not how the patient also speaks. Match the patient and use their language, especially when they use unique words that seem to capture the nuance of their experience.

Nonverbal and Paraverbal Use with Restatements, Paraphrases, and Summaries

Restatements, paraphrases, and summaries serve as the backbone of patient/provider conversations because of their utility in ensuring mutual understanding. These skills also have the power to do much more, however, such as demonstrating curiosity and validation, when used in conjunction with nonverbal and paraverbal behaviors that emphasize key components of their content. Some students share fears that their patients will respond poorly to these skills, and they are hesitant to use them. These fears are usually allayed when they see how skillful combination of nonverbal, paraverbal, and verbal skills lead these to be well-received by patients. Let us consider an extreme example to illustrate the power of nonverbal and paraverbal influence:

Scenario

A physical therapist is meeting with a patient who has missed several post-surgery physical therapy appointments without explanation.

Version One

PROVIDER: I'm glad you're here today, Leslie. I haven't seen you in a few weeks.
PATIENT: Yeah, I finally got a ride from my daughter-in-law. She's waiting out in the car while I'm in here.
PROVIDER: It sounds like you were having a difficult time getting a ride to appointments. [*Neutral face, monotone pitch, not making eye contact with the patient but rather looking off in the distance.*]
PATIENT: Yes, my husband works a lot and there aren't many other people who can bring me here. I don't want to be a bother to my friends or my kids either. They have a lot on their plates. I was so dependent on everyone before my surgery because of my limited mobility and although it's better now on a day-to-day basis, I feel guilty for still needing their help with things like rides and stuff.
PROVIDER: You feel guilty for prioritizing your health. [*One eyebrow raised, mostly expressionless face otherwise, monotone pitch.*]
PATIENT: I feel like I'm trying to do what I can at home to take care of myself. I've been doing the at-home exercises you gave me because I know they're important. I'm ready to get to work today though.
PROVIDER: Okay, I hear that you've missed several appointments and have been doing the exercises at home, but are ready to get to work today. [*Neutral, expressionless face and monotone voice.*]

How do you imagine the patient feels in this scenario? It would be reasonable to guess that she feels ashamed and potentially patronized. Let us now see how these same words could be combined with different nonverbal and paraverbal behavior to convey empathy, curiosity, and compassion.

Version Two

PROVIDER: I'm glad you're here today, Leslie. I haven't seen you in a few weeks.
PATIENT: Yeah, I finally got a ride from my daughter-in-law. She's waiting out in the car while I'm in here.
PROVIDER: It sounds like you were having a difficult time getting a ride to appointments. [*Head tilted to the side, making eye contact, slight head nodding, and expression of mild sadness.*]

PATIENT: Yeah, it's been hard for me because I know these appointments are important, but I've felt like I've already been asking for so much from everyone in my life for the past several months. I don't want to be a burden to people and asking for a ride to these appointments seems like a lot to ask.

PROVIDER: Oh, you feel guilty for prioritizing your health? [*Slight look of puzzlement and sadness on face, subtle nodding, somewhat lower volume and gentle tone with upspeak.*]

PATIENT: Yeah, yeah, I guess I do. I know I shouldn't feel guilty. No one has ever told me that I'm being a burden, but sometimes it's just easier for me to try to do the exercises at home than to deal with the guilt of having to ask someone to rearrange their day to help me. I'm glad I was able to get past that though today and get here. I want to do good work today.

PROVIDER: Okay, I hear that you've missed several appointments and have been doing the exercises at home but are ready to get to work today! [*Slight smile, eye contact, raising eyebrows at end of sentence and increasing volume.*]

How do you imagine the patient feels in this second scenario? Maybe you considered that she feels understood and encouraged. The changes in paraverbal and nonverbal behaviors convey empathy and greater curiosity. Slight mirroring of patient emotions via one's own facial reactions is a subtle way demonstrate empathy while also conveying understanding of the core content that the patient is expressing. The use of up-speak also takes a paraphrase and turns it into an inquiry, which conveys curiosity about what the patient expressed. Paraphrases do not need to be used with up-speak, but they are an effective adaptation to gather more information without asking a question.

A consistent lack of displayed curiosity (via nonverbals and paraverbals) runs the risk that the provider is the arbiter of what is valid and real. In general, lack of interest in the patient's story is counterproductive if the goal is to develop and strengthen a trusting working alliance with the patient. This becomes even more likely when the provider fails to use qualifiers and accuracy checks with their paraphrasing. Consider the example above when the provider makes a paraphrase about feeling guilty about prioritizing her health. Stating, "You feel guilty about prioritizing your health," with a monotone pitch, neutral face, and no qualifiers or accuracy checks suggests that the provider has some special, accurate insight into how the patient is feeling. On the other hand, "It sounds like you might be feeling guilty about prioritizing your health?" with changes in pitch, a subtle expression of sadness in the face, and the use of a qualifier (i.e., "It sounds like...") conveys a reasonable hypothesis with curiosity to know if this accurately captures what the patient is expressing. Note too that the phrasing incorporates identification of the emotion that was embedded in the patient's communication. This balance of confidence to make a guess with curiosity serves to invite patients to offer their perspectives and deepen the conversation. Although the provider may feel confident in their in their assessment of the patient's circumstance, a consistent lack of curiosity can set up the aforementioned dynamic in which the provider is the expert on the patient's reality, which usually does not lead patients to feel empowered in their own self-assessments.

Conclusion

A humanistic view of helping relationships assumes that patients inherently pursue their own actualization and have expert knowledge of themselves. Humanistic-aligned providers will use the skills in this chapter extensively given their capacity to encourage patients to share deeply about themselves and their lives. These skills also support the development of rapport with patients. A close and intimate bond with a patient then allows for the safety and invitation of deeper conversation, potentially of topics that are uncomfortable, avoided, and make the patient feel vulnerable. These same topics may be of central importance to effectively addressing the patient's concerns. Keep in mind that providers need to give their patients a service that they cannot access elsewhere. The service that providers can often give is their listening, non-judgmental ear. Don't assume that patients have such spaces in their daily lives, remember the power of your attention and validation. The skillful combination of para; phrasing, silence, and nonverbal behavior communicates to patients the following message: *"I'm not going to judge what you think and feel; I'm not offended, disgusted, or afraid of what you have to say; I want to know more about you; I'm listening."* If patients perceive these messages from us and accept our invitation to share further, then we are bestowed the opportunity to get to know our patients at deeper levels. The upcoming chapters will explore skills that guide provider behavior in response to this deeper and emotional sharing from patients.

Questions for Class Discussion

1 What are your reactions to the chapter material about silence and its role in a counseling session? Discuss with your classmates.
2 Practice paraphrasing in a small group.
3 Share with your classmates some experiences you have had with someone using minimal encouragers excessively with you. How did you discern whether the person was really listening?
4 Practice summarizing in a small group.

References

Hofstede, G. (2001). *Culture's consequences* (2nd ed.). Sage Publications.

Macduff, I. (2006). Your pace or mine? Culture, time, and negotiation. *Negotiation Journal*, 22(1), 31–45. doi:10.1111/j.1571-9979.2006.00084.x.

McKay-Semmler, K.L. (2017). High- and low-context cultures. In *The International Encyclopedia of Intercultural Communication*, Y.Y. Kim (Ed.). doi:10.1002/9781118783665.ieicc0106.

Templeton, E.M., Chang, L.J., Reynolds, E.A., Cone LeBeaumont, M.D., & Wheatley, T.(2022). Fast response times signal social connection in conversation. *Proceedings of the National Academy of Sciences of the United States of America*, 119(4), e2116915119.

Trompenaars, F. & Hampden-Turner, C. (1997). *Riding the waves of culture: Understanding cultural diversity in business*. Nicholas Brealey Publishing.

Chapter 7

Helping Behaviors: Verbal Skills to Understand and Connect

Chapter Six reviewed paraphrasing and summarizing which focus upon the spoken content of a person's message, or the overt information being shared. In this chapter, we will turn our attention to other levels of understanding what someone is expressing: emotion reflection and meaning reflection. These techniques comprise two of the most foundational skills in active listening. Reflection of emotion and meaning are ways of responding that most explicitly enable a listener to communicate to the speaker a deep, accurate, empathic reception of the speaker's message. One challenge to developing these reflective skills is that information communicated between people usually happens simultaneously in both overt and indirect ways. In Chapter Five, we looked at forms of indirect communication through behavior we can observe in our patient – verbal spoken content, which is the overt communication and paraverbal and nonverbal content, which indirectly express information. Becoming skillful in reflecting feelings and meaning requires becoming a careful observer/listener, integrating all we have observed and heard, and then sharing our observations with the person to whom we are listening. The title of this chapter refers to understanding and connecting; the skills presented in this chapter are among the most essential techniques for establishing and cultivating authentic communication and connection between a provider and their patient.

Given that the focus of this chapter is on reflecting the deeper components of patient expressions, we will look first at an overview of emotions and associated theories. Then, we will present suggested components of an effective emotion reflection. Our focus will then move to cognitive appraisal and meaning making – these provide a framework for understanding and reflecting the deeper content of a patient's expressions. When integrated effectively, these two components (i.e., emotion reflection and meaning reflection) can have a beneficial impact on the empathic resonance that can develop between patient and provider. These skills provide a level of shared meaning and feeling that promote a sense of being seen, which is extremely important to relationship development.

DOI: 10.4324/9781003217589-9

Emotion Reflection

We start this discussion with an examination of emotions in general to ensure that you have a clear conceptualization of the terminology. As you read this material, we invite you to compare the objective content to your own lived experiences. To what extent do these descriptions seem to ring true for you, based on your own experiences? Consider the following: *What are some of the ways you would describe feeling "sad?" Try to identify at least two descriptors that reflect your physical experience of sadness, your mental experience of sadness, and your emotional experience of sadness. Now try to do the same for "relaxed" and "joy."*

In the professional counseling literature, there are several related terms commonly used: *feeling, emotion,* and *affect*. In general, when a provider refers to a patient's *affect*, they are talking about the patient's *displayed emotions*, the outward expression of feelings and emotion. As a side note, there are numerous other definitions of "affect." Hoffman and Doan (2018, p. 3) define "affect" as "the subjective experience and the valence of an emotional state." On the other hand, *emotions* and *feelings* refer to one's *internal, subjective experience* of emotional arousal, including the physiological experience and the non-physical aspects of having a particular emotion.

Most of the commonly used models and treatment approaches in counseling and psychology place emotions and emotional functioning front and center regarding their importance to the outcome of clinical work. Regardless of whether you are a mental health professional or a professional in another helping field, the ability to attune to and acknowledge, the emotions being expressed by your patient will enhance your relationship with them. Authors of similar counseling skills texts (e.g., Cavanaugh, 1982; Ivey & Ivey, 2007; Poorman, 2003; Seligman, 2004; Young, 2005) have noted that emotions are catalysts for growth. Countless others who have preceded them, including some of the most well-known authors in the field of psychology, such as Freud and Rogers, have postulated similarly that emotional processing is a central component of growth and development.

Regardless of how frequently we talk to others specifically about our feelings, our emotional experiences are a significant aspect of being alive. Our emotions are one of the ways that we are internally self-aware of existing as human beings. What's more, our feelings are often the force that prompts us to make changes in our thoughts and behaviors.

Perhaps you recall the psychosocial model of human development established by Erik Erikson. Erikson's psychosocial stages of development identify seven developmental stages that cover the human lifespan, beginning with infancy, all the way through old age. His model rests heavily on the concept of "developmental crisis," which is a process whereby situational circumstance change requires us to develop new ways of coping with environmental or internal challenges. Emotions are a core aspect of discomfort, and then subsequent change and growth. For example, when a child begins kindergarten, there are new routines and expectations for their behavior, which disrupts whatever daily routine they had prior to school. The discomfort of needing to learn new routines ultimately results in the child learning new skills and behaviors – these new skills and behaviors are what we refer to as "growth." Thus, in order to grow, we must experience some level of emotional discomfort or unmet need. Similarly, the Transtheoretical Treatment Model developed by Prochaska, DiClemente & Norcross (1992) articulates the concept that a significant level of emotional discomfort needs to be felt before a person is sufficiently motivated to develop new strategies for coping with unhealthy behaviors, such as substance abuse. We believe that this same process of change, starting with unmet needs or uncomfortable emotions becoming evident, and subsequent motivation for modifying our behavior to change that state, is a foundational description of stages and processes by which we move from one stage to the next.

Some variation of felt experience of emotions is universal; emotions are inherent to being alive with a brain, central nervous system, and peripheral nervous system. It follows, then, that when we suppress our experience of emotions, growth likely will *not* occur, and in some cases, problems will emerge because our needs are not being met, or there remain unprocessed or unacknowledged emotions. There are a host of physical conditions that are exacerbated by stress, suppressed emotions, and other forms of emotional distress: cardiac conditions, gastrointestinal conditions, skin conditions, circulatory problems, and so on. Thus, the importance of helping people gain awareness of their emotions extends beyond the immediate benefit of relationship enhancement; it can support their optimal physical functioning, too.

The Importance of Empathy in Helping Relationships

In professional helping fields, empathy is a *crucial* ingredient to developing rapport with a patient. Wiseman (1996) denotes four attributes of empathy:

1 Seeing the world from the other's perspective
2 Holding a non-judgmental stance about that perspective
3 Understanding the other's feelings
4 Communicating understanding to the person

In order for us to engage in empathic understanding, it requires feeling *with* the patient. This can be emotionally fatiguing and yet, it also demonstrates a willingness to connect with their uncomfortable and painful experiences. When a provider is willing to understand and connect with the emotions of the patient, they can provide care that is appropriate to the patient's emotional state. In addition, "staying with" the emotions within a conversation versus bypassing them in favor of focusing on solutions or next steps communicates the message that the patient's emotions are important, and by extension, the patient themselves are important. Focusing on emotions also adds a deeper level of understanding to the concern at hand and can help a patient gain new perspectives on a situation. Consider the following two conversations between a provider and patient. The first conversation is devoid of emotion reflections, and thus minimal empathy, whereas the second conversation is full of emotion reflections and thus, explicit empathy.

Scenario 1: A client talking with their clinical mental health counselor about career indecision

CLIENT: Taking this time off work because of my knee surgery was just supposed to be for my physical recovery, but I actually think it's helping me re-evaluate my career.

COUNSELOR: Mmhmm. (*Nodding head.*)

CLIENT: I feel so much happier that I'm not pressuring someone to buy something that they don't really need. I used to like the challenge of being in a sales position, but the older I get, the more I feel like I'm taking advantage of people. It's kind of gross actually when I think of how happy I would be to lock someone into a contract even when I could tell it was outside of their budget.

COUNSELOR: I hear that you don't want to do that job any more.

CLIENT: Right, it doesn't feel right any more to do that kind of work. I'm actually thinking about applying to some jobs in these next few weeks just to see what might be out there. I think if I could find a job in this industry and that wasn't in the sales part of it then I'd feel better.

COUNSELOR: So you're thinking about looking for a new job?

CLIENT: I guess so! The problem is that the commission with my current job is so good. It really puts me in a financial place that is comfortable. I don't know if I'm ready to give that up.

Scenario 2: A client talking with their clinical mental health counselor about career indecision

CLIENT: Taking this time off work because of my knee surgery was just supposed to be for my physical recovery, but I actually think it's helping me re-evaluate my career.

COUNSELOR: Mmhmm. (*Nodding head.*)

CLIENT: I feel so much happier that I'm not pressuring someone to buy something that they don't really need. I used to like the challenge of being in a sales position, but the older I get, the more I feel like I'm taking advantage of people. It's kind of gross actually when I think of how happy I would be to lock someone into a contract even when I could tell it was outside of their budget.

COUNSELOR: Oh, hmm, the distance from your work is allowing you to get in touch with the conflict you feel in this type of work. It sounds like you feel some guilt about both the work and how "success" feels in sales?

CLIENT: Ugh... yes, actually. I do feel sort of guilty. And I think the reason I feel guilty is because I can see the customer right in front of me and I can imagine how their overstretched budget is going to affect their life. It kind of makes me sad to think about it, like I'm somewhat responsible for any financial problems they start to have.

COUNSELOR: Oh gosh, feeling responsible for the financial troubles of clients must give you feelings of regret. I also hear that you see clients as whole people, not just customers, which humanizes them too you, and leads you to feel some disappointment in yourself.

CLIENT: Yeah... yeah, it does. I actually think that's my strength, that is, that I see clients as whole people. I wish I had a job that valued that quality in me.

As you can see in scenario 1, the lack of emotion reflection led the conversation to move quickly to the client's desire to find a new job, bypassing a rich emotional component to the current issue. In scenario 2, the reflection of emotion also led the client to think about a new job but with greater insight into what his strengths were and what motivated him to want to move out of a sales position.

Frameworks for Understanding Emotions

One model for conceptualizing how emotions are generated is referred to as the cognitive appraisal approach. The essence of the cognitive appraisal approach is that events in and of themselves hold no meaning – through our perception of the event and our subsequent interpretation (appraisal: what we tell ourselves about the event) we then experience particular feelings about it. The author most commonly identified as first articulating this approach is Arnold (1960), although this idea goes all the way back to Greek philosophers like Socrates. Numerous foundational authors (i.e., Beck, Ellis, Meichenbaum) in the past century identified cognitive appraisal as a key element in treating individuals who experience excessive, negative, emotional experiences.

The Affect Circumplex

Emanating from the field of management comes a helpful way to conceptualize emotions and their relationships to one another, referred to as the "affect circumplex." This model provides a visual representation of the broad range of discrete emotions that exist in the context of overall emotional experience (see Figure 7.1). Emotions are in a continual cycle of flux and change in the same way that our other needs, like hunger and sleep, also cycle regularly. In the case of emotions, there is a need for some form of expression in order for emotions to be metabolized. In your careful observation of the patient while they are speaking, you may notice some shifts in their paraverbal communication, such as rate of speech or vocal underlining and subtle shifts in facial expression or body posture, that change, which can suggest the presence of emotional energy. When you notice these shifts, try to determine whether the emotional energy valence appears to be on the positive or negative end as well as whether the level of activation is at a typical level of energy given the person's baseline, or if it is significantly higher or lower than typical for that individual. Some authors who have carefully examined the affect circumplex model have identified relative positioning of various feeling words. It is relevant to our discussion here because it is a visually based means of talking about ambivalent emotions.

Ambivalent Emotions

When we simultaneously have emotions in different quadrants, our resultant internal experience can be one of intensely mixed feelings, confusion, or distress. Mixed or contradictory feelings can be especially hard for people to acknowledge if the emotions felt are not expected or desirable in their social/relational context of family or community. For example, consider a family situation in which an elder family member who was often judgmental and unkind to one of their children in particular, becomes terminally ill and dies. Family members are grief stricken with the loss; usually, grief is a socially expected emotional response. However, the adult child who was in disfavor with the deceased parent might also feel relief, or even some satisfaction (or some other positively valanced emotion) related to the parent's death. Yet, they may be unwilling to share (or even admit to themselves internally) those positive feelings, owing to shame or fear of being negatively judged. Thus, the person may suppress or disregard that aspect of their emotions, leading to an incomplete metabolization, and residual, unprocessed emotional energy. This unprocessed emotional energy remains as unexpressed energy, which can then become apparent in one of several ways. Sometimes unexpressed energy manifests in the form of physical symptoms ranging from minor aches and pains to

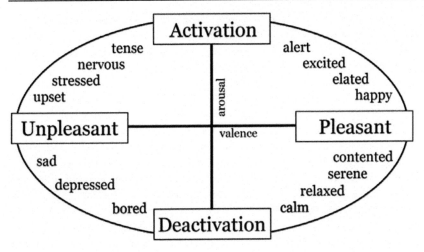

Figure 7.1 The Affect Circumplex

insomnia, debilitating migraines, gastrointestinal distress, hypertension, etc. Other times that energy is simply suppressed by pushing it out of our ordinary awareness. This is a strategy that can be costly emotionally, and yet, it also can be functional in the short term. The ability to shut off one's emotional experiencing to focus on the cognitive and objective aspects of a situation enables us to bracket our experience and make decisions that allow for forward movement.

Emotions and Cultural Display Rules

Some researchers interested in the universality of emotions and of emotional expression have worked to identify consistency across cultures; in particular are Ekman and Friesen (1971), who were discussed in Chapter Five. As you might recall, Ekman and Friesen (1971) identified six easily recognizable facial reactions that reflect emotions seen across diverse cultures. The universal facial expressions are surprise, anger, disgust, fear, happiness, sadness, and contempt. Universal emotional experiences offer us a broad way to understand a wide range of people from diverse backgrounds.

Human beings are capable of a wide range of emotions, and in many instances, there are multiple, sometimes contradictory, emotions people experience simultaneously. Consider the term "bittersweet," which is the way people sometimes describe a major life experience such as graduating college. This descriptor exemplifies the co-existence of seemingly opposite emotions. Many life experiences result in a similar process of generating multiple emotional experiences simultaneously.

People differ in how aware they are of their internal emotional state and how able they are to accurately and thoroughly express their emotions. The sources of variability around this process are nuanced. Some individual difference might be the result of inherited temperament along with inherited resting neurological arousal, how the person is "hard-wired."

Beyond the heritability aspect of emotional awareness, two other factors, closely related, contribute to individual differences. These two factors are 1) culturally based expectations and socialization about acknowledgement and expression of emotions; and 2) each family systems' norms and rules. A large body of literature exists that establishes the construct of Cultural Display Rules (e.g., Matsumoto). Cultural Display Rules (CDRs) are the norms and expectations about how, and how much, emotional experiences are expressed to others. While Ekman and Friesen established that some facial expressions are highly recognizable even when the viewer and the person being viewed are culturally dissimilar, there is a big difference between recognizing emotion in another person and expressing emotion ourselves. Some authors (e.g., Hutchinson et al., 2020) have identified a number of socially constructed rules that define emotional expression. Some culture-based rules about emotional expression tell members they should:

- express emotions directly as experienced with no effort to change the valence or intensity (complete emotional transparency);
- amplify the intensity of the feelings beyond what is actually felt (exaggerate emotions);
- diminish the intensity of the feelings (downplay emotions);
- disguise the feelings by making them look like something other than what they really feel (pretend emotions);
- downplay the emotion or qualify it in a way that cancels it out (discredit their entitlement to emotions);
- express no emotion at all (avoid emotions).

Personal Reflection

Consider the following: What were the Cultural Display Rules in the household where you grew up? How were those rules communicated to you? What kinds of reactions do you notice internally as you read about each of the Display Rules that were not part of your own cultural conditioning?

In some cultural groups, it is considered disrespectful or an indication of weakness to disclose emotions such as sadness, despair, desperation. These perceptions of emotions may be tied to other rules, possibly related to gender. For example, straight and cisgender men can sometimes feel it is unacceptable to express emotions such as vulnerability and sadness. Thus, in a relational context that prohibits certain emotional expression, when a person feels an undesirable emotion, they may secondarily have shame that they are feeling it, or they may experience a strong need to suppress that prohibited emotion to maintain the balance and order in the social system. From a culturally responsive stance, it is important not to identify any one of these CDRs as "pathological" or something that needs to be fixed. It can be meaningful to explore with a patient how CDR is working for them and to the degree to which they consciously want to adopt it.

Identifying and Categorizing Emotions

It can be surprisingly helpful to verbalize our feelings even when there are no external circumstances or situations that are changed because of the feeling expression. The process of unpacking, acknowledging, and coming fully into contact, with our full range of feelings, can help those feelings to be metabolized and resolved. There are two important foundational skills needed in the process of identifying and categorizing emotions: *recognition* and *labeling*.

Prior to being able to label an emotional experience, we need to be able to *recognize* an emotional experience within ourselves or others. The ability to sense an internal emotional experience can be difficult for people who lacked sufficient exposure to role modeling of this type of self-awareness. For many people, emotions are felt in a manner that is physical/visceral in the body. A person might have their stomach "in knots," experience lethargy in their arms and legs, or feel tension in their shoulders and jaw or heat in their face. This ability to notice internal, visceral experiences and connect them to an emotion is a learned skill and for some of us takes practice. Other people may observe their own behaviors and thoughts and be able to recognize how those thoughts and behaviors are being influenced by an emotion within themselves. Regardless of where our self-observation originates, the crucial skill in recognition is the ability to be self-observant regarding one's internal experiences and notice their fluctuations.

If someone can recognize emotional experiences within themselves, the next step is that of *labeling*. To label one's own emotions in a meaningful way, or the emotions of someone else, a person needs a sufficient 'emotional vocabulary' – that is, a set of words that can describe emotional experiences. Much like developing vocabulary in a foreign language, the ability to develop a rich and effective emotional vocabulary first requires exposure to emotion words. Our level of exposure to emotion words varies widely and is influenced by the amount and type of emotions expressed and discussed in the environments where we spend time.

Take a moment to reflect on your exposure to emotion words. What emotion words were used the most to describe feelings in your home growing up?

134 Helping Skills for Counselors and Health Professionals

It is common for students to recognize that their emotional vocabulary is lacking and in need of expansion. A "feeling wheel" is a helpful tool for increasing one's emotional vocabulary. A feeling wheel provides a simple diagram for understanding common emotions and providing nuanced emotion words that can more accurately describe someone's experience (see Figure 7.2; Roberts, 2022). Of course, simply looking at a feeling wheel is not sufficient for expanding one's emotional vocabulary. Like learning a foreign language, reading a set of new words once will not result in those words becoming permanent fixtures in one's vocabulary. We need to use these words regularly in our lives to make them accessible when we need to draw on them in our professional work. When teaching students, we encourage them to print out a feeling wheel and place it in a place in their home that they visit regularly (i.e., the refrigerator door, a bathroom mirror) and take a moment to identify their emotions using the wheel each time that they pass it. Another method that we recommend is to keep the

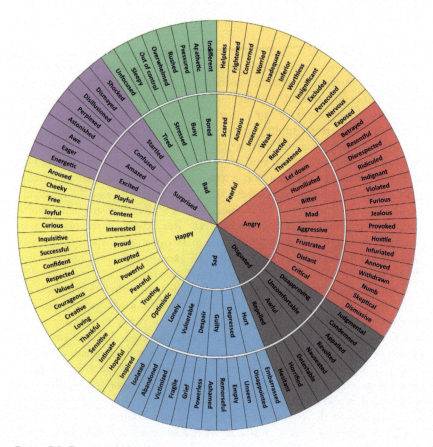

Figure 7.2 Emotion Wheel

feeling wheel handy while watching a TV show and take a moment to identify the emotions that the various characters are experiencing throughout the episode. Simple practices such as these can improve your ability to accurately recognize and label your emotions, and the emotions of others.

Emotions and Needs

Another way to deepen your understanding of emotions, beyond expanding your emotional vocabulary, is to understand how emotions are often connected to human needs. We will discuss human needs in more depth later in this chapter, but for the moment, review the lists of emotions seen in Figures 7.3 and 7.4 that are categorized by needs either being met or unmet. This list was created by the Center for Nonviolent Communication (2005) and is both comprehensive and atheoretical. As you listen and observe your patients, and yourself, listen and watch for expressed or implied needs as well as expressed or implied feelings.

The Skill of Emotion Reflection

Take a moment to think of a time you were trying to express something important to you, yet the listener did not understand or perhaps did not acknowledge your intended message. What kinds of thoughts and emotions were generated for you in that situation?

The purpose of the above self-exploration is to illustrate the primacy of someone feeling heard, seen, and understood. People often experience a sense of relief, validation, value, and connection when they know a listener is accurately perceiving them and their experience. The skills we will focus on in this chapter are very instrumental as you develop the skill to intentionally cultivate the other person's experience of being heard.

The components of an emotion reflection are:

Entry qualifier + emotion identification + accuracy check

The entry qualifier and accuracy check provide a tentative stance that lets the patient know you are basing your emotional identification on what you are observing, and that you're open to correction. The core of an emotion reflection is stating an emotion word that you think accurately fits what the person is expressing. Here is an example of a full emotion reflection:

I hear you saying that you feel betrayed by their behavior, did I get that right?

In the above example, "I hear you saying that..." is the entry qualifier. It establishes the tentative tone and the source of your conclusion about their

Feelings when your needs are satisfied

AFFECTIONATE	CONFIDENT	GRATEFUL	PEACEFUL
compassionate	empowered	appreciative	calm
friendly	open	moved	clear headed
loving	proud	thankful	comfortable
open hearted	safe	touched	centered
sympathetic	secure		content
tender		**INSPIRED**	equanimous
warm	**EXCITED**	amazed	fulfilled
	amazed	awed	mellow
ENGAGED	animated	wonder	quiet
absorbed	ardent		relaxed
alert	aroused	**JOYFUL**	relieved
curious	astonished	amused	satisfied
engrossed	dazzled	delighted	serene
enchanted	eager	glad	still
entranced	energetic	happy	tranquil
fascinated	enthusiastic	jubilant	trusting
interested	giddy	pleased	
intrigued	invigorated	tickled	**REFRESHED**
involved	lively		enlivened
spellbound	passionate	**EXHILARATED**	rejuvenated
stimulated	surprised	blissful	renewed
	vibrant	ecstatic	rested
HOPEFUL		elated	restored
expectant		enthralled	revived
encouraged		exuberant	
optimistic		radiant	
		rapturous	
		thrilled	

Figure 7.3 Satisfied Emotions

emotion, in this case, what the person is saying. The word "betrayed" is the emotion identification component and the provider's best attempt to capture emotions they heard being expressed. "...did I get that right?" serves as the accuracy check. This final component invites the patient to confirm, modify, or deny what the provider stated.

Helping Behaviors: Verbal Skills to Understand and Connect   137

Feelings when your needs are not satisfied

AFRAID	**CONFUSED**	**EMBARRASSED**
apprehensive	ambivalent	ashamed
dread	baffled	chagrined
foreboding	bewildered	flustered
frightened	dazed	guilty
mistrustful	hesitant	mortified
panicked	lost	self-conscious
petrified	mystified	
scared	perplexed	**FATIGUE**
suspicious	puzzled	beat
terrified	torn	burnt out
wary		depleted
worried	**DISCONNECTED**	exhausted
	alienated	lethargic
ANNOYED	aloof	listless
aggravated	apathetic	sleepy
dismayed	bored	tired
disgruntled	cold	weary
displeased	detached	worn out
exasperated	distant	
frustrated	distracted	**PAIN**
impatient	indifferent	agony
irritated	numb	anguished
irked	removed	bereaved
	uninterested	devastated
ANGRY	withdrawn	grief
enraged		heartbroken
furious	**DISQUIET**	hurt
incensed	agitated	lonely
indignant	alarmed	miserable
irate	discombobulated	regretful
livid	disconcerted	remorseful
outraged	disturbed	
resentful	perturbed	**SAD**
	rattled	depressed
AVERSION	restless	dejected
animosity	shocked	despair
appalled	startled	despondent
contempt	surprised	disappointed
disgusted	troubled	discouraged
dislike	turbulent	disheartened
hate	turmoil	forlorn
horrified	uncomfortable	gloomy
hostile	uneasy	heavy hearted
repulsed	unnerved	hopeless
	unsettled	melancholy
	upset	unhappy
		wretched

Figure 7.4 Unsatisfied Emotions

Although an entry qualifier and accuracy check are not required, they communicate your openness to be corrected and avoid positioning you as the authority on the patient's emotional experience. When using an emotion reflection without an entry qualifier or accuracy check, it's important to demonstrate openness to correction through our paraverbal behavior. For example, if we said, "You're scared about the results of the test?" we might want to raise our pitch at the end of the sentence (i.e., upspeak) to indicate our curiosity as to whether the statement fits with the patient's experience. Review the exchange between a provider and patient below to see the impact of emotion reflections on the depth of conversation.

Scenario: A physical therapist is meeting with a patient for a second appointment. In the first appointment, the physical therapist asked the patient to practice some exercises at home between appointments

PROVIDER: How did the exercises at home go, Mr. Jackson?

PATIENT: Oh, you know, I tried a little bit but I don't know, they seemed a little silly. My grandson even laughed at me when I was trying them — would you believe that? I would have never laughed at my grandpop when I was a kid! That would've gotten me into some deep trouble.

PROVIDER: Oh yeah? Your grandson laughed at you?

PATIENT: Yeah, he said what I was doing looked so easy and he thought it was funny that it was my "homework."

PROVIDER: You mentioned that the exercises seemed silly?

PATIENT: Yeah... [*sigh*]... yeah. I'm just wondering if they're really going to help. How could gripping those rubber ball things actually help? It seems like I've lost so much of my abilities in so many areas — how is *that* gonna be the thing that helps?

PROVIDER: Ahh... I hear that you're feeling a bit skeptical of the exercises, does that sound right?

PATIENT: Yes, yes... I'm sorry. I don't mean to say you don't know what you're doing but c'mon — how could that little exercise ever get me back to how I was before the stroke?

PROVIDER: It sounds like you might feel somewhat hopeless about your recovery process?

PATIENT: [*Nodding*]

PROVIDER: Gosh, I wonder if that hopelessness keeps you from doing the exercises as much as prescribed because it feels pointless?

PATIENT: It does, actually. I get the worksheets out that you gave me and the supplies and then I think to myself, what's the point?

Helping Behaviors: Verbal Skills to Understand and Connect   139

In the interaction above, you'll notice that the provider provided two emotion reflections that highlighted the client's expression of feeling skeptical and hopeless. If the provider had not reflected the emotions of the patient, where do you think the conversation may have gone? What do you think the value of highlighting the patient's emotions is to their recovery process?

Meaning Reflection

As we've been discussing, the goal of these techniques for responding is to communicate a deep, empathic understanding of the patient's experience. Thus far we have focused on the patient's emotional experience; we turn now to a person's thought process and cognitive aspects of the emotions they are feeling and exhibiting.

When an event happens in our lives, many of us perceive our feelings at the exact same time that we observe or hear it. Many of us are aware of our emotional reaction even before we become aware of our thoughts or self-talk about that event. Our thoughts and internal dialogue about the event are referred to as cognitive appraisal, and as mentioned earlier in the chapter, this idea that we create our emotions through our cognitive appraisals dates all the way back to Greek philosophers. While experiencing and being aware of emotions is a fundamental aspect of being alive, so is the process of meaning making as a fundamentally connected aspect of those emotions. Meaning making is the experience of interpreting and making sense of life experiences. The meanings that each of us make are influenced by factors like our personality, previous life experiences, values, and cultural identities.

Meaning making is fundamental to the human experience. Therefore, the microskill of meaning reflection can become an especially important strategy in therapeutic relationships after there has been enough of a relationship established that you have a strong sense of knowing the patient well. Each of our styles of cognitive appraisal is a process so personalized and contextual that in a first meeting, or even in the early stages of relationship development, it is almost impossible for us as providers to fully grasp our patient's cognitive process. Many of us have had the experience of meeting someone and discovering a great deal of interests, preferences, and thoughts in common. There can be an immediate sense of familiarity when we encounter someone who is highly similar to us on some important variable. However, when we meet someone highly similar in a professional helping context, we must be careful not to over-identify or to assume we are completely familiar with their situation, feelings, and thoughts. Even though well-intentioned, to assume that we know exactly what another person is thinking and why can be very minimizing for them. It is also potentially ethnocentric in the broadest meaning of this word. Even when the person we are talking to appears to be very similar to ourselves, it is critical to the relationship development that we take the time to listen and understand their appraisal process – that is, we must not assume that our way of making meaning is exactly the same as theirs.

It takes considerable time with another person to learn enough about them to be able to accurately reflect the meaning they ascribe to a particular circumstance in their life. Often a person's meaning making is implied, but like feelings, meaning making may not be explicitly stated in the course of a typical social conversation. Nevertheless, developing the skill of listening for implied meaning, or actively inquiring about implied meaning, can be done early in a helping relationship. The meaning we attach to an event is determined by many contextual factors. We will take a look at some of the variables contributing to meaning making, that combine to create an infinite number of constellations. Each of our cognitive frames from which meaning arises are unique because our frames come from the totality of our life experiences, including the systems in which we exist, the spaces in society we occupy, the particulars of our living environments, and the extent of emotional injuries and trauma we have experienced. We are going to examine some of these factors with an eye toward how those factors influence our cognitive appraisals. Having this understanding will assist you as you develop this active listening skill of reflecting meaning.

Schemas

The term "schema" is derived from cognitive theory. A schema is a mental framework that enables us to interpret and understand information. Schemas help us make sense of our world by comparing new information to previously existing schemas, or frameworks, for the relevant concept. For example, if you go to a corner drug store and notice a device at the front of the store with a computer screen, scanner, and bagging area but with no employee, you might accurately conclude that this is a self-checkout station. If you've previously seen or used a self-checkout at another store, then you have a schema for what a self-checkout entails: a computer screen, a scanner, an area for bagging. When you see this at your corner drug store for the first time, and it looks similar to your existing schema, but with inconsequential differences (i.e., different colors or shapes in the design of computer screen, slightly different bagging area set-up) then you'll likely accommodate your schema to include this new, slightly different self-checkout station but still understand that it is a self-checkout and understand the general process for using it. If you had never encountered a self-checkout before, you would be lacking a schema for a self-checkout and might experience confusion regarding what it is or what you're expected to do with the set-up.

This example of a schema for self-checkouts is quite concrete and simplistic. In reality, we have schemas for just about everything in our lives, including intangible and abstract concepts. For example, we hold schemas for concepts around romantic relationships, civic duty, war, and illness. The process of comparing new experiences to existing schemas is the process of making meaning in our lives. Sometimes our new experiences don't adequately fit with our existing schemas, so we build an entirely new schema for the experience. Other times we can modify the existing schema to include new information. Regardless, from a cognitive perspective, we're making sense of our world by organizing our experiences in relation to our previous experiences.

These schemas, while they are foundational aspects of all our cognitions, are not necessarily something we think much about. Nevertheless, they can definitely become apparent with some exploration. Values clarification exercises can be a good way to access our deeply held beliefs and values, which can be closely linked to our schemas. We cannot overemphasize the importance of not judging or criticizing your patient's schemas, even when they appear to you to be distorted, incomplete, or faulty. Those distortions may become one focus of your later work with them, but identifying a distortion too early in a helping relationship can be detrimental to your patient's sense of feeling understood and accepted by you.

The term "cognitive triad" refers to the schemas and beliefs each of us hold about ourselves, the world, and the future. Beck, Rush, Shaw, and Emery (1987) first identified this triad as central to understanding the cognitive components of clinical depression. Since that time, many studies have corroborated the finding that the cognitive triad is generalizable cross-culturally as well, with evidence being identified in Taiwan (Lai et al., 2014), South Africa (Cortina et al., 2016), Egypt, Canada (Beshai et al., 2012), and Turkey (Erarslan & Işikli, 2019). We will consider the cognitive triad in the context of nested systems.

Influences on Meaning Making

The microskill of meaning reflection can be difficult to learn because it requires putting oneself into the mindset of another person without actually having lived that person's life, so that we can articulate how they seem to be understanding a circumstance in their life. This is also a difficult skill because the meaning that a person is making is not always reflected in their non-verbal behavior, which is different from the way that emotions can be observed even if they're not explicitly stated. If you better understand the factors that can influence meaning making, it can increase your ability to extrapolate from the concrete details of what a patient is saying and take a tentative guess at the deeper message you hear them conveying.

Ecological Systems

Bronfenbrenner's ecological systems model offers us a way to have a contextualized understanding of someone else that allows for cultural responsiveness and trauma-informed considerations. The ecological systems model views human development as a complex interplay of multiple spheres of influence. The essence of Bronfenbrenner's model is that we learn how to perceive ourselves on the basis of how others behave toward us. We learn whether we are loved (and therefore lovable), trustworthy (and therefore sincere) and given responsibility (and therefore competent), unsafe (and therefore in danger), valued (and therefore valuable), etc., from our interactions at all levels of nested systems. The systems with the most concentrated impact upon our perceptions of ourselves and the world are our microsystem and mesosystem.

Microsystem level

The microsystem is comprised of dyads and triads of an individual in face-to-face interaction with one or two others; this is the most proximal level of influence. These dyadic interactions occur between people in a household, friends, or teachers. Beginning at the microsystem, the quality of the interpersonal contact between ourselves and other individuals in our immediate (home) environment has a high degree of influence over how we come to see ourselves. Our perception of how people behave toward us informs us about how they see us. We conclude that our perception reflects the actual truth, and this "truth" in turn becomes the basis upon which we see ourselves.

Self-perceptions and beliefs about who we are and how we are, which gradually develop over our childhoods, are highly susceptible to all kinds of environmental influences, ranging from facilitative to detrimental, during early stages of development. As we move through adolescence, our self-perception gradually becomes more stable and resistant to contradictory information as we move into adulthood. Understanding a person's unique nested systems, both past and present, can provide a window to gaining an accurate picture of the meanings they use as they make sense of their worlds.

Mesosystem level

The mesosystem is a web of many microsystem interactions, which consists of interconnections between the dyads and triads of the microsystem. Examples here could include extended family such as grandparents, aunts, uncles, clergy members who are close to the family, as well as other members from their religious community.

Besides the micro and meso systems, differences in religiosity and spiritual beliefs, the geographic location and associated sociocultural characteristics of that area, prevailing political events, and subsequent acceptance or rejection of people based on diversity variables, can have a very strong influence on the decisions and internalized beliefs in all three domains of the cognitive triad. Religious beliefs have been identified as protective factors in depression (Wei & Liu, 2013; Berzengi et al., 2017; Newton & McIntosh, 2010) perhaps because religious teachings enable a person to have meaning for their existence and for their suffering.

Exosystem level

The exosystem is comprised of environments that have indirect influence on a person's internal experience, such as parents' place of employment, policies in a school, and local politics. Values and rules are expressed within these environments, and although they may not be consciously or individually adopted by an individual, they reflect prevailing norms for understanding and evaluating situations.

Macrosystem level

The macrosystem is the broadest level of system that exerts influence on the individual. This includes a person's ethnicity, culture, social or political systems, belief systems, and lifestyle. Similar to the exosystem level, the macrosystem reflects norms and values that influence meaning making. For example, if a woman sought a medically necessary abortion in the recent past, but lives in a state where abortion access was recently curtailed because of a Supreme Court decision, she may begin reflecting on her experience and making new meaning of the past experience.

Let us consider a brief case example for illustration of how this model can help us with client understanding. Please note that this is not intended to be a comprehensive case analysis of the client situation but rather a brief example of how the model can help organize our understanding of Larry's current experience.

Larry is a 40-year-old White divorced father who has primary custody of his 8-year-old daughter. He is seeking counseling for assistance with parenting, as he questions his ability as a father and is aware that he does not know how to have fun. Larry was the oldest of five boys in his family of origin and was raised on a working farm with a father who had an additional job away from the farm. Larry was put in charge of managing the farm animals, keeping their stalls cleaned out, and other chores. Although he was interested in wrestling and track, his parents demanded he devote himself to his role as eldest son. He had no school friends and spent all his time working the farm or doing homework. His father was addicted to alcohol and was often physically and emotionally abusive to Larry and

Larry's mother. Larry internalized his father's messages of being no good, lazy, and stupid. Larry's mother, who was religiously oriented, advised Larry to follow his father's directions and try to meet father's expectations although they were unreasonable. As an adult, Larry became aware that he was unable to laugh and have fun in the way he observed other people do. In addition, he came to counseling verbalizing that he was being taken advantage of by his boss because he was unable to say no when his boss insisted that he work overtime at the machine shop where he'd been employed for the previous 14 years.

Now we can take the elements of Larry's background that set the stage for some of his current difficulties. At the microsystem level, his father instilled in him worthlessness, while his mother instilled putting other's emotional needs before his own even when being victimized. Representing the mesosystem level interactions between his parents and his paternal grandparents who were similarly harsh and critical about childrearing, and Larry perceived that his siblings made no effort to either help him with his chores or defend him against his father. This lack of support informed him that he was not worth their effort and was therefore worthless. At the exosystem level are the teachings of their church, which state that children must always respect and obey their parents.

These schemas of worthlessness, not being entitled to joy, love, and unconditional nurturance, became the eyeglasses through which he saw himself. Much of the meaning-making he did was based on his perceived reality of worthlessness. He was understandably depressed and experiencing hopelessness about being a good enough father to his daughter.

By having this contextualized understanding of Larry's developmental experiences, we can more readily empathize and try to approximate his view as we offer to him reflections of the feelings and meaning he is expressing. This in turn will deepen his experience of being heard and held, which is fundamental to the process of helping.

The Skill of Meaning Reflection

Like so many other aspects of culturally responsive helping, hearing another and understanding what they are communicating is a nuanced process. There are multiple layers of meaning that may be communicated simultaneously, and in some cases, the meta-message that becomes apparent to you as the listener may be outside of your patient's conscious awareness. Depending on how well we know the person and what the content is, we can choose how concrete or abstract we want to be with our reflection of meaning.

Meaning reflections do not follow a particular format or composition in the same way of an emotion reflection. Rather, a meaning reflection is simply a paraphrase that reflects the provider's best attempts to ascertain the deeper meaning of what the patient has expressed. There is a degree of interpretation that is necessary and there is always some risk that the provider will be inaccurate in their meaning reflection. Recall that a paraphrase closely aligns with the specifics of what a patient stated. Compare this to a meaning reflection, which steps further away from the specifics of what the patient said and rather, attempts to capture a larger and more profound reflection of what the patient expressed. Consider the following example and spot the subtle differences between a paraphrase and a meaning reflection in response to the patient's disclosure.

PATIENT: I'm not going to do it any more. I'm not going to drive up to her house whenever she needs me, at the drop of a hat. I have my own life and I can't keep doing this. I've got my own life to deal with too, ya know!? She acts like her problems are so much more pressing than mine.

Provider (paraphrasing): It sounds like you're not going to accommodate her in the way that you have been any more.

Provider (meaning reflection): It sounds like you see your needs as just as important as hers, and that sacrificing for her so often is downplaying the importance of your own needs and wants.

Overt and Covert Communication Patterns

There are a host of nonverbal and paraverbal cues that accompany a spoken message, which then inform the context and support accurate exchange of intended and received meaning. We talked at length in Chapter Five about attunement to those cues. These are the subtle aspects of the other person's communication pattern that will inform our perception of the emotions the other is feeling as they are expressing the content of their message. We mention it again here because there is a fair likelihood that a speaker will not specifically use feeling words as they are describing a situation to you. However, you may have enough information by observing their affect and paraverbals in combination with the content of their message to proceed with your feeling reflection and make a highly educated guess about their underlying feelings.

There is not a specific formula to follow when engaging in the skill of meaning reflection, but you can keep in mind the importance of the components of emotion reflection that were discussed earlier in this

146   Helping Skills for Counselors and Health Professionals

chapter. With a meaning reflection or emotion reflection, maintain a stance of tentativeness and openness to correction; this skill requires making some assumptions about a person's feelings or views that are not yet fully articulated by the person themselves. Below are examples of what a person states (and how they state it), the verbal content of their message, the implied content of their message (which incorporates the paraverbal content), and then most broadly, the meta-message (which reflects the deeper meaning).

Scenario: Parent speaking about their 17-year-old child

PARENT'S STATEMENT AND NON-VERBAL BEHAVIOR: I heard Bob come in the house from Jayla's graduation party at 3:00 am even though his curfew is midnight. He thought I was asleep, but the dog barked and then I heard him tiptoeing up the stairs. Now there's another graduation party tonight.

[*As the speaker rolls her eyes and shakes her head back and forth in a "no" gesture.*]

VERBAL CONTENT: Bob violated his curfew by three hours and he didn't volunteer that information. There's another party happening tonight.
IMPLIED MESSAGE: Since Bob didn't follow the rules and was trying to be sneaky coming in the house, you are making him stay home tonight.
META-MESSAGE: Bob once again showed you that he is not trustworthy when he is given adult privileges.

Scenario: A patient is talking about a situation in their life related to work

PATIENT'S STATEMENT AND NON-VERBAL BEHAVIOR: Well, finally after three other times I was turned down, I got the promotion at work! You are looking at the new assistant manager of our store. It's been a heck of a thing and I was ready to give up, now I'm glad I kept trying.

[*Patient is smiling broadly and nodding their head.*]

VERBAL CONTENT: I'm hearing that you were persistent and eventually you experienced success.
IMPLIED MESSAGE: I can hear by your tone of voice as you share that you are feeling satisfied and perhaps relieved that your persistence has led to a better job with more money and responsibility.
META-MESSAGE: I can see how pleased you feel that all this hard work over these years has finally been recognized and valued by your employer. They are telling you that you have proven yourself, and the quality of your work justifies you moving up in the organization!

The process of communication is an interactional pattern of message transmission and retrieval. Communication theory has much to offer us as we consider counseling interactions, particularly considering that the entirety of counseling is predicated on accurately perceiving what another person is attempting to communicate. This idea of a completely objective, accurate perception of another person's message is a goal, not a true possibility, because we can never be free of our brains and bodies. Our own humanity and subjectivity are part of what make each interaction with someone a completely unique experience that can never be duplicated. In a conversation with anyone, be it a social conversation or a professional therapeutic interaction, when we speak, we are expressing an intended message. We assume that what the listener perceives in our message is consistent with the message we are intending to communicate. Conversely, when someone tells us something, we assume our perception of their message is indeed the message they intended to send. Unless there is a secondary conversation to examine the message intended and message received, we cannot know for sure that explicitly accurate communication is occurring.

Long before a person begins metabolizing feelings or making changes in their thinking and behavior, the process of explicitly accurate communication must be well established. The great thing is that relationship development blossoms and thrives when one (or both) parties are striving to listen. Taking the time to really understand what a person is communicating to us is of tremendous benefit to the relationship because in taking that time, we are communicating, "You're worth my time." When we listen to understand, rather than to reply, we open ourselves to empathically resonate with the other person.

Conclusion

This chapter has covered material that is literally central to the process of relationship development with our patients. We looked at emotions with an eye toward the purpose they serve each of us as humans, and we emphasized the importance of professional helpers being emotionally literate. Our clients and patients will potentially have an enhanced experience of our help if we are able to perceive and support the emotions that are evident in our interactions with them. Equally important in this process of developing emotional literacy, we as helpers need to have a solid understanding of cultural display rules, if we wish to be truly culturally responsive.

Another important microskill that was presented and explained is the skill of meaning reflection. Helping people to articulate their perceptions and to understand the connection between their meaning making and their felt emotions is an important aspect of professional helping. Even in those cases where the focus of our help is not specifically counseling, understanding and reflecting our patient's meaning making can be very helpful in establishing a helpful, productive relationship with them. This naturally may lead to better outcomes. These two types of reflection, feeling and meaning making, comprise some of the most fundamental building blocks of a solid helping relationship.

Questions for Class Discussion

1 How comfortable are you with your feeling word vocabulary? What are some strategies you can think of to expand it?
2 Talk with your classmates about what kinds of thoughts and feelings you experience when you are conversing with someone who is expressing intense feelings of anger, sadness, or other feelings that are uncomfortable for you.
3 Discuss a time when you shared some private feelings with another person and felt truly heard and honored. What did that person say and do that facilitated your sense of being completely validated?

References

Arnold, M. (1960). *Emotion and personality: Volume 1, Psychological aspects*. Columbia University Press.

Beck, A.T., Rush, A.J., Shaw, G.F., & Emery, G. (1987). *Cognitive Therapy of Depression*. Guilford Press.

Berzengi, A., Berzenji, L., Kadim, A., Mustafa, F., & Jobson, L. (2017). Role of Islamic appraisals, trauma-related appraisals, and religious coping in the posttraumatic adjustment of Muslim trauma survivors. *Psychological Trauma: Theory, Research, Practice, and Policy*, 9, 189–197. doi:10.1037/tra0000179.supp.

Beshai, S., Dobson, K., & Adel, A. (2012). Cognition and Dysphoria in Egypt and Canada: An Examination of the Cognitive Triad. *Canadian Journal of Behavioural Science*, 44(1), 29–39. doi:10.1037/a0025744.

Cavanaugh, M.E. (1982). *The counseling experience: A theoretical and practical approach*. Waveland Press.

Center for Nonviolent Communication. (2005). Feelings Inventory. www.cnvc.org/training/resource/feelings-inventory.

Cortina, M., Stein, A., Kahn, K., Tintswalo, M.H., Holmes, E., & Fazel, M. (2016). Cognitive styles and psychological functioning in rural South African school students: Understanding influences for risk and resilience in the face of chronic adversity. *Journal of Adolescence*, 49(1), 38–46. doi:10.1016/j.adolescence.2016.01.010.

Ekman, P. & Friesen, W.V. (1971). Constants across cultures in the face and emotion. *Journal of Personality and Social Psychology*, 17, 124–129.

Ekman, P., Sorenson, E.R., & Friesen, W.V. (1969). Pan-cultural elements in facial displays of emotion. *Science*, 164(3875), 86–88.

Erarslan, Ö & Işikli, S. (2019). Adaptation of the Cognitive Triad Inventory into Turkish: A Validity and Reliability Study. *Noro Psikiyatr Ars*, 56(1), 32–39. doi:10.29399/npa.19390.

Hofmann, S.G. & Doan, S.N. (2018). The social foundations of emotion: Developmental, cultural, and clinical dimensions. American Psychological Association. doi:10.1037/0000098-000.

Hutchinson, A., Gerstein, L., Millner, A., Reding, E., & Plumer, L. (2020). Counseling Psychology Trainees' Knowledge of Cultural Display Rules. *The Counseling Psychologist*, 48(5) 685–671. doi:10.1177/0011000020915968.

Ivey, A.E. & Ivey, M.B. (2007). *Intentional interviewing and counseling: Facilitating client development in a multicultural society* (6th ed.). Thomson Higher Education.

Lai, C., Zauszniewski, J., Tang, T.-C., Hou, S.-Y., Su, S.-F., & Lai, P. (2014). Personal beliefs, learned resourcefulness, and adaptive functioning in depressed adults. *Journal of Psychiatric and Mental Health Nursing*, 21(3), 280–287. doi:10.1111/jpm.12087.

Newton, A.T. & McIntosh, D.N. (2010). Specific Religious Beliefs in a Cognitive Appraisal Model of Stress and Coping. *International Journal for the Psychology of Religion*, 20, 39–58. doi:10.1080/10508610903418129.

Poorman, P. B. (2003). *Microskills and theoretical foundations for professional helpers*. Allyn & Bacon.

Prochaska, J.O., DiClemente, C.C., & Norcross, J C. (1992). In search of the structure of change. In *Self Change* (pp. 87–114). Springer.

Roberts, G. (2022). Emotion Wheel. https://imgur.com/q6hcgsH.

Seligman, L. (2004). *Technical and conceptual skills for mental health professionals*. Merrill/Prentice Hall.

Wei, D. & Liu, E. (2013). Religious Involvement and Depression: Evidence for Curvilinear and Stress-Moderating Effects Among Young Women in Rural China. *Journal for the Scientific Study of Religion*, 52(2), 349–367. doi:10.1111/jssr.12031.

Wiseman, T. (1996). A concept analysis of empathy. *Journal of Advanced Nursing*, 23(6), 1162–1167. doi:10.1046/j.1365-2648.1996.12213.x.

Young, M.E. (2005). *Learning the art of helping: Building blocks and techniques* (3rd ed.). Prentice Hall.

Chapter 8

Helping Behaviors: Verbal Skills to Invite Exploration

We will begin this chapter with a discussion of the inherent power differential that exists in any professional helping relationship. When someone in need comes to see you, they are seeking your services because you have been trained and hold a license to provide services. These credentials place you in a position of power. Why is it important to speak of the professional relationship in this way? Many people who seek our services come with aspects of their identity or experiences that result in disempowerment in some spaces of their lives. Medical mistrust, as discussed in earlier chapters, can have a detrimental impact on treatment outcome. This can result from a patient withholding important information, not following through on suggestions their provider is offering, or simply not keeping or rescheduling an appointment. Therefore, being conscious about the power we have over our patients is critical. Providers should be aware of their paraverbal and nonverbal behavior when asking questions of their patients. Later in the chapter we will discuss specific techniques for questioning that can enhance relationship development.

This chapter on questioning takes us further along the trajectory of provider directiveness; the questions you ask, if you ask any, steer the focus of your interaction with your patient in a particular direction. Throughout this chapter we will also discuss questioning patients from a trauma-informed perspective. In a counseling context, some models of helping emphasize the therapist exerting significant influence over the choice of topic, breadth of scope, and depth of disclosure. Examples of directive models include cognitive behavioral and brief solution focused. In contrast, other models of counseling, such as person-centered, conceptualize that same directiveness as contraindicated and detrimental to the person's growth. In other health professions, there may be very specific pieces of information a provider must acquire from a patient. In these contexts, the provider may have a clearly conceptualized agenda as to what is necessary and sufficient intervention to assist the patient in attaining their goals.

Regardless of your theoretical orientation, questioning is a skill that can be tremendously effective, or tremendously unhelpful, depending on when

DOI: 10.4324/9781003217589-10

and how it is used. Often, beginning students in classroom practices tend to rely on asking question after question to keep their partner talking, without differentiating between information that is beneficial to the process from simply talking for the sake of keeping the other person talking. Regardless of your profession or the context in which the questions are being asked, we strongly encourage you to develop your questioning skills with mindfulness. When using questioning in a counseling session, it is important you do so with a clearly articulated model or goal and from a trauma-informed perspective.

Questioning from a Trauma-Informed Perspective

Earlier in the textbook, we discussed the four Rs of trauma-informed systems created by the Substance Abuse and Mental Health Services Administration (2014). The Rs of trauma-informed systems realize the impact of trauma, recognize the signs and symptoms associated with trauma, respond accordingly through a trauma-informed lens, and resist re-traumatization of the patients whom we serve (Substance Abuse and Mental Health Services Administration, 2014). When questioning patients, it is imperative to ensure that we avoid traumatizing or re-traumatizing them in the settings where we serve them. Helpful questioning behavior includes asking them questions that help to empower them in the space where they may feel vulnerable, owing to physical or mental health concerns, asking them to describe what they need to feel safe in your space when they come in for treatment, and being transparent about the process of treatment. Unhelpful questioning behaviors include asking for *unnecessary* details of past trauma experiences and asking leading questions that imply responsibility for their past traumatic experiences.

Empowering patients gives them an opportunity to open up and share information and ask questions that they may have. In some situations, patients may feel powerless, owing to their mental or physical health concerns. As a provider, when getting patients to open up we want to create spaces for them to feel empowered to use their voices to answer questions and to ask questions to get the services that they need. The second component is to ensure that patients feel physically and emotionally safe sharing information and asking questions within the professional space. One effective way to see if patients feel safe in your space is to simply ask them what they need. Sometimes, as practitioners we assume that we know what patients need in order to feel secure, but what we may find relaxing and comforting may not be the same for our patients. So, it is key to ask patients what they need in order to feel protected when opening up, sharing, and asking questions. The last component is to be transparent about services that the patient will receive and give them an opportunity to reflect and ask questions about treatment that they will receive. When providing services to patients, transparency is an important component to ensuring that you are operating through a trauma-informed lens.

Effective Questioning

Effective questioning is predicated on a clear purpose and rationale before actually using the skill; we need to be cognizant of our intention before we ask a question. Skilled providers use questions to serve a variety of purposes. Some of those purposes include:

1   Gathering information during an intake or assessment appointment
2   Beginning a counseling session
3   Clarifying a patient's statement
4   Sharpening the focus in a particular way (e.g., on content or on affect)

Our first step will be to look at specific mechanics of asking a question. The subsequent discussion is organized around each of the listed purposes. Each discussion section will provide dialogue examples of how that purpose is accomplished.

Open and Closed Questions

One way that questions can be categorized is open-ended versus closed-ended. An open- question is one that will likely result in a person answering with an elaborated response. The answer to an open question is usually not one that can be given in a single word. In contrast, closed questions seek a specific response, often one that can be offered in a single word or by a "yes" or "no" answer. Novice providers may erroneously assume that open questions are *always* better than closed questions. This is not necessarily true; in some circumstances closed questions are preferable. An example would be when a provider needs to solicit a particular bit of information from the patient. Open questions begin with the following words: *How, What, When, Where, Who,* and *Why.* Closed questions begin with words such as: *Is, Are, Do, Did, Could, Would,* and *Have.*

Generally speaking, open questions will result in the patient continuing to talk and giving more material, some of which may be pertinent to the intended focus, and some of which may not. Among the open-ended question stems, "what" questions are likely to result in a person giving facts and details, whereas "how" questions are more likely to yield process or sequence information. For example, "What happened?" will be answered with a factual recounting of an incident; "What was the movie about?" will result in a summary of the movie plot. In contrast, "How did that situation come about?" or "How was the movie?" will be answered with responses that are more process oriented, that is, describing how the situation unfolded and what the feelings and internal experiences were.

Mechanical Aspects of Questioning

Regardless of whether a provider's questions are open or closed, asking questions is directive because the patient's response will take the focus of discussion in a particular direction. One basic choice you will make as you ask questions will be whether you wish to place the focus on the content of the patient's story, or on the subjective experience about the story, which will take the discussion in a process-oriented direction.

The actual wording of the stated question is your overt message to the patient. Also present and affecting the interaction will be the covert message of the question; the covert message is communicated in part by your paraverbals and in part by the focus of the question. As you have noticed, the paraverbal aspect of the interaction between you and your patient has been a recurrent topic of discussion. That emphasis on paraverbals continues in this present discussion of how to ask effective questions. Your voice tone and the mechanics with which you speak will make all the difference between a respectful, thought-provoking inquiry and a stern, judging, or critical demand for a piece of information.

Personal Reflection

Can you recall a time when someone asked you a series of questions, one after the other, before you had a chance to respond? How did that feel? How did those feelings influence the way you responded to them?

Avoiding an ambiance of interrogation can be accomplished if you do two things. First, ask only one question at a time. Sometimes in our eagerness to help, we ask more than one question in rapid succession before the other person can answer our first question. Keep in mind that if a client feels interrogated, there will be less likelihood of a shared process of exploration and change, which is the overall goal of our work with our patients. One well-timed and well-worded question is far better than three mediocre questions asked in rapid sequence. Here is an example of an ineffective series:

CLIENT: I'm so glad to be back here to see you. My visit with my sister was okay, I guess, but it's a relief to be back home and coming for counseling.
COUNSELOR: So, the trip wasn't good? What was the problem? You seem upset. Did she say something that upset you?

This counselor response could leave the client feeling bewildered or overwhelmed by which question to answer first, even though it seems clear that the counselor is asking these questions out of genuine concern for the patient. Take a moment to think about what you want to ask, and then word your question briefly in a way the patient will be able to answer you. After you've asked the question, stop talking, sit back, and wait. If your question is one that provokes introspection, your patient may not be able to immediately produce a response. This is where your comfort with silence will come into play. Here is an example of a more effective question in response to the client's statement:

CLIENT: I'm so glad to be back here to see you. My visit with my sister was okay, I guess, but it's a relief to be back home and coming for counseling.
COUNSELOR: I get the sense your visit wasn't perfect. What was the visit like for you?

The second thing you can do to minimize an "inquisition" is to take time to respond to the client's response to a question before asking another one. After using your attending skills to attune yourself to their response, take the time to acknowledge the answer before asking another question. An acknowledgement could take the form of a paraphrase, a reflection of feeling, or a reflection of meaning. If the acknowledgement is done with intent, not perfunctorily but rather with a moderate rate of speech, the person will experience being heard by you, which is necessary for the relationship to deepen. Besides the obvious benefit of rapport, this reflective technique will also slow down the process and minimize a conversational pattern of rapid-fire questions.

CLIENT: Well, she was busy with friends the whole time. I don't think we went out for lunch or dinner even once all weekend without a whole bunch of her friends coming along, and they drank the entire time and got really loud. She never asked me anything about my life or my new job or anything.
COUNSELOR: It sounds like she was busy with friends and you didn't feel that she was focused on you. I recall that you haven't had any chance yet to tell her about all the changes happening in your life and were hoping to tell her about those things. Did I hear you correctly?

One way to imagine the questioning process is like fishing. You can either cast a net or drop a line; a dropped line may or may not result in catching a single fish, depending on where the line is dropped. On the other hand, a widely cast net will catch a variety of fish as well as other creatures - or even unwanted objects.

Sometimes when novice counselors begin working with clients, they are so conscientious and concerned about being helpful that their counseling sessions consist mainly of directly focused questions that result in the patient correspondingly giving one discrete piece of information. Then, as the question-and-answer conversational pattern becomes established, and the client becomes accustomed to the counselor setting the agenda and direction. By sparingly asking open-ended questions and remaining open-minded about what the client should be talking about, we are best able to follow the client based on what appears salient to them.

In some cases, the circumstances of the patient's referral for counseling might be such that it is appropriate for the provider to be structuring the interaction. For example, if a client has been referred to a mental health clinic for an anger management counseling program, the counselor may need to ask a specific set of questions. Similarly, if a patient is seeking health services, there may be a circumscribed set of questions pertaining to that aspect of their physical or emotional functioning. This is why providers need to consider the overall goal of the interaction with the patient and use questioning behavior accordingly to achieve the goals.

Ineffective Questioning Behaviors

Here is a dialogue example of a string of inappropriate, directive questions:

COUNSELOR: Lisa, I'm so glad you came to see me today. So how are things going in school?
CLIENT: Pretty good, I guess.
COUNSELOR: That's great! What were your grades on your last report card?
CLIENT: I had an A in math, a B in language arts, a B in social studies, and Cs in art and gym.
COUNSELOR: Well done! And how about your behaviour grades?
CLIENT: I had S's for satisfactory on everything.
COUNSELOR: Excellent! Are things going pretty well with your friends?
CLIENT: Some of them.
COUNSELOR: Are you still going to the movies and practicing your dances?
CLIENT: I guess.

So far, the counselor has been the individual directing the focus, and although her questions have been answered, she still has no information as to what the client might actually want to discuss. If a client has no prior experience with counseling, they may feel comfortable deferring to the authority of the counselor. Some people may have expectations that counseling will be like going to visits with other healthcare providers, which might tend toward greater provider directiveness. In Western medicine, when we go to a physician, we expect the physician to ask questions we will answer before the physician then gives us a diagnosis and recommendation for how to treat our problem. In those interactions, the physician is the person responsible for doing the asking, thinking, diagnosing, and treating. Naïve counseling clients cannot be faulted for assuming that a similar pattern would exist in a counseling session.

If you are working with someone who has never before been a client, it is possible that they will hold similar expectations about the counseling process. So, if you lapse into a pattern of interaction like the one above, you become the one doing the work, meaning that you are thinking, reasoning, processing, and the client's role will only be to receive your mental efforts. Ideally, the client should be making at least the same degree of mental and emotional effort in the interaction as you are. We refer to this as the client "working," and a general guideline is that you as the counselor should strive to never work harder than your client. In the dialogue example above, the counselor is definitely working harder than the client.

Here is another dialogue example using the same client, but with the counselor placing the onus of work responsibility on the client:

COUNSELOR: I'm so glad to see you today, Lisa. What's been going on that you asked to see me?
CLIENT: I'm really upset about Mary's birthday party. All the other girls are invited except me, and they're being mean to me too.
COUNSELOR: I want to hear more about this birthday party invitation thing. What happened?
CLIENT: Well ...

By asking these two open-ended, yet focused questions, the counselor got right to the heart of Lisa's concerns and reason for requesting counseling. This gave Lisa the opportunity to establish some control over the interaction, and also saved considerable effort on the counselor's part.

Something else important to recognize is that the meta-message in these focused, open-ended questions is that this is the client's work to do, not the counselor's. If the counselor had been asking a whole string of closed questions, and then at the end said, "You know, this is your counseling session and you'll be the one working toward the solution," the spoken message would not match the counselor's behavior. This would constitute a mismatch between the counselor's words and actions, which could create dissonance for the client. The client might become distrustful of the counselor because of the misalignment between the counselor's words and behaviors.

Another ineffective questioning behavior is asking multiple-choice questions. A multiple-choice question entails asking a question and then immediately offering up possible answers before the patient could answer.

This usually occurs when a provider feels like it would be helpful because it could signal that the provider anticipates the patient's answer, thus suggesting they understand the person and their concerns. An example might be, "What stopped you from accepting the invitation? Was it because you had a headache or because you didn't like the other people who would be there?". However, multiple choice questions eliminate the opportunity for the patient to express themselves fully and independently. The best practice is to ask an open question and simply await the patient's response.

The Problem with "Why"

Questions that start with "why" are open questions; however, they carry with them a unique consideration for their use. "Why" questions are particularly tempting for those of us who are psychologically minded and want to understand a person's underlying motives. However, when we ask a why question, it puts the other person in the position of needing to provide a reason. What we're essentially doing is requiring a justification. "Why are you angry at your partner?" is asking a client the reason for their anger. Asking for justification can evoke defensiveness from the client. Additionally, "why" questions can be difficult for a client to answer because they themselves may be unsure of what led them to think or behave or feel a certain way. Lastly, asking why subtly carries a covert implication that we as counselors are in a position to judge whether the person is entitled to their reaction, behavior, etc. This implication is clearer with another example of a commonly asked question: "Why did you do that?"

Asking a child "why" may result in a literal, concrete response. One of the authors (K.M.) was once working with a boy who had run away from the treatment center where she worked. When the police picked him up, he gave them his correct name but his incorrect birth date. After he returned to the treatment center, she asked him why he had given his wrong birth date, and he replied, "That's my alias!" While this was true, that in his mind the incorrect birth date was his disguise, it didn't help her understand his motivation for lying. It would have been more effective for her to comment on his behavior by saying, "I saw in the police report that you gave them the wrong date of birth. What was going on for you that you decided to do that?"

If you ask an adult why they did something or feel a certain way, the most likely outcome is either some type of justification or a defensive reply of "I don't know." This might be the truth too, perhaps the person really doesn't know why they did something or has a particular feeling. Asking why in the manner described can be detrimental to your efforts to establish and maintain a therapeutic alliance. For that reason, we encourage novice counselors to studiously avoid using "why" when they use questions. Consider the following alternatives to these "why" questions in Table 8.1.

Table 8.1 Alternatives to Why Questions

Why question	Open-ended alternative
Why didn't you call her when you knew he was upset?	How did you feel about communicating with him once you found out he was upset?
Why did you drop out of the program?	What brought you to your decision to drop out?
Why didn't you use the new re-direction technique when she got angry and yelled at you?	Tell me about how you decided to manage the situation when she got angry.

With the final example you may notice that the alternative open question isn't technically a question at all. The statement "tell me..." is actually a directive but functions as a question. It is important to retain gentle and curious paraverbal and nonverbal behaviors with "tell me..." directives so that the provider does not come across as demanding.

Dialogue Examples of How to Achieve Specific Purposes

At the beginning of the chapter, we listed numerous purposes that can be served by the judicious use of questions. Now we will return to that list and give you some dialogue examples of how questions could be used to accomplish each purpose.

Gathering Information at an Intake or Assessment Appointment

When a patient is seen for a first session, it is necessary for the provider to gather information. Depending on the setting (e.g., school, hospital, community agency), the degree of comprehensiveness of background information will vary. Note that Chapter 9 of this text is devoted almost entirely to basic mental health assessment, so we won't go into great detail here about the breadth of information that might be gathered in a first session. What is relevant to discuss here is that even in a first meeting, when you don't know a person very well, a couple of well-phrased questions interspersed with other microskills will be more conducive to relationship development than a lengthy series of questions. Here is an example of a good opening that uses one well-phrased question.

COUNSELOR: Let's start by talking about what's been going on with you that led you to schedule this appointment with me today.
CLIENT: Well, I just found out my wife is going to move out of the house, and she is filing for divorce.

COUNSELOR: Okay, so you just got this information about your wife leaving you. Tell me about how this is affecting you.

Here is another example of a gentle, open-ended question that therapists often use to begin a counseling session.

COUNSELOR: It's very nice to meet you, Mrs. Flowers. How can I help you?

Beginning a Counseling Session

A common way that novice providers begin a session with a patient they've been seeing is to ask, "What's been going on lately?" Here's an example of how an interaction might transpire when you initiate a counseling session this way:

PROVIDER: Hi Roberto, what's been going on?
PATIENT: Well, let's see. The motor on my car has been making a funny noise, so I took it to my brother-in-law who owns a dealership over on the west side. Turns out it's something with the timing chain and the air intake valve, and he's giving me a good deal on the repair bill.

This type of opening question is fine if you wish to hear the patient recount what has happened in their life in the recent past. Sometimes that is what you are hoping for, but the disadvantage is that it may take the focus of discussion in a direction that does not really pertain to the patient's main reason for seeking your services.

Alternatively, you can begin the session with a question that immediately focuses the patient's attention in a relevant direction. Consider the following example:

PROVIDER: Roberto, the last time we met, we were focusing on some things you could try doing to help you parent your daughter and not give in to her when she argues with you. Were you able to try any of them?
PATIENT: Yes.
PROVIDER: Tell me about that.
PATIENT: Okay. You know how you said I could try...

Clarifying a Patient's Statement

Sometimes a patient will say something that is confusing to you, or that will seem to have ambiguous meaning. Where a paraphrase could be helpful, sometimes it just is easier and makes more sense to ask a question that clarifies what the patient is trying to communicate.

PATIENT: So, there we were walking around at the market, and all of a sudden Kai turned to me and said, "Cut it out right now or I'll just leave you here and drive by myself." I ended up taking the bus home.
PROVIDER: Do you mean she left you at the mall?
PATIENT: No, she didn't leave me there. But I got tired of her attitude, so I left on my own.

Another way to clarify what a patient has expressed is essentially the technique we talked about in the previous chapter in which you paraphrase and then do a checkout to verify that you correctly understand what the client is communicating. A question can be used the same way at the end of a paraphrase, that is, adding on "...do I have that correct?" or "...am I understanding you?"

Sharpening the Focus

Questions can be used to home in on a particular aspect of the patient's concern. Let's take a look as some example dialogue between a patient and provider to explore how different questions direct the patient to discuss different components of her concern.

PATIENT: So, there we were walking around at the market, and all of a sudden Kai turned to me and said, "Cut it out right now or I'll just leave you here and drive by myself." I ended up taking the bus home.
PROVIDER: Do you mean she left you at the mall?
PATIENT: No, she didn't leave me there. But I got tired of her attitude, so I left on my own.
PROVIDER: So basically, she got mad at you, but you were also mad at her, and so you took matters into your own hands and left and rode the bus home? Am I getting that correct?

In the dialogue example above, the clarifying question focused on the content of the patient's concerns: the details of the story. The question sharpened the focus on the sequence of events. That same discussion about the patient's concerns would go in a completely different direction if the provider chose to ask questions that emphasized the process rather than the content. Here is an example of how that might unfold:

PATIENT: So, there we were walking around at the market, and all of a sudden Kai turned to me and said, "Cut it out right now or I'll just leave you here and drive by myself." I ended up taking the bus home.

PROVIDER: How did that feel when Kai said that to you?
PATIENT: Oh, who cares? What kind of a friend is she anyway if she'd just leave me like that?
PROVIDER: It sounds to me like you're asking yourself whether you really have a friendship with someone who would threaten to strand you at the market. Let's talk about how you think a "good friendship" might look different from this one. Could that be helpful?

In this second example, the question directed the patient to discuss their thoughts about the friendship itself, not the details of the situation. Let us now explore some common habits that can easily develop without a provider's mindful attention to their own behavior.

Developing Good Questioning Habits

There are some common pitfalls in questioning behavior beyond those already discussed (i.e., back-to-back questions, multiple choice questions). Some other common "bad" habits include poor timing and leading questions. Leading questions come in a variety of forms that will be discussed shortly. Regarding poor timing, a poorly timed question can have a negative impact on a patient and the dynamic in the moment. As an example, imagine a patient tearfully sharing that his father had died a week prior, and the counselor responding, "Didn't you tell me you were adopted?" Not only is the provider not responding to the patient's expressed emotions, but they are centering the interaction on the provider's desire for information rather than on the patient's need for acknowledgement and empathy. Even worse, that question could be perceived as implying that if they were adopted, their grief would somehow be different: less painful or severe. The helpful questioning habit to develop is to ensure that when used, questions should pertain to the most salient aspects of what the patient is sharing, including observing and honoring their expressed emotions.

Another bad habit in questioning behavior is asking a question in a leading manner. A leading question is any type of question that attempts to elicit a particular answer from someone. Leading questions can come in several forms including assumption of a solution, reflection of implicit bias, and desire for patient to agree with your own perspective. Let's explore each of these.

Assumption of Solution

As you are listening to someone you're helping, there may be times when the solution to their problem or concern will appear to be completely obvious. Unless being aware that we are doing it, we may ask questions that imply a client should have acted in some way. This can be detrimental to the working relationship for a couple reasons. For one thing, what seems like a viable solution to you may not feel viable to them. Second, it presumes that you know better what that person needs than they do. Third, even if it is a viable option, if the person has been unable to take those steps, they may think you are judging or criticizing them and be even less likely to explore what is preventing them from taking steps. Patients often know what they "need to do" to resolve their concerns; however, they are seeking your guidance because they are struggling to do that thing.

The most frequent example of this is in a counseling context is when a person is describing an interpersonal conflict, which is a very common topic in counseling, and the counselor asks, "Have you talked to ___ about ___?" On the surface this seems like a perfectly reasonable action to ponder - holding an assertive, direct conversation with another person about uncomfortable feelings, thoughts, or behaviors might help resolve the issue. However, lots of people don't do that - either because of their cultural beliefs about self-disclosure, or because they are conflict avoidant, or unassertive, or a variety of other reasons. Regardless of the reason for their not initiating that conversation, asking the question in that way implies covertly that they should have done it already, or should do it in the future. It is dangerous to make that assumption because we do not yet know what has prevented it. This is a valuable place for exploration! Thus, a more effective way to invite exploration is to ask, "What have you tried to manage this problem?" If they have initiated that direct conversation, they'll tell you. If they have not initiated it, you'll learn more about their conflict resolution style without shaming or directing them toward behavior that might require incongruence culturally or otherwise personally for them. Taking it a step further, advising action that is contrary to a person's inclination potentially represents an overstepping of the ethical principle of autonomy.

Reflection of Implicit Bias

As discussed in previous chapters, most people hold some number of beliefs about people and groups that are based on stereotypes and not the actual diversity of people within that group. It is not surprising that people develop such judgements because these often result from living in an environment in which those views were commonly held and routinely expressed. However, as people go about their lives, they often realize that they hold a limited or stereotyped view of a particular group and that they may have been unaware of such a bias until it was brought to their attention. Implicit biases are the judgement and beliefs that we hold of others that are often beyond our conscious awareness. Implicit biases can lead providers to ask a leading question that reflect the bias.

Imagine that a provider held the stereotyped and inaccurate belief that people with disabilities were inherently asexual. The following dialogue example reflects a conversation in which a counselor's implicit belief is reflected in his questioning behavior with a client that uses a wheelchair.

CLIENT: It's been pretty tense in our relationship since she started her new anti-depressant medicine. She was originally worried about the side effects related to concentration, but it turns out the thing that's bothering her the most is that she doesn't feel much sexual desire any more. It's been hard on me too, but I didn't want to say anything because I don't want her to feel even worse.
COUNSELOR: Oh, okay, so this is hard for you? (counselor has furrowed brow and appears confused)
CLIENT: Uhh, yeah, I mean, I miss being intimately connected with her in a sexual way.
COUNSELOR: Ah, okay, uh-huh. [*Counselor is nodding and his eyes are wide.*]

The counselor responded in a way that seems to question why this is a concern for him. The underlying assumption that the client might perceive is "You assume that I'm a person without sexual desires." Patients often pick up on these implicit biases that find their way into leading questions. There may be implicit biases you hold that influence the way you are asking questions. Take a moment to consider for yourself, *what are groups about which you have a limited or stereotyped view? What would it look like to ask a leading question that reflected your implicit bias?*

The more helpful questioning behavior that counteracts this problematic one actually doesn't necessarily involve crafting different questions. Rather, it involves exploring one's views and assumptions about people, groups, and situations to interrogate them for inaccurate biases. Take time to expand your views and conceptualizations of groups with which you are less familiar and then the likelihood of asking implicitly biased questions will decrease.

Desire for Confirmation

The last type of leading question is that which seeks confirmation from the patient but is stemming from a circumstance in which the power differential might lead the patient to simply agree with the provider, even though they feel otherwise. These leading questions rely on the perceived authority of the provider to make a statement but frame it as a question that assumes the patient will agree. Consider the following example.

CLIENT: I've been wanting to talk with him about his marijuana use, but I'm just so nervous about it. I know I'm his mother but now he's an adult I just think that he doesn't really care about my opinion any more.

I'm afraid that he's going to use this as another reason to say that he can't be open and honest with me, because he'll think that I'm judging him. I just don't know what to do. I'm not sure if I should just let it go and let him learn his lesson on his own, or if I should say something.
COUNSELOR: You're not going to let his hurt feelings get in the way of this important conversation, are you?

In this question from the counselor, it is apparent that the counselor is discounting the apprehension that the client feels about having this conversation with her son. The counselor's statement makes the assumption that hurting her son's feelings is not an adequate reason for avoiding the conversation. A more effective response to this client might simply be a paraphrase and an emotion reflection. If the counselor were to ask a question, it should not be one that judges the client's behavior.

Conclusion

One of the commonly recurring themes in this text involves the inherent power imbalance in helping relationships and the critical need for a professional helper to maintain acute awareness of that. In this chapter, we looked at multiple purposes that can be served by asking questions. At the same time, however, we emphasized that damage to the working relationship can be done if questions are not worded and delivered properly. Misuse of questioning can contribute to an exacerbation of the omnipresent power imbalance. Even if harm is not done, the overuse of questioning simply sets up a dynamic in which patients lack agency to drive sessions.

Questions for Class Discussion

1 How did the material in this chapter fit with what you've previously thought about questioning in counseling?
2 What do you see as the main disadvantages of keeping questions to a minimum?
3 To what extent do you associate asking clients questions with being in an "expert" role? How does this relate to your self-expectation about your responsibility and role as a professional counselor?

References

Substance Abuse and Mental Health Services Administration. (2014). *Trauma-Informed Care in Behavioral Health Services: A Treatment Improvement Protocol*. U.S. Department of Health and Human Services, Substance Abuse and Mental Health Services Administration, Center for Substance Abuse Treatment.

Section III

Putting Helping Skills to Work

Chapter 9

Basic Mental Health Assessment

The foundational information (i.e., ethics, cultural diversity, human development) and helping skills you've learned across the previous eight chapters have prepared you to combine this learning into action with patients. One of the first opportunities for using these skills may occur when you meet with a patient for the first time. During the first meeting, a provider typically places special emphasis on getting to know the patient through a trauma-informed lens to ensure that the patient can get the services they need without being traumatized or re-traumatized in the setting. This focus on assessment is pragmatic given that diagnoses may need to be rendered and treatment plans created – both of which require learning wide ranging information about a patient.

Provider focus on learning a lot about a patient also serves to develop rapport between the provider and patient. This is a first opportunity for the patient to learn the clinical style and personality of their new provider. The nature of initial meetings between patients and providers varies widely depending on the discipline of the helping field, the context of the first meeting, organizational practices, and the approach taken by the provider. There are common threads across most initial patient meetings and within this chapter we will explore the *how* and *what* of assessment. This chapter will focus on the assessment of the mental health functioning of a person and will be most relevant to providers who work in the mental health fields such as counselors, social workers, and other therapists. For those readers who are providers in other fields, we hope that this chapter expands your understanding of relevant mental health variables in your patient's life that may impact your work and treatment with them.

Assessment Timing and Goals

Assessment involves gathering vital information about a patient and evaluating the patient's functioning on the variables that are relevant to the provider's scope of practice. Assessment provides clarity of diagnosis and treatment needs, and because this is an essential, foundational step in

DOI: 10.4324/9781003217589-12

receiving care, it usually occurs at the outset of a helping relationship. Appointments focused on assessment have varying terms in the mental health field, including diagnostic assessments, intake appointments, and mental health assessments. These appointments differ from subsequent appointments because of the need to collect a vast amount of information about the patient's current and historical mental health functioning. Owing to the nature of these appointments, transparency about the process should be discussed. Many times, these information gathering appointments are saturated with provider inquiry (i.e., questions, statements with upspeak), and it is crucial that other basic counseling skills are used to balance the conversation. When a provider asks too many questions without also offering some amount of reflection of content (i.e., basic content, emotions, meaning), the patient may feel like they are the subject of an interrogation by someone who doesn't care about their responses. The other benefit of balancing inquiry with content reflection skills is the development of rapport; the patient will feel heard and understood. Although gathering sufficient information is crucial to initial treatment decisions, building rapport, perhaps at the expense of missing some minor information, is a wise expenditure of session time. The growing rapport may increase the likelihood that the patient will return for a future appointment because they felt understood, trusted the process, and felt validated.

As your patient continues to return for subsequent appointments, then the process of assessment becomes subtle and peripheral to the work with the patient. Diagnoses, treatment plans, and the overall conceptualization of the patient will become increasingly refined as the provider continues to learn more about the patient. There may be times in which there is a relevant need for a targeted assessment of the patient, depending on the particular symptoms or presenting problem. Separate psychological testing may be warranted if the patient is deteriorating or plateauing in functioning or there is a particular area of functioning that requires expert assessment (e.g., intelligence testing, neurological testing, etc.). These instances may require referral to a specialist, and the specialist will complete an assessment battery and a report to communicate their findings back to the provider and patient. The information from the report will likely inform the provider's continued work with the patient and hopefully illuminate previously unknown or misunderstood concerns so that treatment can be adapted accordingly. Consider the case example below of when targeted assessment provided clarity to the mental health treatment of a patient.

A mental health counselor was working at a community mental health agency that treats adults. The provider, Ms. Carpenter, recently began working with Mrs. Wright. Mrs. Wright is a 43-year-old White, cisgender woman. Mrs. Wright presented with symptoms of depression. She is unemployed, separated from her spouse, and is struggling to care for her three children. Ms. Carpenter approached her work with Mrs. Wright in a similar manner to other clients with similar presenting concerns which included heavy emphasis on Cognitive Behavioral Therapy (CBT). Ms. Carpenter explained CBT concepts to Mrs. Wright and sent her home with worksheets as homework to further implement CBT interventions. Week after week, Mrs. Wright would not bring back the completed worksheets and state that she forgot them or that they got lost. Ms. Carpenter was frustrated and perceived that Mrs. Wright was not putting adequate effort into her therapy. Ms. Carpenter decided that they would complete one of the worksheets together in session and was surprised to see that Mrs. Wright was struggling to spell some basic words. Ms. Carpenter referred Mrs. Wright to a psychologist in the agency for testing to clarify the client's level of cognitive functioning.

The psychologist completed a battery of tests and provided the written report to Ms. Carpenter. Ms. Carpenter was surprised to learn that Mrs. Wright's intellectual functioning was below average and that she was functionally illiterate. Mrs. Wright was ashamed of her difficulties with reading and writing and often hid these from people for fear of judgment. Without the specialized testing, Ms. Carpenter would have continued to interpret Mrs. King's behavior as a sign of resistance to treatment. Ms. Carpenter discussed the results with Mrs. Wright, and they were able to discuss Mrs. Wright's feelings of shame and how illiteracy impacted her life. Ms. Carpenter subsequently adapted her approach to treatment to be aligned with Mrs. Wright's level of cognitive functioning.

Assessment processes range from informal and unstructured to formal and standardized. The previous example highlights how the informal assessment of the patient's functioning, based on Ms. Carpenter's conversations with Mrs. Wright, were not adequate in accurately understanding Mrs. Wright's cognitive functioning and reading/writing capacities. Formal assessment, conducted by a specialist, provided important clarity that impacted the course of treatment. The current chapter will focus on unstructured and semi-structured basic mental health assessment. Learning how to conduct structured and standardized assessments require reading and training beyond the scope of this textbook. Thus, let us turn our focus to the overall goals of assessment, which are common across most assessment processes.

Assessment Goals

The primary goal of assessment is to increase a provider's knowledge of the patient's history, vital information, and their functioning on variables of interest to that provider's scope of practice. This information is gathered in several ways, which may include initial forms/documents that a patient completes as a part of becoming a new patient. Much of this information may be provided via self-report in an initial appointment. Other information might be gathered via patient completion of formal assessments such as those specific to symptoms. For example, a new parent might complete the Edinburgh Postnatal Depression Scale (EPDS) during their infant's scheduled appointments, or a therapy client might complete a Beck Anxiety Inventory (BAI) at their first appointment with a therapist. Gathering this information at the outset of treatment provides a baseline for their level of functioning which can inform the providers' thoughts about the overall process of treatment and allows the clinician to make adjustments if the client is not improving adequately. The information gathered informs the initial diagnosis and treatment planning process.

The areas of assessment are wide ranging and include the following: presenting concern (including their subjective level of distress and the degree of functional impairment); history of presenting concern (frequency, intensity, duration, onset – abbreviated as FIDO); presence of other mental health symptoms; family information; relationship history and social support; legal history; employment history; school/academic history; trauma and adverse childhood event history; current living arrangements; suicidal and homicidal ideation, plan, and intent; current and past psychotropic medications; current alcohol and drug use and history of use; legal history, and history of previous mental health treatment. Within each of these areas there are a multitude of areas to be further explored and the depth of that exploration will be informed by the patient's presenting concern. For example, if a patient presents with distress related to their family relationships, it will be imperative to gather a full picture of the family's functioning, which could include the following: who is in the patient's family, the nature of the relationships among family members, the presence of mental health concerns among family members, and the living arrangements of family members. The options for inquiry are almost endless; the provider needs to make decisions about the most relevant information to gather at the starting point of treatment.

A secondary goal for initial assessment is for the patient to experience empathy, trust, and validation from their provider. Patients are in a vulnerable state given their need for help and their reliance upon the provider for such help. A provider who is overly focused on inquiry can fail to provide compassionate and empathic responses to the patient. Although a robust amount of data might be gathered, the patient might leave feeling unheard or uncared for. As stated previously, inquiry must be balanced with empathic responses that promote trauma-informed practices to support the patient. Not only do such reflective statements (i.e., paraphrases, emotion, and meaning reflections) convey empathy, they also provide opportunity to confirm mutual understanding. Especially in these early stages of relationship development, when the provider and patient are getting to know one another, offering paraphrases and reflections ensures that the communicated message intended by the patient is in fact aligned with the message the provider has received.

A third goal of assessment is to create a sharable document that summarizes all the information gathered from the appointment. This skill of such clinical writing will be covered in other places in your professional curriculum but remembering the goal of creating a shareable document will likely inform the questions asked within the initial appointment. It can be helpful to consider what an outside observer might be curious about when reading the summary of the appointment and then gather that information while still in session with the patient. We emphasize also that the document should be shareable, meaning that it should use clinical language that is common across health professions and avoid slang and idioms. Idioms are culturally linked and may not be discernible to professionals from other cultural groups.

A fourth and final goal for assessment is to empower the patient. Patients seek help from a provider because the provider has the expertise and skill to assist the patient in improving their functioning. It is unlikely that the patient's problems will be "solved" by the end of the initial appointment; however, a skillful provider offers the patient reassurance that they can be helped. As an initial assessment is nearing completion, we have two suggestions for final questions that are both very useful both diagnostically and relationally. The first question is, "Is there anything I have not asked you about that you think is important for me to know about you?" Asking this question opens the door for the patient to designate what is "important," which might be very different than what the provider thinks is important. Honoring their perspective on their own concerns and their contribution to the relationship development is an indirect way of communicating our respect for them.

One other very important query might be prefaced like this: "For the past 60 minutes, I've been asking you a whole lot of questions about many things. I want to also give you time to ask questions of me – what questions do you have for me?" An extremely common question patients present is some version of "have you seen people like me before?" and, "are you going to be able to help me?" Essentially what they are asking is whether you believe they can "get better" and whether you can help them get better. They are seeking hope. Hope has been identified as one of the four common determinants of treatment outcome (Duncan, Miller, Wampold, & Hubble, 2010).

This is sometimes called *instilling hope*. While we as providers can never say for certain what the outcome of treatment will be, we can still offer a response that allows room for hope. As a clinician, one of the authors (S. D.) has sometimes said the following to her patients: "I know we just met today and I'm only just getting to know you, but I want you to know that I've worked with people who had have similar struggles as you described, and I've seen them get better because of therapy. I'm looking forward to working with you so that things can change and feel better." This message communicates that even though the patient may not feel hopeful, the provider is optimistic. Provider optimism coupled with communication of an initial understanding of the presenting concern can empower the client. The empowered client is aware of what the concern is and knows what they need to do to improve the situation, and in the case of mental health therapy, that usually means attending and engaging fully in the treatment provided by the therapist.

Assessment of Pathology, Impairment, and Distress

Initial assessment has multiple complimentary goals that when done well results in informed providers and empowered patients who feel connected to one another. Although many topics will be discussed during initial contact with a patient, there will be a clear focus on the presenting concern. The presenting concern is the issue that caused a patient to seek treatment from a provider. The presenting concern is usually the first topic of discussion and providers may inquire in several ways such as, "Tell me about what brings you in today" and, "What is the concern that you're having in your life?" Patients will typically speak for an extended period to describe the issue of concern and the provider will then make decisions about where to inquire further to fully understand the concern. Providers will ask follow-up questions that help them in determining the presence and degree of pathology, as well as the level of impairment and distress.

Psychopathology

Psychopathology is the scientific study and classification of mental health disorders. Providers will collect information from their patient to decide what psychopathology may be present so that an appropriate diagnosis can be rendered. Rendering a diagnosis is the first step in treatment planning because a course of treatment is dependent on complete understanding of psychopathology. The ability to inquire about the presence of relevant symptoms requires adequate understanding of psychopathology, and the ability to differentiate between differences in conditions that may present similarly but represent two different processes of disturbance and impairment. This skill set is beyond the scope of this textbook. Mental health professionals are required to complete graduate coursework on diagnosing psychopathology and will combine this knowledge with their helping skills to gather information in a non-judgmental and compassionate manner.

Not all patients present with psychopathology although they may be experiencing notable subjective distress; they may present with non-diagnosable concerns that still may be uncomfortable but are not considered to be a mental health disorder. For example, a patient may seek mental health counseling after a breakup-up with a romantic partner. Another patient might seek mental health counseling for assistance in making a career decision. Both examples are non-pathological and yet may elicit uncomfortable feelings and conflict for a person.

The Socially Constructed Nature of Psychopathology

The American Psychiatric Association (APA) is the publisher of the Diagnostic and Statistical Manual of Mental Disorders (DSM-5-TR). The DSM is the commonly used classification system of mental health disorders to provide diagnoses across providers using a unified taxonomy. The larger medical community utilizes the International Classification of Diseases – 11th Revision (ICD-11), which is published by the World Health Organization (WHO) for the diagnosis and classification of disease, beyond (but still including) mental health disorders. Both texts function similarly for healthcare providers; the DSM is simply specific to mental health disorders. Diseases of mental health involve greater subjectivity in their classification compared to diseases of the rest of the body, although mind-body dualism overlooks the complex and interrelated nature of mind-body functioning. The DSM is updated on a regular basis to reflect diagnostic criteria that are supported by the most recent scientific literature of mental health disorders. Some diagnoses that were present in past versions of the DSM were eliminated (e.g., same-sex sexual behavior) and others have been added (e.g., Prolonged Grief Disorder). Some of these changes come from societal evolution and recognition of the inappropriate pathologizing (labelling a behavior as pathological) of normal behavior and confirmatory literature, while others stem from updated scientific understanding of phenomena that were not previously well understood.

The other challenge to the classification and conceptualization of mental health disorders is that mental health symptoms cannot often be seen via objective tests such as diagnostic imaging (e.g., MRI, PET scan, X-ray) or other tests of organ and bodily functioning (e.g., presence of bacteria, blood pressure, cholesterol levels, etc.). Many mental health disorders rely on the self-report of the patient, along with provider observations of the patient's behavior, and as was discussed previously, patients vary in their ability to be an accurate historian. Another added layer of complexity with regard to creating a taxonomy of mental health disorders is that the very definition of "unhealthy behavior" varies across cultures. Some cultures may interpret having visions of deceased loved ones as positive spiritual omens to be celebrated, whereas other cultures may view this as a symptom of a psychotic disorder. A third complicating factor in the subjective interpretation of patient behavior is that it's influenced by provider biases, both conscious and unconscious. For example, children with minority racial and ethnic identities are more likely to receive a diagnosis of a disruptive behavior disorder instead of diagnosis of ADHD when compared to white, non-Hispanic children (Fadus et al., 2020). The provision of mental health diagnoses requires training beyond the scope of this book for the reasons just discussed, but providers will be better prepared for such training if they are aware of their own values and biases as well as the potential impact of identifying and classifying behaviors that comprise subjective aspects of mental health disorders.

Impairment

Impairment is the negative impact of a problem or concern on a patient's functioning. When we talk about "impairment," we are referring to the patient's ability to engage in the activities of daily living that are developmentally expected in their culture. The presence and degree of pathology does not correlate perfectly with the level of impairment. Impairment is influenced by factors like a patient's coping capacity and the presence of social support and other resources. Resources and circumstances that can mitigate impairment include financial and housing stability as well as access to and utilization of support services. Particularly in an initial assessment, providers can and should explore the person's different major life roles to better understand the manifestation of impairment across multiple aspects of their life. Most people have several major life roles that include caring for themselves, caring for others (e.g., children, parent, other family member), and fulfilling their worker or student obligations. The act of caring for oneself and others comprises a large set of activities that includes personal hygiene, feeding, and maintaining a place of living. Severe impairment may mean that someone is struggling with activities of daily living (ADLs) such as bathing and feeding themselves. Not being able to work or attend school, or being fired or receiving failing grades, are also probable indicators of not fulfilling socially expected roles and which may suggest severe impairment. Unfortunately, severe impairment can beget greater distress because losing one's job and being unable to care for oneself create new challenges and demoralization.

Distress

Distress is a person's subjective experience of suffering. Like impairment, distress levels do not correlate exactly with the degree of pathology present. Therapists may denote that a client's concern is "objectively mild but subjectively severe." By this they mean that the presenting concern does not correspond to a diagnosable level of pathology, yet the client is greatly distressed by the concern. For example, the first author has conducted therapy in university counseling center settings. Romantic relationship break-ups with high school partners were a semi-common presenting concern for freshman students. These students would often be highly distressed (e.g., frequent crying, skipping class, making frantic efforts to rekindle the relationship, feeling lonely and adrift); however, from a clinical perspective, the concern is developmentally typical for college students and is not a diagnosable disorder. Even though this dichotomy may be present for patients it does not mean that providers should be dismissive or invalidating of their distress. A lack of coping skills and difficulty with perspective taking can lead patients to have outsized reactions to their concerns. Treatment sometimes involves assisting patients in developing the skills and accessing the resources to mitigate their distress, even when concerns are objectively mild. There is an opposite and somewhat more concerning dichotomy between pathology and distress though.

Occasionally, a patient might have a high degree of pathology but a low level of distress. This is not inherently problematic, but it requires further exploration to determine the cause of the low distress. Some encouraging possibilities for the dichotomy may be that the patient is coping effectively with the concern and is utilizing available resources to mitigate their distress (i.e., seeking support from family and friends, engaging in religious or spiritual practices to make meaning of their difficulty). In this case, the patient understands the gravity or severity of their concern and has been able to manage the concordant level of distress in a healthy way. Another possible explanation for such a dichotomy is more concerning for a patient's prognosis. Patients might have low insight into the severity or gravity of their concern, or they may be emotionally disconnected, owing to feeling overwhelmed or hopeless. These scenarios require that a provider attempt to motivate the patient to engage in the necessary actions to remedy their circumstances even when the distress isn't present.

Distress is a common motivation to seek help and the goal across many helping professions is to help a patient "feel better." However, clients might arrive to treatment not because they are distressed themselves, but owing to some outside circumstances. For example, the first author provided psychotherapy for a client who was encouraged to attend psychotherapy by their academic advisor after they exhibited unusual behavior during an academic semester. The client failed their coursework for the semester but still wanted to remain in school, so they acquiesced and came to psychotherapy. The patient was diagnosed with Bipolar I Disorder, and their most recent bizarre behavior was due to a manic episode. The client did not personally find their behavior in the manic episode to be concerning and rather had an opposite interpretation; they saw the behavior as a positive manifestation of their personality and enthusiasm for life. Although psychopathology was present and impairment was moderate to high (e.g., failing out of school, lost job, relationships were strained), the client's subjective distress was low. They lacked insight into the severity of their diagnosis and the gravity of implications of their recent behavior.

Given the low distress, the client lacked motivation to remain in voluntary psychotherapy and dropped out of treatment.

Approaches to Mental Health Assessment

The nature of initial mental health assessments with patients will depend on the standard procedures of the setting. Large mental health agencies and practices will likely have a regimented and comprehensive process whereas a clinician in a small private practice may utilize an individually developed approach that is adapted to each new patient. Despite the wide variation there are broad categories that classify the method and the data sources. While the method and data sources are important, ensuring that you as the practitioner are assessing through a trauma-informed lens is integral. There are screening tools and methods to screen for trauma. The National Center for PTSD (2021) has compiled a list of screening instruments that are used to help assess patients to determine if they been exposed to traumatic events. Also, *ACES Aware* via the State of California Department of Health Care Services (2022), provide guidance on available screening tools. One of the most widely utilized screeners is the Adverse Childhood Experiences Questionnaire.

The Adverse Childhood Experience Questionnaire is composed of questions to assess exposure of traumatic experiences throughout childhood (Felitti et al., 1998). Five of the questions specifically are concerned with personal events that happened to the client, such as the three types of abuse (physical, verbal, and sexual) and neglect (physical and emotional). The other five questions are related to the primary care giver or family members in the home. The questions ask about if a parent has ever been incarcerated, was there domestic violence in the home, did a parent abuse substances, did a parent have a mental illness, and did the child experience a loss of a loved one (e.g., divorce, death).

While screeners or questionnaires can help with gathering information pertaining to your patient, it is essential to remember the four R's (realize, recognize, responds, and resist re-traumatization) by the Substance Abuse of Mental Health Services Administration (2014). When assessing we must consider the potential impact that trauma has had on our patients. Sometimes these realizations happen during initial intake appointments and other times through regular interactions we may realize the impact. Also, we must recognize the signs and symptoms that may be spoken or unspoken that signal the impact of trauma when working with patients. Responding in a way that is trauma-informed is important. Many times, as practitioners we interact with patients, and we notice policies, procedures, and practices that may not align with trauma-informed practices. It is our job to respond to patients through a trauma-informed lens and to bring attention to policies, procedures, or practices that may not support patients from this perspective. Lastly, as practitioners we must resist re-traumatizing when assessing the needs of patients. Paying attention to tone, body language, personal space and other factors are key when assessing to ensure that we as practitioners are not traumatizing or re-traumatizing patients.

Initial contact with a patient is a time in which a patient may need to disclose about past traumatic experiences, but this does not mean that they need to retell every detail of a past trauma. Rather, the provider should collect information about traumatic experiences in a way that obtains only the necessary details and does not ask a client to retell a trauma narrative if they do not want to or it is not necessary at that time. Discussing a traumatic event in detail can be very emotionally destabilizing for some patients and may be a component of trauma treatment, and may not be necessary at the initial outside of assessment. We also must provide our patient's adequate time to emotionally regulate themselves if they become intensely emotionally aroused when discussing traumatic experiences. This means watching the clock to ensure that there is enough time in the session for the patient to decompress before they must return back to their daily life.

Methods

Structured

Structured interview approaches are the most rigid among the three method categories. Structured interviews provide each patient the same experience regardless of the provider, and as such, provide uniformity across patients and providers. The Structured Clinical Interview for DSM-5 (SCID-5) is a well-known option and is rigorous and comprehensive. The SCID-5 specifically aims to collect data that assists a provider in making a mental health diagnosis using the DSM-5. A benefit of structured approaches, like the SCID-5, is that they collect data in a manner that avoid the influence of provider bias. For example, a structured interview is a standardized experience and regardless of the provider's perception of the relevance of a question, it is still asked of all patients. This means that information that might be overlooked otherwise is collected. Structured interviews, however, can be experienced as impersonal and inflexible by both patients and providers. As discussed earlier, a goal of initial contact with a patient is to express empathy and validation which in turn, builds rapport. Unfortunately, structured interviews can feel mechanical and may not allow for nimble and empathic responses to patient disclosures. Structured clinical interviews are more common in research settings where standardization is needed to ensure fidelity in data collection processes.

Semi-structured

Semi-structured interviews incorporate the frameworks of structured interviews but allow for flexibility in direction and focus. Semi-structured interviews typically follow a format, either self-created or provided by other professionals, that guide the areas of assessment. Many clinicians enjoy the loose framework provided and the option to discuss topics as they naturally arise in conversation compared to the fixed nature of structured interviews. A semi-structured interview does orient a provider to topic areas to be discussed that might be overlooked otherwise, which guards against provider bias. The benefits of flexibility and provider responsiveness make semi-structured interviews an appealing choice for many providers.

Unstructured

Unstructured interviews, as the name implies, have no formal organization and are often driven by the patient. A provider may start an unstructured interview with a simple prompt (e.g., "What brings you in today?") and then allows the patient to direct the focus of topics discussed. A provider will still ask follow-up questions and may intentionally ask about areas that have not been discussed, but the valuing of flexibility is paramount, and some topics may not be inquired about or discussed. Unstructured interviews can feel free-flowing and responsive but sometimes lack the comprehensiveness needed to make initial clinical decisions.

Data Sources

Subjective

Sources of data are differentiated by a subjective/objective dichotomy. Subjective data sources are influenced by people's feelings and thoughts, whereas objective data sources are unaffected by the feelings and thoughts of people. Most information about patients in mental health settings comes from subjective sources of data, the primary source being patient self-report. Patient self-report is possible through two main avenues: what they verbally share in appointments and what they report on paperwork and tests/assessments. Many tests and assessments that utilize standardized scoring are still reliant on patient self-report and therefore are influenced by a patient's capacity for accuracy and insight into their experiences. As discussed in previous chapters, children and those with cognitive impairments may not be accurate historians and will require collateral information to evaluate the accuracy of their self-reports. In addition, patients may distort their self-report to achieve the outcome they seek. For example, a patient who is being forced to receive psychological intervention (e.g., court-mandated counseling) may downplay or deny their current psychosocial concerns. In an opposite scenario, a person who seeks some type of benefit (e.g., financial support, emotional support) might malinger, that is to exaggerate or feign symptoms, to achieve their desired outcome. These are just a few examples of situations that exemplify how self-report is subjective.

Given the subjective nature of patient self-report, it is important to consider how the patient's report aligns with other available information. Providers will benefit if they hold a stance of trust *and* curiosity in patient self-report. What is more common than outright, intentional misrepresentation is the likelihood that patient self-report is biased, owing to unintentional factors, such as maladaptive thought patterns or skewed worldviews. A provider who remains curious and skeptical will be able to identify when patient self-report does not align with other available information and gently address those discrepancies with the patient. Despite the pitfalls of the subjective nature of self-report, it is the only means of accessing the type of information that mental health providers rely upon to diagnose and treat patients. Patients' report of their emotions and thoughts are the foundation of many symptoms for mental health diagnoses, and therapists must determine if the self-report of the patient is trustworthy. Some of the factors that providers consider in determining trustworthiness include the patient's cognitive capacity, the patient's motivations, and the context of the self-report.

Objective

Objective sources of information about patients come from methods that are not impacted by human thoughts and feelings. For example, if a therapist works in a court-mandated counseling environment for people with histories of substance use disorders, the patients may take a urinalysis test to detect the presence of substances. The result of these exams exemplifies their objective nature in that they cannot be influenced by patient thoughts or feelings. These types of physical tests are less common in the mental health assessment realm though. Other sources of objective data might include test and assessment results that rely on behavioral observation of the patient. Although there is room for potential manipulation or bias, such tests and assessments are more objective compared to those based on self-report. For example, IQ, achievement, aptitude, and memory tests rely on patients to engage in tasks or solve problems in a standardized manner. Although it is possible for a patient to intentionally do poorly on these tests, assessors may be able to detect this behavior. Some tests contain validity scales and others can be paired with other assessments to detect malingering, such as the Test of Memory Malingering

(TOMM) that appears to be a test of memory capacity but in reality, is a test of memory malingering.

Collateral

The third source of data can be either objective or subjective in nature, but it comes from sources other than the patient. Collateral data is information from outside sources, such as family and friend disclosures and records from other professionals (e.g., legal records, academic records, medical records). Collateral information can reinforce or call into question the accuracy and completeness of patient self-report. For example, a patient with a substance use disorder might underreport their symptoms, owing to shame and stigma; however, collateral information from their spouse might provide a more complete picture of the nature of their substance abuse. Of note though, the trustworthiness of the spousal report needs to be considered as well, as their report is vulnerable to the same pitfalls as all other self-reporting from the patient. Seeking collateral information is a common practice when working with children because of the potential that they lack the insight, awareness, or communication skills to convey information about themselves. Several common assessments of childhood behavior rely upon reporting from caregivers and teachers to report on their functioning in various facets of their life.

For example, if assessing an eight-year-old child for possible attentional problems, a thorough evaluation would include having not only the parents complete a behavioral rating scale, but also the child's classroom teacher, and possibly their after-school childcare provider. In this case, the provider would be looking for consistency of certain behaviors across a number of different adults and different environments. If there is inconsistency across environments and/or raters, then a problem formulation might involve something other than a diagnosable attention deficit in the child.

Providers do not always have easy access to patient records from other professionals. In some settings it might be easy to access records from other providers (e.g., hospital settings, community mental health), whereas more self-contained practices may require a patient to sign a "Release of Information" that provides consent for the provider to seek records from another source. Once again, collateral data strengthens the validity of a provider's assessments of the patient because it is triangulated. Triangulated data is data that is observed across multiple sources, such as the patient's self-report, the provider's observation, and a third (or more) source that is collateral, such as a previous provider's records. Collateral information is not always available or easily accessible and, in this case, providers should listen for patient self-report that is inconsistent with previous self-reported data. Consider the scenario below as an example of potential inconsistency across patient self-report.

Ellen is a counselor who works in a private practice, and she recently began seeing a new client named Danny. Danny is a 19-year-old Latino, cisgender man who is seeking therapy because of relationship issues with his family and academic stress. Danny reports that he recently began his freshman year of college and is living away from home for the first time. Danny stated that his family is "toxic" and that he's really glad to be living away from them because they were not "supportive." Danny aspires to become a surgeon and said that he has been joining various clubs and organizations at college to build a professional network. He described college as the time to "finally get away" from his hometown and family. He described feeling depressed and overwhelmed though and attributes these emotions to the difficulty in his coursework as a pre-med major. When asked about his friendships in high school and at college he stated that they were unsatisfying. He described past friendships as intense and short-lived and that he longed for "better friends."

Ellen inquired about other collateral records, but Danny stated he has never sought therapy in the past and has only recently seen nurse practitioners for physical exams so that he can participate in team sports. Ellen noted that several recent disclosures from Danny have not seemed to fit with his narrative as described thus far. For example, Danny recently dislocated his shoulder during a softball game at an on-campus event. When describing the incident, he stated that both his parents drove the four-hour drive to campus to be with him at the hospital and then stayed in town for several days to coordinate his aftercare. Danny also recently mentioned that his roommate moved out of his dorm room because they "didn't get along well." Lastly, Danny said that he's feeling anxious that he won't be offered the opportunity to join any of the college's fraternity chapters. He said the "brothers" in the various fraternities have not been welcoming. With all the stress of his first semester of college, Danny said he was considering transferring schools so he could be around a group of more "mature" college students.

If you were the therapist in this circumstance, how would you conceptualize this information? All this information is subjective and self-reported, and yet you might be curious about how his perceptions align with events that he reported. An important part of being a provider is maintaining a degree of skepticism and curiosity around patient self-report. This does not mean that providers should take the perspective that patients are lying about everything in their life but rather, patients may lack insight into parts of their lives or may misrepresent parts of their life to get their needs met. In the case of Ellen's work with Danny, she might find it helpful to "hold loosely" the narrative that Danny has provided that suggests that everyone else in his life is the problem (i.e., other people are toxic, unsupportive, immature, not welcoming) and remain open to the possibility that Danny's behavior contributes negatively to interpersonal relationships.

Mental Status Exam

Another important component of assessment with patients is gathering information about the patient's functioning in areas where they lack insight or awareness but can be observed by a professional. A Mental

Status Exam (MSE) aims to assess a patient's appearance, speech, attitude, behavior, mood, and affect. Providers vary in the comprehensiveness of their assessment of a patient's mental status, particularly based upon the setting for their contact. Inpatient settings in which patients have more severe concerns usually require attention to all aspects within a MSE, whereas low-severity outpatient care may require less rigorous assessment of MSE variables. Table 9.1 provides guidance on the areas assessed in a typical MSE and questions to consider that help a provider arrive to

Table 9.1 Mental Status Exam

Category	Facets and Example Descriptors
Appearance	• Hygiene and grooming (e.g., well-groomed, unkempt) • Appropriateness of clothing for the weather and situation
Speech	• Normal, pressured, tangential, circumstantial?
Attitude and Behavior	• Calm, agitated, cooperative, uncooperative, belligerent?
Mood	• Euthymic, irritable, elevated, anxious, depressed?
Affect	• Within normal range, constricted, flat, labile, blunted, reactive, mood congruent?
Thought Process and Content	• Spectrum of goal-directed/logical to disorganized
Orientation	• Aware of time (i.e., date) and place (i.e., where they are currently)?
Perception	• Presence of hallucinations, delusions, and/or obsessions?
Memory	• Can the patient remember past events? • Can the patient remember very recent events? • Can the person retain new information at the current assessment?
Fund of Knowledge	• Is the person aware of current events? • Does the person know the name of the current president?
Concentration	• Can the person complete simple concentration tasks (e.g., counting by 7's or 3's, spelling a common word backwards and forwards)?
Abstract Thought	• Is the person able to interpret culturally familiar proverbs (e.g., "People who live in glass houses shouldn't throw stones")?
Insight and Judgment	• Level of insight into their condition? • Does the person show sound judgment?

detailed descriptions of patient functioning (Washington State Department of Social and Health Services, 2022).

The areas assessed in a MSE do not always require explicit inquiry but rather can be determined from provider observation of the patient, such as appearance and the nature of their speech. Other areas can be ascertained via the typical conversations that would occur during a first interaction with a patient, such as insight, mood, and thought processes. Other areas will need to be explicitly assessed if the clinical situation warrants, such as concentration and fund of knowledge. When the patient's functioning is typical and doesn't demonstrate any signs of psychopathology, then a provider might simply describe their mental status as "within normal limits."

Risk Assessment

An important component of any initial clinical interaction is assessment of risk, which refers to a patient's potential for suicidal and violent behavior. This is a topic that can be fraught with uncomfortable emotions for novice providers for a variety of reasons. Risk assessment can be scary, and anxiety-provoking given the potential for catastrophic consequences if managed inappropriately. Many people, providers included, have been impacted by suicide or violence in their life and thus discussing the topic with patients can be personally upsetting. Most mental health providers have ethical obligations to ensure the safety of their patients when patients demonstrate levels of risk to themselves or others that pose an imminent threat. Providers who feel competent assessing and managing patient suicidal and violence risk will likely feel empowered and less anxious. The majority of the following discussion of risk assessment will focus on suicide risk versus violence risk. Suicide risk is more common; however, advanced training on violence risk assessment is warranted for providers who work with populations where patient violence is more likely. A brief review of violence risk assessment will be provided along with suggestions for further reading.

Terminology

Language is always changing, and the way that providers discuss risk assessment should be reflective of up-to-date clinical terminology as opposed to outdated or colloquial language. When discussing suicide risk, there are terms to definitely avoid, both of which are outdated and/or confusing. One phrase to avoid is one that is commonly used: "to *commit* suicide." The word *commit* is frequently used when discussing the perpetration of crime (e.g., commit robbery, commit a felony) and carries stigma with it. Some more accurate phrases that can be used instead are "to attempt suicide," "to die by suicide," and "to complete suicide." These phrases also offer greater specificity to the action taken by the person in addition to being free of the criminal assumptions underlying the word *commit*.

Another phrase to avoid is "suicidal tendencies." This phrase is unhelpful because the word *tendencies* is non-specific and can mean different things to different providers. Instead of using tendencies, it would be clearer to describe the action such as *thoughts, attempts,* or *desires,* and so on. Another vague phrase to avoid is "hurt oneself." This phrase is sometimes used in a question such as, "Have you been wanting to hurt yourself?" However, the issue with the phrase is that it means different things to different people. To "hurt oneself" may reference suicide for one person but refer to self-injurious behavior to another person. It is advisable to be explicit in one's language with a patient instead (e.g., "Have you been wanting to kill yourself?"). The clinical and specific manner of referencing self-injurious behavior that is not intended to be lethal is non-suicidal self-injury (NSSI).

Personal Reflection

What kinds of feelings and thoughts emerge for you as you think about suicide? How has suicide impacted you in your life, and how do you imagine that might impact your work in your discipline when you have patients who are experiencing with suicidal ideation?

Myths and Facts

Misinformation around suicide is dangerous because it can give people a false sense of security or lead them to avoid taking action to help someone with suicidal thoughts or behavior. Accurate information about suicide empowers providers to make sound clinical decisions related to risk assessment. Here are some key pieces of information about suicide.

- Fact: Suicide is a leading cause of death for all age groups and is particularly high for adolescents and young adults (Centers for Disease Control and Prevention, 2022a).
- Fact: Some populations have higher rates of suicide, including: Native American/Alaska Native and non-Hispanic White populations, veterans, people living in rural areas, and LGBTQ individuals (Centers for Disease Control and Prevention, 2022a; Grant et al., 2011).
- Fact: Cisgender men are more likely to die by suicide more often than cisgender women, but cisgender women make more non-fatal suicide attempts than cisgender men (Centers for Disease Control and Prevention, 2018).

- Myth: Talking about suicide with someone will make them more likely to attempt suicide.

  Fact: Talking with someone about suicide reduces their likelihood of attempting suicide (Mayo Clinic Health System, 2021).

- Myth: Suicide occurs without warning.

  Fact: Although some suicides may occur without warning, most people who attempt suicide also demonstrate clear warning signs that will be discussed below (Mayo Clinic Health System, 2021).

Risk Factors and Warning Signs

When providers recognize that suicide poses a serious risk, particularly within some demographic and cultural groups, and that it can often be prevented by proper intervention, then they can prepare themselves for detecting suicidal risk and assessing of the level of risk. Suicidal behavior is more likely among certain groups, as mentioned previously, and among people who have known risk factors. Risk factors and warning signs are different from one another, and a simple analogy will illustrate their difference. Consider the example of a heart attack: there are risk factors for heart attacks (i.e., factors that increase the likelihood someone will have a heart attack) and warning signs (i.e., signs that a heart attack is imminent). Risk factors for a heart attack include high blood pressure, high blood cholesterol, and smoking, whereas warning signs include chest discomfort, upper body pain, shortness of breath, and nausea (American Heart Association, 2022b; Centers for Disease Control and Prevention, 2022). Presence of a risk factor does not mean that a heart attack is imminent but rather that the provider should be aware that the condition is more likely for that person compared to people without the risk factor. Risk factors for suicide span different aspects of a person's life and are provided in Table 9.2 (Centers for Disease Control and Prevention, 2021c).

The risk factors for suicide are wide-ranging and commonly present in patients who are seeking mental health counseling. As risk factors accumulate, so does the level of risk. Some risk factors cannot be changed or are not within individual control, but those that are malleable can be areas of clinical focus to decrease a patient's risk. In addition, building up protective factors can decrease the risk for suicide. Protective factors include having coping and problem-solving skills, supportive interpersonal connections (i.e., relationships with friends, family, community), supportive relationship with providers, access to healthcare, lack of access to lethal means, and holding cultural or religious beliefs that discourage suicide (Centers for Disease Control and Prevention, 2022c. The protective role of

Table 9.2 Suicide Risk Factors

Individual	Relationship	Community	Societal
Previous suicide attempt	Adverse childhood experiences	Barriers to accessing healthcare	Stigma associated with mental illness or help-seeking behavior
Substance abuse disorders	Bullying	Cultural or religious views that suicide is noble	Easy access to lethal means
Mental illness	Family history of suicide	Suicide cluster in community	Unsafe portrayals of suicide in media
Serious physical illness	Relationship problems (e.g., breakup, violence, loss)		
Social isolation	Sexual violence		
Criminal problems			
Financial problems			
Legal problems			
Job problems or loss			
Aggressive or impulsive behavior			

healthcare and supportive relationships in a healthcare setting underscore the importance of access to healthcare services and culturally congruent helping skills that facilitate supportive relationships with clients who have been historically marginalized and excluded from accessing healthcare.

It is crucial that providers know the signals of immediate potential for suicide so they can act accordingly. Some warning signs may be observable to outsiders, whereas others may require inquiry into how a person is feeling and what they are thinking. Warning signs are distributed into categories in Table 9.3 (Centers for Disease Control and Prevention, 2018).

Assessment

Suicide risk should be assessed at the first meeting with any new patient. The future assessment of suicide risk beyond the first meeting is dependent on the presence of risk factors and warning signs. The presence of any warning signs warrant assessment. Providers should always err on the side of caution, which means assessing for suicide risk, versus assuming there is

Table 9.3 Suicide Warning Signs

Talk	Behavior	Emotions
Talking about or posting on social media about wanting to die	Being isolated and withdrawn	Feeling like a burden
	Increased substance use	Increased anxiety
	Seeking access to lethal means	Feeling trapped or in unbearable pain
	Making plans for suicide	Increased anger or rage
	Sleeping a lot or very little	Extreme mood swings
		Feeling hopeless

no risk present. Providers will find that "there is no pillow so soft as a clear conscience." The act of initiating an assessment of suicidal risk also requires that the provider become more directive. The provider needs to gather a large amount of sensitive information in a timely manner so that there is time to act, if needed, to ensure the patient's safety. It might also seem like beginning a risk assessment is a shift to the flow of the conversation, and indeed, it is. Providers can ease into the assessment process with frankness and concern. A provider might say, "I hear you sharing a lot of feelings of hopelessness. Sometimes when people are hopeless, they consider killing themselves. I'd like for us to talk a bit about that." Let us now discuss the specific areas of inquiry to make a sound assessment of someone's level of suicide risk.

Ideation

Ideation refers to simply thinking about suicide. A provider can simply ask "Are you thinking about suicide?" or "Are you thinking about killing yourself?" It is important that providers use explicit language (e.g., kill oneself, suicide) because it removes the ambiguity of colloquialisms (e.g., hurt oneself, end it all). Patients who report having thoughts of suicide may have active thoughts (e.g., "I want to die") or passive thoughts (e.g., "I wouldn't be upset if I didn't wake up tomorrow), or a combination of both. Providers should follow up to understand the nature of the thoughts (i.e., what they are specifically thinking), the frequency of the thoughts, and when the thoughts are occurring. Inquiry regarding suicidal ideation should be explored for both the present time, the recent past, and historically in their life. If a patient reports that they are not having current thoughts of suicide, then the provider should inquire if they ever have had them in the past. If the patient is currently having thoughts of suicide, or has in the past, then the provider should inquire about the presence of a plan.

Plan

Inquiry about the presence of planning explores the extent to which they have thoughts about a means of completing suicide or engaged in preparatory behavior. Providers can ask something like, "I hear that you've been having thoughts of suicide; what plans have you considered?" As you can see, this is a leading question because it implies that they have thought of a plan. This leading question gives the client tacit permission to acknowledge plans they have considered. If they truly have not ever considered a plan, then they will respond as such. Patients may express vague plans that they've hardly considered or merely heard of, and others will express detailed plans. It is crucial to continue to inquire about all conceived plans because people may have multiple methods in consideration.

Providers should inquire about their current access to the means and their ease/difficulty obtaining accessing means, including firearms, even if they have not mentioned considering firearms. Firearms are the leading method used in completed suicides (Centers for Disease Control and Prevention, 2022d). Providers also need to explore the extent that the patient has acquired or prepared means. For example, patients may have researched how to purchase a firearm in their state, may be saving up medication, or may be researching different means on the internet. Beyond this, patients may have rehearsed some methods or devised a series of steps they need to take in preparation to carry through with their plan.

Providers should be familiar with the degree of lethality of various means even though the lethality of the patient's potential plans will not be explicitly discussed with them. Some methods of suicides are highly lethal (i.e., firearms, suffocation by ligature, drug overdose, and jumping from high structures), and many may vary in their chance for rescue. Some plans may include precautions against being discovered or rescued. The specific details and context of their plan can vary the likelihood of death. Almost all methods have some degree of lethality and should be taken seriously.

Intent

Suicidal intent is the degree to which a person aims to carry out their plan. Intent is more difficult to assess because it is less binary compared to the presence or absence of ideation and plan. Intent fluctuates, and there is no universally agreed-upon measure of intent. Some providers use a scale of 0–10 that is reflective of the likelihood they will carry through with their plan with zero meaning a 0 percent chance and ten meaning a 100 percent chance. A provider might ask the patient, "As of today, on a scale of 0–10 where zero is a 0 percent chance of carrying out your plan and ten is a 100 percent chance of carrying out your plan, where would you be?" Tracking intent via a scale such as this can be useful when assessment occurs regularly and can alert both the provider and patient to fluctuations toward increased risk.

Risk & Protective Factors

Research-supported risk and protective factors exist for many patients as well as those that are idiosyncratic to their unique circumstances. Providers need to inquire about the conditions in their life that increase and decrease their level of risk. For example, a patient might report that a pending decision at work (e.g., being fired) is a potential risk factor and that their risk will increase if there is an unfavorable outcome. Protective factors often center around important relationships in their life and the desire to not emotionally hurt loved ones. We have encountered many patients over the years that cite a desire to not emotionally hurt their romantic partner, parents, siblings, children, friends, and pets as protective circumstances in their life.

A balance of helping skills should be used throughout the suicide assessment process. Although question asking behavior will be prominent, it must be balanced with reflection of content, emotions, and meaning. Reflection of content can be difficult for providers when discussing suicide because they fear that acknowledging their thoughts is somehow an endorsement of them. Providers can use the previously discussed skills to ensure that they hear what their patient is expressing while also not inadvertently endorsing suicidal behavior. For example, a provider might say, "I hear that you feel hopeless and like killing yourself is the only solution," or other stems such as, "It sounds like you think/feel…" As a reminder, talking about suicide does not increase their risk and similarly, acknowledging that you hear their emotional pain and hopelessness does not suggest that you sanction suicide.

Consultation

Consultation is the process of discussing a clinical circumstance with a professional peer or supervisor. When providers are under the training and supervision of an advanced provider, they should seek consultation with their supervisor and/or other advanced professionals when working with patients with suicidal risk. Consultation assists the novice provider with guidance on how to proceed with the patient given their level of suicidal risk. Initially, we recommend that prior to any clinical work, novice providers speak with their supervisors proactively about how they should handle suicidal risk in patients; different settings will necessitate differing levels of response and protocol. In general, though, providers should err on the side of caution and not hesitate to step out of a meeting with a patient for a quick consultation with an available advanced provider. The novice provider should be prepared to briefly describe the patient's current and historical level of risk (e.g., thoughts, plans, intent, history of attempts, risk and protective factors) and provide their tentative plan to ensure patient safety. An advanced provider can bring an objective perspective and insight to ensure sound decision making. They can provide guidance on a proper course of action, or simply confirmation that the novice provider's clinical assessment and plan are reasonable.

Acceptable provider response to patient risk is wide-ranging. At the lowest levels of risk, it might be sufficient to provide emotional validation and support for the client with continued monitoring for changes in their suicidal risk. On the upper level of a continuum, a patient might require immediate, involuntary hospitalization to ensure their safety. Not all helping professionals have legal authority to impose involuntary hospitalization, and providers should be aware of what their options are within their place of practice. The middle ground of responses includes creating safety plans, working with patients to reduce access to means, and increasing their level of care (e.g., connecting with more intensive and targeted mental health care services). Novice providers should familiarize themselves with the expected approaches to managing and decreasing risk within their setting prior to working with any patients. Ultimately, providers should be prepared to discuss suicide with patients, both to determine and manage risk, as well as to understand their experience and integrate this aspect of their thinking into the larger conceptualization of the patient's treatment needs.

Documentation

A necessary component of suicide risk assessment is documentation after a meeting with a patient. Comprehensive clinical notes ensure that a provider can recall all details upon the next meeting with the patient as well as protect a provider by establishing thorough documentation of their clinical assessment and action. In the unlikely and tragic circumstance that a patient dies by suicide, a provider would take some relief if they ensured that they fully documented how they managed and responded to the patient's suicidal risk to guard against accusations of malpractice. Providers should document all information that was learned from the patient regarding their ideation, plan(s), intent, risk and protective factors, history of suicidal risk, and exactly what actions were taken to reduce risk and manage their safety. Even when a patient denies that they are having suicidal thoughts, it should be documented (e.g., "Patient reported they have never experienced thoughts of suicide, currently or in the past") because as the adage goes, "If it wasn't written down, it didn't happen." Although documentation of suicidal risk can be tedious, it is an important part of the process that benefits both the patient and the provider. In addition, when suicidal ideation and intent is a focus of concern and/or intervention, on-going periodic notation about the current level of suicidality is advisable.

Here is a dialogue example from a suicide assessment of a 34-year-old single mother of two children who is struggling with financial instability, chronic pain, and depression:

COUNSELOR: I'm so glad you were able to get a ride and keep your appointment today. I've been wondering how you've been doing.
ANNA: Well, you're about to get your wish. My life is one unending battle and I think about not going on.
COUNSELOR: The constant struggles are totally wearing you down. Tell me more about "not going on."
ANNA: You know what I mean. When I look into the future all I see is more of the same forever. I'm stuck in a game where the rules are in everyone else's favor and the only way to win is to quit.
COUNSELOR: So what exactly would quitting look like?
ANNA: Do we have to go there? OK, I think about going to bed and not waking up.
COUNSELOR: It would be a huge relief to just go on sleeping forever?
ANNA: Yep, like literally never wake up. Every night when I go to bed I pray I'll die in my sleep.
COUNSELOR: How often are you thinking about just taking matters into your own hands and killing yourself?
ANNA: I try to push that idea out of my head every day; it's there a lot.
COUNSELOR: I hear that this is a pretty constant thought. [*Brief silence.*] What ideas do you have about how you might carry out that task of killing yourself?
ANNA: I'd do sleeping pills and alcohol.
COUNSELOR: Tell me more about that idea.
ANNA: Well, this is where I sort of get stuck. I can't leave the kids with John; he'll be mean to them. My mother isn't well enough to take them, and if I just go, they might end up in foster care. Bad things happen there.
COUNSELOR: So your love and concern and commitment to Joy and Heath is preventing you from considering more seriously how to actually kill yourself. I hear that you recognize how incredibly important you are to them, and how devastating it would be for literally the rest of their lives if you did it. Have you considered any other plans, like getting access to a gun?
ANNA: Oh gosh no... no way to the guns. I've just thought about pills because I have those at home.

COUNSELOR: Okay, it sounds like pills and alcohol are the only plan you've considered? [slight upspeak]. Your kids really keep you going through each day though.
ANNA: Yeah, it's the only thing that keeps me going.
COUNSELOR: That makes a lot of sense.
ANNA: This is why I feel so hopeless, it's like, I don't think anything will get any better but I also feel like killing myself isn't an option either.
COUNSELOR: It doesn't feel like an option?
ANNA: [*Sigh*] No, yeah, it's like, even though I want to die. I wouldn't actually ever do it. I can't do that to the kids.
COUNSELOR: I hear you, you're saying you really would like to die, and equally strong though is your conviction to stay alive for your children.
ANNA: Yeah, yeah. That's it. So it's like, where do we go from here?
COUNSELOR: I was hoping we might circle back to some things you said earlier about two things; one is about you not having any friends in your support system, and the other was about the rules being stacked against you....

Violence Risk Assessment

The assessment and prevention of violent behavior is also referred to as homicide risk assessment. Given that violence against a third party with intention to kill is obviously a matter of public safety, possible violent outcomes should always be assessed as part of an intake. Other forms of violence that may be assessed by providers include violent behavior toward family members and sexual violence. The nature of the violence and the intended target determine the potential that a provider holds a *Duty to Warn*. The findings of the Tarasoff case (*Tarasoff v. Regents of the University of California*, 1976) determined that providers have an obligation to both assess for violence risk and also to inform third parties who are the intended target of the violence. Across areas of practice, providers consistently have a duty to protect vulnerable populations (e.g., children, older adults, people with a disability who rely on the care of other adults). For this reason, a variety of dangerous actions against these populations may need to be assessed beyond simply homicidal violence. Violence risk assessment is difficult because violent behavior has a low base rate and thus, provider prediction accuracy may be lower. In addition, patients who are planning violence may simply withhold that information even when asked directly about their intentions.

Like assessment of suicidal risk, the goal of violence risk assessment is not simply to *predict* a behavior but also to *prevent* it. Providers have historically used unstructured clinical interviews, and these have been criticized for their low validity and inter-rater reliability. Actuarial instruments have also been utilized, and such instruments rely on predicting violence risk based upon an algorithm that excludes the provider's judgement. Actuarial instruments have pitfalls as well; they have been criticized for their overreliance on historical and static variables, and their lowered prediction accuracy to populations beyond a narrow scope of focus (Haggård-Grann, 2007). The literature recommends that providers utilize *structured clinical judgement* which combines the strengths of clinical judgement (e.g., nimble inquiry of fluctuating variables) and actuarial instruments (e.g., comprehensive assessment and increased consideration of variables that should be weighted heavily based on statistical findings).

In summary, Haggård-Grann (2007) recommends consideration of risk factors, similar to the process of suicide risk assessment, with attention to factors that are static as opposed to dynamic, and those that are individually based versus contextual. Factors that are static are those which will not evolve and shift over time. Recalling that providers are not only aiming to predict violence to protect others but also to prevent violence, attention to dynamic, or malleable, factors (e.g., emotional maturity, substance use) can be targeted to reduce risk. Utilizing structured clinical judgment involves assessment of risk factors, such as the ten historical risk factors found in the Historical, Clinical, and Risk Management Violence Risk Assessment Scheme (HCR-20; Webster et al., 1997) as well as provider inquiry into nuanced situational factors present for the current circumstance. Haggård-Grann (2007) also recommends use of specialized assessment instruments such as those for family violence and sexual violence, when indicated. Providers should seek out collateral data when possible. Further reading on violence risk is necessary for providers, and they should seek further reading on violence risk assessment (c.f., Douglas & Otto, 2020) as well as literature on the best practices for the populations for whom they provide services.

Conclusion

The journey of forming a relationship with a new patient is both exciting and even daunting at times. There is a vast amount of information to learn about a patient while also placing equal emphasis on building rapport, two seemingly opposite tasks. Careful balance of helping skills will help providers gather needed data on a patient while also demonstrating understanding and empathy. Even when clinical circumstances warrant in-depth assessment of vulnerable areas, such as suicide and violence risk, these inquiries are experienced as humane when providers can remain focused on being connected with their patient, not simply gathering information from them. When patients feel heard and understood, they are more likely to become empowered co-conspirators with the provider in the efforts to help them heal.

Questions for Class Discussion

1 What is your reaction to the idea that everyone has a threshold for violence? Where does your own threshold lie?
2 What are your thoughts about diagnosis? To what extent will you need to diagnose your clients in your intended professional position, and to what extent are your thoughts at odds with what your job may require?

References

American Heart Association. (2022). Warning signs of a heart attack. www.heart.org/en/health-topics/heart-attack/warning-signs-of-a-heart-attack.
Centers for Disease Control and Prevention. (2018). Suicide rising across the US. www.cdc.gov/vitalsigns/suicide/index.html.
Centers for Disease Control and Prevention. (2022a). Facts about suicide. www.cdc.gov/suicide/facts.
Centers for Disease Control and Prevention. (2022b). Heart attack symptoms, risk, and recovery. www.cdc.gov/heartdisease/heart_attack.htm.
Centers for Disease Control and Prevention. (2022c). Risk and protective factors. www.cdc.gov/suicide/factors/index.html.
Centers for Disease Control and Prevention. (2022d). Suicide and self-harm injury. www.cdc.gov/nchs/fastats/suicide.htm.
Douglas, K.S. & Otto, R.K. (2020). *Handbook of violence risk assessment*. Routledge.
Duncan, B.L., Miller, S.D., Wampold, B.E., & Hubble, M.A. (Eds). (2010). *The heart and soul of change: Delivering what works in therapy* (2nd ed.). American Psychological Association. https://doi.org/10.1037/12075-000.
Fadus, M.C., Ginsburg, K.R., Sobowale, K.Halliday-Boykins, C.A., Bryant, B.E., Gray, K.M., & Squeglia, L.M. (2020). Unconscious bias and the diagnosis of Disruptive Behavior Disorders and ADHD in African American and Hispanic youth. *Academic Psychiatry*, 44, 95–102, doi:10.1007/s40596-019-01127-6.
Felitti, V. J., Anda, R.F., Nordenberg, D., Williamson, D.F., Spitz, A.M., Edwards, V., Koss, M.P., & Marks, J.S. (1998). Relationship of childhood abuse and household dysfunction to many of the leading causes of death in adults. The Adverse Childhood Experiences (ACE) Study. *American Journal of Preventive Medicine*, 14 (4), 245–258. doi:10.1016/s0749-3797(98)00017–00018.
Grant, J., Mottet, L., Tanis, J., Harrison, J., Herman, J., & Keisling, M. (2011). *Injustice at every turn: A report of the National Transgender Discrimination Survey*. National Center for Transgender Equality and National Gay and Lesbian Task Force.
Haggård-Grann, U. (2007). Assessing violence risk: A review and clinical recommendations. *Journal of Counseling and Development*, 85, 294–301. https://doi.org/10.1002/j.1556-6678.2007.tb00477.x
Hubble, M.A., Duncan, B.L., & Miller, S.D. (1999). *The Heart & Soul of Change: What Works in Therapy*. American Psychological Association.
Mayo Clinic Health System. (2021). Eight common myths about suicide. www.mayoclinichealthsystem.org/hometown-health/speaking-of-health/8-common-myths-about-suicide.

National Center for PTSD. (2021). PTSD screening instruments. www.ptsd.va.gov/professional/assessment/screens/index.asp.

State of California Department of Health Care Services Aces Aware. (2022). Screening Tools. www.acesaware.org/learn-about-screening/screening-tools.

Substance Abuse of Mental Health Services Admininstration. (2014). SAMHSA's Concept of Trauma and Guidance for a Trauma-Informed Approach. https://ncsacw.acf.hhs.gov/userfiles/files/SAMHSA_Trauma.pdf.

Tarasoff v. Regents of the University of California, 17 Cal. 3d 425, 551 P.2d 334 (1976).

Washington State Department of Social and Health Services. (2022). Mental status exam guidelines. www.dshs.wa.gov/sites/default/files/forms/pdf/13-865add.pdf.

Webster, C.D., Douglas, K.S., Eaves, D., & Hart, S.D. (1997). *The HCR-20 scheme: The assessment of dangerousness and risk* (Version 2). Burnaby, BC: Simon Fraser University and Forensic Psychiatric Services Commission of British Colombia.

Chapter 10

Evidence-Based Practice

Introduction

Current students in the health and counseling fields are likely exposed to evidence-based practice (EBP) from the inception of their training. Students may be familiar with terminology surrounding the EBP movement and likely have a nascent understanding of the concept; however, a deeper comprehension is necessary to be effective as a provider with diverse populations. This chapter will demystify the EBP movement for the novice provider so that this foundational knowledge can be used as a springboard for advanced learning in areas of practice that are relevant for that provider.

History of EBP Movement

The evidence-based practice movement recognizably began in the early 1980s when a group of epidemiologists published a series of articles that advised physicians how to utilize scientific literature in clinical practice (Sackett, 1981). However, the roots for the EBP movement began in the 1950s and 1960s in the US when the medical field was rapidly expanding with regard to facilities, providers, scientific advancements, and insurance availability. This period was known as the Era of Expansion, and a confluence of factors led to greater scrutiny on the practices deployed by medical providers (Kowalski & Chung, 2013). What was termed "evidence-based medicine" by the originators is known as evidence-based practice more broadly and has since expanded to many other fields including nursing, psychology, a variety of health fields, and beyond. In simple terms, evidence-based practice is the use of data derived from the scientific process to evaluate the efficacy of a practice. It may appear to be common sense to consider scientific data in the process of determining an appropriate treatment, although in the recent past many providers relied upon tradition as the guiding force in deciding treatment. The concerning example that stimulated Dr. Sackett's work in the EBP movement was the

DOI: 10.4324/9781003217589-13

finding that a determining factor for treatment type for hypertension was the year of graduation of the treating provider. That is, providers were basing treatment upon the prevailing practices at the time of their training versus adopting newer methods and deciding among methods depending on their scientific support (Kowalski & Chung, 2013).

The EBP movement relies on the scientific method as the basis for understanding what works for whom and is the best tool that currently exists for providers to pursue this knowledge (American Psychological Association, 2005). The aim of EBP is to increase the likelihood of desirable treatment outcomes for patients, which can include both reduction of troublesome symptoms as well as increased quality of life and functionality (Tolin et al., 2015). Working from an EBP approach may seem like a labor-intensive process for a provider, however, continued efforts will reduce the cognitive load of the task because of increased familiarity with the literature and the process of seeking out evidence. Operating from an EBP framework gets easier over time.

Terminology

Many fields have taken the Institute of Medicine's (2001) definition of EBP and modified it slightly to fit the specifics of their own field. The working definition that will be used in this chapter is one the comes from the American Psychological Association: "the integration of the best available research with clinical expertise in the context of patient characteristics, culture, and preferences" (American Psychological Association, 2005, p. 5). Given that the EBP movement has been applied to a variety of fields, the remainder of the EBP discussion in this chapter will focus on the mental health fields such as counseling, social work, and psychology. First, we will define the three components of EBP as well as EBP's benefits and drawbacks (see Figure 10.1).

Research Evidence

The first component of the tripartite definition of EBP is the best available research evidence. Research evidence is data that comes from peer-reviewed, scientific studies that have been published in reputable outlets. This source of data has greater reliability and validity compared to informal sources of data such as hunches, intuition, conclusions drawn from casual observation, and opinion. Research that is published in peer-reviewed scientific outlets has followed the scientific process and has been scrutinized by knowledgeable peers who can evaluate the soundness of findings against the data and methodology. Alas though, one singular research finding is typically not enough to suggest that a treatment "works." Treatment efficacy is evaluated when the extant body of research

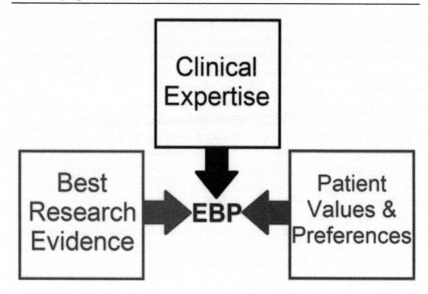

Figure 10.1 Empirically Based Practice Components

findings is considered so that conclusions can be drawn from all of the available evidence.

The best available research evidence is captured by a term that is similar but not the same as EBP, which is empirically supported treatment (EST). EST is sometimes, and inaccurately, used in an interchangeable fashion with EBP. Empirically supported treatments are a smaller part of the EBP equation: ESTs are "clearly specified psychological treatments shown to be efficacious in controlled research with a delineated population" (Chambless & Hollon, 1998, p. 7). ESTs are also known as empirically validated treatments and evidence-based treatments. A treatment cannot simply be found effective in one study and thus be identified as an EST. Chambless and Hollon (1998) established the first set of criteria that determine if a study achieves the moniker of EST. These criteria were more recently updated by Tolin et al. (2015) and aimed to address prevailing critiques of guidelines for determining EST. Beyond the best available research evidence are two other components that are integrated together to determine EBP.

Clinical Expertise

The second component of the EBP equation is the expertise of the provider. Providers obtain competence via their specialized education and training, which is combined with their practice experience (American Psychological Association, 2005). The EBP definition highlights the need for provider expertise because of the advanced capacity for reasoning that experts have obtained. Experts, compared to novices, can:

> recognize meaningful patterns and disregard irrelevant information, acquire extensive knowledge and organize it in ways that reflect a deep understanding of their domain, organize their knowledge using functional rather than descriptive features, retrieve knowledge relevant to the task at hand fluidly and automatically, adapt to new situations, self-monitor their knowledge and performance, know when their knowledge is inadequate, continue to learn, and generally attain outcomes commensurate with their expertise.
> (American Psychological Association, 2005, p. 10)

The expertise of a provider can make decisions that cannot be simply generated by a decision tree or a list of recommendations. Providers are not infallible to bias and cognitive errors, though.

Personal Reflection

Consider for yourself a time in which you felt confident about your conclusions or assessment of a circumstance, only to later learn you were incorrect. What led you to feel confident in your conclusion at the time? Was there evidence you overlooked? How did emotion potentially sway your thinking? How did you learn that you were incorrect? What did you learn about your own thinking process from that experience?

Given human fallibility to thinking errors and bias, the American Psychological Association (APA) (2005) have identified a set of comprehensive areas of competencies that encompass clinical expertise. These competencies are wide-ranging and encapsulate expected domains that are relatively objective in nature (e.g., assessment, diagnostic judgment, systematic case formulation, treatment planning, clinical decision making, treatment implementation, and monitoring of patient progress) as well as those that are more subjective (e.g., interpersonal expertise; continual self-reflection and acquisition of skills) (American Psychological Association, 2005).

Patient Variables

The first two components of the EBP approach encapsulate evidence-supported treatment and the expertise of the provider. However, consideration must always be given to the unique person for whom the treatment is intended. Sue and colleagues (2019) encapsulate the variability of humans with reference to the East Asian saying: "All individuals, in many respects, are a) like no other individuals; b) like some individuals; and c) like all other individuals" (p. 32). From this perspective, providers can recognize the universality of many human qualities and needs. This perspective also highlights that attention must be given to the facets of patient's identity, both in group membership and those that are individual-specific, to fully understand a patient's treatment needs (Sue, 2001). See Figure 10.2 for a summary of the identities, experiences, and capacities that encompass each level of the self.

Mental health treatments must be tailored to a patient's unique constellation of identities, both individual and group level, which include their "specific problems, strengths, personality, sociocultural context, and preferences" (American Psychological Association, 2005, p. 14; Norcross, 2002). Other patient variables that must be considered include their "values, religious beliefs, worldviews, goals, and preferences for treatment" (American Psychological Association, 2005, p. 15). The consideration of these patient variables allows the provider to examine how their patient

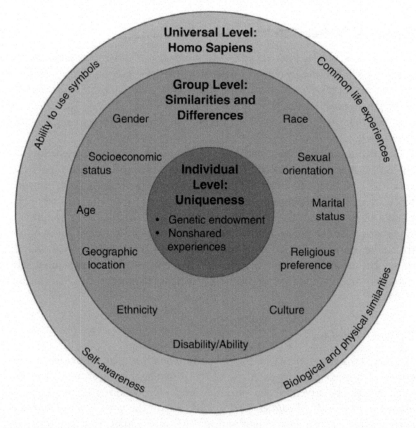

Figure 10.2 Levels of Self

varies from the sample patients within the EST research that is being considered. Indeed, adaptations of ESTs are sometimes needed to make treatment relevant and fit the needs of the patient at hand.

The aim of the provider is to modify the treatment in a manner that retains fidelity to the effective components of the treatment while adapting to the needs of the patient. Sue et al. (2019) note areas of possible adaption such as: 1) a match between spoken language and racial/ethnic backgrounds of the patient and provider; 2) integration of cultural values into treatment strategies; 3) use of cultural sayings and metaphors in treatment; and 4) examination of the impact of environmental variables (e.g., acculturation conflicts, discrimination, income status) upon the presenting concern and treatment. Each of these example areas is not an automatic adaptation though simply because a patient differs in notable ways from the samples used within the relevant EST literature. Rather, a provider must use their expertise and knowledge of the patient to develop adaptations that are needed, relevant, and likely to have a positive impact on treatment.

Benefits of the EBP Movement

The clear benefit of the EBP movement has been a focus on empiricism to guide clinical decision making. A focus on empiricism means that providers are asked to look at empirical evidence to make decisions versus intuition or anecdotal evidence. The EBP movement has resulted in advancements in understanding what works and what does not. This means that students in training programs have their education guided by the insights provided from the EBP movement. In addition, the public can access information regarding what constitutes empirically supported practices and thus be informed seekers and consumers of treatment (Tolin et al., 2015).

Critiques of the EBP Movement

The noble aims of the EBP movement do not shield it from justified criticisms. A full exploration of the challenges and critiques of the EBP movement are beyond the scope of this text. Readers can explore discipline-specific scientific literature for in-depth discussion of these challenges, and possible solutions, from scholars in their fields. We will briefly review some common critiques of the EBP movement to emphasize that no effort toward treatment optimization is without shortcoming.

There are several critiques of the scientific research process used to identify empirically supported treatments within the mental health treatment fields. One line of critique explores the limitations of the research methodologies used to identify efficacious treatments. Randomized controlled trials (RCTs) are one of several acceptable methodological approaches to identifying treatment outcomes; however, given the rigor of RCT design they are "high-quality evidence," according to Tolin et al. (2015, p. 14), and thus have important implications for determination of efficacious treatments. RCTs require that researchers define a specific population for study and utilize a treatment approach that is regimented and replicable, usually using a treatment manual. A narrowly defined sample (e.g., minimal to no co-occurring disorders, people with life circumstances to participate in a research study) and a treatment that easily lends itself to replication (e.g., cognitive behavioral therapies) can limit both generalizability to broader populations as well as the approaches to treatment that can be studied.

Another critique of efficacy research is the tendency toward focusing on symptom reduction versus patient functionality. That is, a treatment might provide a reduction in symptoms of a disorder but not meaningfully impact the person's functionality in important realms of their life. This issue is linked to critiques that efficacy research may find statistically significant beneficial outcomes, but those may not translate to clinically significant differences for a patient. In addition, most research on EST only follow patients for a brief period and thus the long-term efficacy of ESTs are lesser known. A final critique is on the lack of clarity as to what constitutes the active ingredient(s) within a specific EST. All of these are worthy concerns and scholars have proposed solutions to improve the EST movement (Tolin et al., 2015).

Additionally, some scholars have contended that adaptations intended to align an EST with the individual and cultural factors that differentiate the patient from the samples in efficacy research are inadequate (Gone, 2009). That is, the perspective is that the original treatment was developed through the lens of the values and preferences of the majority cultural identities, and thus adaptations are insufficient to make the treatment relevant to groups that vary from those with majority cultural identities. An alternative area of focus is upon the therapeutic relationship and its specific components that positive impact treatment outcomes, known as Empirically Supported Relationship (ESR) variables. Some identified ESR variables include goal consensus and collaboration, empathy, therapeutic alliance, and provider management of countertransference (Ackerman et al., 2001). The intention of identifying ESR variables is a recognition that these factors can exist, and be impactful to treatment outcomes, across a variety of cultural groups without curtailing cultural adaptability.

Treatment Planning

Treatment planning maps an appropriate set of interventions that align with a patient's diagnoses and treatment goals. The foundational helping skills learned within this text provide the basis of a provider's ability to carry out clinical work with their patient. The larger process of determining a plan for treatment for a patient will require integration of several competency areas, including diagnostic skills, ethical behavior, application of theory, and the skills needed to utilize an EBP approach. Taken together and with appropriate supervision and consultation, the novice provider can engage in the process of treatment planning.

The primary step in the treatment planning process is determining the patient's clinical needs. This process is facilitated by collection of vital information via an initial meeting with a patient, as was discussed in the previous chapter. Providers must identify relevant diagnoses as well as circumstances that warrant clinical attention. This process requires that a provider acknowledge both their scope of practice and the available resources within their location of practice. A provider's scope of practice encompasses the clinical activities that a provider has the authority and competency to perform. The location of a provider's practice determines the range of services available to a patient. Patients with severe pathology likely have greater clinical needs that can only be met by a practice with a comprehensive range of services, such as individual therapy, group therapy, psychiatry, and case management. Some patients may even require inpatient or residential care if they are medically unstable or a risk to themselves or others. The initial determination of a patient's needs will determine if the provider and the setting are an appropriate fit for further treatment, and if they are not, then the provider will support the patient in connecting with the appropriate services.

Goal Creation

If the provider determines that the patients' needs are an appropriate fit for their scope and location of practice, then it is paramount that they jointly determine treatment goals. Treatment goals need to align with a patient's diagnoses as well as reflect their desired outcomes. Patients occasionally need assistance in the identification and conceptualization of their goals, and providers can assist them in crafting goals that are appropriate for the context of current treatment. Some basic requirements for successful goal setting are as follows: 1) the goal is within the patient's control; 2) the goal is achievable within the timeframe of treatment; 3) the goal aligns with the provider's scope of practice. Goals can be further refined by using the SMART acronym to increase their clarity and achievability.

SMART stands for: Specific, Measurable, Achievable, Relevant, and Time-bound. Specific goals are explicit and clear in their definition of the desired outcome. A vague outcome for a mental health patient might be "feeling better," but a specific outcome would be a "decrease in symptoms of Social Anxiety Disorder." Even greater specificity could be added by denoting the degree of desired decrease, such as to sub-clinical levels. Specific goals lend themselves to the next criteria, measurability. A measurable goal can be tracked with associated metrics. In the mental health field, various tests and assessments exist to track the presence and degree of mental health symptoms. Achievable goals are those that are likely to be attained given the client's condition and available supports. A client with long-standing symptoms of anxiety may never experience complete remission of all feelings of anxiety; however a goal of sub-clinical levels of anxiety would be achievable with adequate clinical support. Relevant goals are ones that the patient sees as meaningful and worth their effort. A patient that is distressed from years of anxiety symptoms is likely to be invested in the efforts to achieve a reduction in symptoms. Lastly, goals should have a clear timeline for achievement. This aspect requires that a provider offers a reasonable timeframe based on their experience working with similar patients with similar goals. In the current example, it might be reasonable for the patient to achieve a reduction in social anxiety symptoms to sub-clinical levels within eight months.

Integration of EBP

After the diagnostic and goal creation processes have concluded, the provider must map out a course of treatment that is appropriate for the patient's needs. This is the time when providers must seek out reliable guidance on what treatment methods are supported by empirical evidence. This process is cognitively draining when a provider is in-training or early in their career because they are still developing familiarity with treatment literature on a wide range of clinical concerns. As providers progress in their training and narrow in on a smaller sub-set of clinical concerns, the process of treatment planning becomes easier and more efficient. In the beginning, providers will need to identify a source of empirically supported treatments that are appropriate for their field, which will be discussed further in the next section. In the case of the patient with social anxiety disorder, the provider might review the American Psychological Association's Society for Clinical Psychology website to identify empirically supported treatments for Social Anxiety Disorder and discover that Cognitive Behavior Therapy (CBT) for Social Anxiety Disorder has strong research support.

The provider will need to compare their client's demographics to those represented in the research samples that support the efficacy of the treatment. The provider finds that her patient is well-represented among the research samples and concludes that prevailing treatment is likely appropriate to use with the client given the similarity between samples and client characteristics. The provider then considers her own scope of practice and expertise. She has worked with other anxiety disorders and is supervised by a clinician with experience with patients with Social Anxiety Disorder. The provider concludes that she has acceptable familiarity with CBT, anxiety disorders, and access to supervision and consultation with other providers to support her work with the current patient. In this example, everything worked out as easily as possible. A known empirically supported treatment existed, the patient was well-represented in the research, and the provider had appropriate training and support to adopt this treatment approach. Providers will encounter scenarios where a patient's treatment needs are not as easily identified through the literature. These scenarios are common, and the following section will explore how to build one's knowledge of empirically based practice when everything doesn't always go this smoothly.

Building Knowledge of EBP

The core focus of this text is building a skillset for interacting with patients in a multiculturally competent and trauma-informed manner. This skill set will become second nature with repeated practice and opportunities for self and other-observation and feedback. Alongside of this development though, you need to develop the ability to find and evaluate professional literature to determine the best course of treatment for your patient. This is also a skill to be utilized across one's entire professional career, because there will be advances in patient treatment and in order to be the most impactful provider you will need to keep abreast of these developments. Recall that Sackett found that a predictor of a physician's treatment approach was the year in which the physician graduated from medical school! Do not assume whatever the current practice during your training years will remain so throughout your entire career.

Sources of EBP Knowledge

Most scholarly journals within a professional discipline contain articles that discuss the origins and development of the EBP movement within that field. Those articles are a great starting point for understanding EBP within one's profession. Some disciplines maintain centralized websites for seeking information about EST whereas others rely on individual providers to seek out the specific EST information needed through databases of empirical research.

There are several high quality, centralized resources within the counseling field for EST information. Two helpful resources are those associated with the American Psychological Association (APA). The APA has various divisions based on subdisciplines and professional interests, two of which are The Society of Clinical Psychology (Division 12) and The Society of Clinical Child and Adolescent Psychology (Division 53). These divisions maintain websites that provide reasonably current databases of EST for diagnoses and concerns in the field of counseling and psychology. The Division 12 resource focuses on diagnoses and treatments for adult populations (https://div12.org/psychological-treatments/) and the Division 53 resources provides guidance on EST for children and adolescents (https://effectivechildtherapy.org). The Division 12 website is geared toward providers whereas the Division 53 website could be used by providers and parents to better understand EST options. Another centralized resource is the website maintained by the Substance Abuse and Mental Health Services Administration (SAMHSA) within the U.S. Department of Health and Human Services (www.samhsa.gov/resource-search/ebp). As providers begin their first field placements, they will benefit from regularly consulting these resources to examine what the current literature says regarding empirically supported treatment of the concerns of their various patients.

Adapting ESTs

Recall the matching an EST to a diagnosis or concern is not the only part of the equation for EBP. EBP also requires that the patient's values and preferences be considered. As the EBP movement has developed, the professional literature has too and holds examples of how EST can be adapted to patient's unique needs. In fact, the *Map of Adaptation Process* is a systematic approach for adapting evidence-supported treatment (McKleroy et al., 2006). As an example of this adaptation process, consider a diagnosis of Posttraumatic Stress Disorder (PTSD). The APA Division 12 website denotes several ESTs with varying levels of support for treatment of PTSD, one of which being Cognitive Processing Therapy (CPT). Adapted CPT has been studied for Spanish-speaking Latine clients (Valentine et al., 2017), Kurdish clients (Kaysen et al., 2013), Bosnian clients (Schulz et al., 2006), and Native American women clients (Pearson et al., 2019), among other groups. In the Pearson et al. (2019, p. 697) example, CPT was adapted by "removing scientific jargon; improving readability; and culturally adapting concepts, definitions, and handout materials." Adapted CPT was found to have positive impacts on mental health and risk behavior outcomes in the study. There won't always be an empirical article to guide the EST adaptation process to a client's unique values and preferences. However, familiarizing oneself with adaptation literature can assist providers in thinking flexibly. Flexible thinking can assist a provider in maintaining fidelity to the core components of an EST while tailoring it to the needs of the patient.

Developing Competency

Recall that the third component of EBP is clinical expertise. Clinical expertise comes from specialized training and experience and allows for a provider to make nuanced decision about the implementation of an EST. A precursor to expertise is competency, the ability to conduct a treatment effectively. Developing competency generally requires a combination of education and supervised practice. During your formal education in your field you will develop competency for a variety of common clinical practices. However, in order to grow as a provider and treat concerns that you did not learn about in your training years, you will need to utilize continuing education and supervision/consultation to develop new competencies, and eventually, clinical expertise.

Continuing Education

Continuing education is a requirement for almost all licensed professionals across health professions. Professional organizations and licensing boards set standards for acquisition of continuing education credits regarding how much and how often. Formal continuing education can be a wonderful impetus for developing competency, but continuing education can be pursued for implicit motivational reasons as well. Providers will find that simply reading high-quality books and articles is an accessible and time-tested method for developing one's competency.

Supervision/Consultation

Receiving supervision and consultation on one's skills in a new area is an invaluable way to build one's competency. As you have learned in this textbook, there is no substitute for outside observation and feedback of one's skill practice. Although formal supervision may come to end when a provider reaches independent licensure, they can still seek out supervision and consultation with advanced peers.

Conclusion

Developing basic helping skills is the pre-requisite for providing empirically based practices with patients. All EBP require that providers have a solid foundation in basic helping skills to implement the treatments that align with the patient's preferences and values, all while integrating in your own clinical expertise. Acquiring knowledge and expertise in EST requires commitment and time from a provider, but the outcome is likely to be greater efficiency and effectiveness as a clinician.

Questions for Class Discussion

1 Any approach has advantages and disadvantages. What will be the barriers for *your* use of EBP?

2   How will you go about getting the latest information on evidence-based treatment approaches?
3   What ethical considerations should be explored when using a treatment strategy that has not yet been researched for effectiveness?
4   In your own perception, to what extent do you think emphasis in treatment should be on relationship versus technique?

References

Ackerman, S.J., Benjamin, L.S., Beutler, L.E., Gelso, C.J., Goldfried, M.R., Hill, C., ... Rainer, J. (2001). Empirically supported therapy relationships: Conclusions and recommendations of the Division 29 Task Force. *Psychotherapy*, 38, 495–497.

American Psychological Association. (2005). *Report of the 2005 Presidential Task Force on Evidence-Based Practice*. Washington, DC: Author.

Chambless, D.L. & Hollon, S.D. (1998). Defining empirically supported therapies. *Journal of Consulting and Clinical Psychology*, 66(1), 7.

Gone, J.P. (2009). A community-based treatment for Native American historical trauma: Prospects for evidence-based practice. *Journal of Consulting and Clinical Psychology*, 17, 751–762.

Institute of Medicine. (2001). *Crossing the quality chasm: A new health system for the 21st century*. National Academy Press.

Kaysen, D., Lindgren, K., Zangana, G.A.S., Murray, L., Bass, J., & Bolton, P. (2013). Adaptation of cognitive processing therapy for treatment of torture victims: Experience in Kurdistan, Iraq. *Psychological Trauma: Theory, Research, Practice, and Policy*, 5(2), 184–192. doi:10.1037/a0026053.

Kowalski, E. & Chung, K.C. (2013). The outcomes movement and evidence-based medicine in plastic surgery. *Clinical Plastic Surgery*, 40(2), 241–247. doi:10.1016/j.cps.2012.10.001.

McKleroy, V.S., Galbraith, J.S., Cummings, B., Jones, P., Harshbarger, C., Collins, C., Gelaude, D., & Carey, J.W. (2006). Adapting Evidence-Based Behavioral Interventions for New Settings and Target Populations. *AIDS Education and Prevention*, 18 (SupplA), 59–73. doi:10.1521/aeap.2006.18.supp.59.

Norcross, J.C. (Ed.). (2002). *Psychotherapy relationships that work: Therapist contributions and responsiveness to patient needs*. Oxford University Press.

Pearson, C.R., Kaysen, D., Huh, D., & Bedard-Gilligan, M. (2019). Randomized control trial of culturally adapted cognitive processing therapy for PTSD substance misuse and HIV sexual risk behavior for Native American women. *AIDS and Behavior*, 23(3), 695–706. doi:10.1007/s10461-018-02382-8.

Sackett, D. (1981). How to read clinical journals: I. Why to read them and how to start reading them critically. *Canadian Medical Association Journal*, 124(5). 555–558.

Schulz, P.M., Huber, L.C., & Resick, P.A. (2006). Practical adaptations of Cognitive Processing Therapy with Bosnian refugees: Implications for adapting practice to a multicultural clientele. *Cognitive and Behavioral Practice*, 13(4), 310–321. doi:10.1016/j.cbpra.2006.04.019.

Sue, D.W. (2001). Multidimensional facets of cultural competence. *The Counseling Psychologist*, 29, 790–821.

Sue, D.W., Sue, D., Neville, H.A., & Smith, L. (2019). *Counseling the Culturally Diverse: Theory and Practice*. (8th ed.) Wiley.

Tolin, D.F., McKay, D., Forman, E.M., Klonsky, E.D., & Thombs, B.D. (2015). Empirically supported treatment: Recommendations for a new model. *Clinical Psychology: Science and Practice*, 22(4), 317–338. doi:10.1037/h0101729.

Valentine, S.E., Borba, C.P.C., Dixon, L., Vaewsorn, A.S., Guajardo, J.G., Resick, P.A., Wiltsey Stirman, S., & Marques, L. (2017). Cognitive processing therapy for Spanish- speaking Latinos: A formative study of a model-driven cultural adaptation of the manual to enhance implementation in a usual care setting. *Journal of Clinical Psychology*, 73(3), 239–256. doi:10.1002/jclp.22337.

Chapter 11

Helping Skill Integration

One commonality about helping across all the health professions is the sizable gap between what students learn in their theoretical and conceptually based courses and their field experiences they have toward the conclusion of their training. You will be learning more about assessment and diagnosis, and ethical behavior in your discipline. Nevertheless, when you move to doing your field-based training, you will likely find that some of your real-life patients are presenting with concerns and issues that are complex and nuanced, to a degree far less defined than we might expect based on the book learning during your coursework.

In this book, we've covered a broad range of topics that all pertain to aspects of relationship development. Factors of human development, intersectionality, and individual characteristics like trauma history have been presented sequentially, with an eye toward what helping looks like in that context. These variables all play a huge role in any given person's life, and in reality, there is a constantly evolving interplay of those variables all the time! Thus, we will use this chapter to present three patient case descriptions as vehicles for discussion of how the variables co-exist and most importantly, how a helper can use their knowledge of those variables to maximize their effectiveness. The case descriptions will be a child, a young adult, and an older adult.

Adriana

Presenting Concern

Adriana is a nine-year old cisgender, multiracial girl of Native American, White, and Latina identities. She is in the 4th grade in public school. She lives with her mother and father in a mobile home community in a rural area. Adriana's mother, Aubrey, works at a warehouse, processing orders. Adriana's father, Jeff, works as a long-haul semitruck driver. Adriana's parents sought out counseling for their daughter when they learned that she had been sexually assaulted by a teenage boy in their neighborhood. Adriana was reluctant to share what happened to her parents, but her

DOI: 10.4324/9781003217589-14

parents were able to get her to open up after they assured her that she would not be punished for telling them why she was behaving unusually. Aubrey and Jeff had noticed that for the past month, Adriana began wetting the bed, was wanting to be driven to school instead of taking the bus, and was complaining of stomach aches.

Patient History

Adriana has met developmental milestones at normative times throughout her life thus far. She is doing well in school and her teachers describe her as "bubbly" and "talkative." She enjoys playing videogames such as Minecraft and also likes "adventuring" in the woods and fields near her home. Adriana was briefly (i.e., 3–4 months) a member of a local children's dance studio but because of family financial strains, she could not continue her lessons. Adriana states that she wants to be a teacher when she grows up.

Adriana describes her homelife as "good" but that she misses her father when he is working. Jeff is typically gone for 4–5 weeks at time and then home for a week or so. Jeff's mother, Lynn, is often a primary caregiver for Adriana when Aubrey is working evening shifts at the warehouse. Lynn has chronic obstructive pulmonary disease (COPD) and isn't able to physically monitor Adriana much because she struggles with shortness of breath and low energy, however, she is able to be a presence at home when Adriana gets home from school and would otherwise be alone.

Adriana is friends with a group of similarly aged peers in her neighborhood, who are also in her classroom at school. Several months ago, a new teenage boy moved into the neighborhood to live with his grandmother. This teenage boy began hanging out with Adriana and her friend group. It was during this time that Adriana was sexually assaulted by the boy several times. Aubrey and Jeff reported the assault to the police and charges have been filed against him. The boy has since moved in with another family member and no longer lives in the mobile home community. A trial date has not yet been set.

Lynn blames herself for the sexual assaults because they happened "on [her] watch," that is, on evenings when she was watching Adriana. Although Aubrey and Jeff don't blame Lynn, they do harbor some anger toward Lynn for letting the teenage boy come over to the home and spend time with Adriana without direct supervision. There has been tension in the home between Lynn and Aubrey for the past month.

Objective Assessment and Level of Functioning

Adriana continues to do well in school and remains interested in her pastime of exploring nature and videogames. She has withdrawn somewhat from socializing with her friends because she feels shameful about what happened to her and fears that the other children will know and will judge her. Adriana's main complaints are stomach aches and wetting the bed, which she says is "embarrassing" because she "isn't a little kid."

Subjective Assessment

Adriana reported feelings of shame, fear, anxiety, and sadness. She reported feeling responsible for the tension in her home between her parents and her grandmother. She says she feels better knowing that the police will "punish" the teenage boy who hurt her, but she says she also feels "bad" because she sees the boy's grandmother in the neighborhood often and feels like that grandmother blames Adriana for him having to go live with another family member.

Mental Status

Adriana presented for her first session of counseling appropriately groomed and with seasonally appropriate clothing. During the meeting, she was oriented to person, place, and time. She was somewhat reserved but opened up by the end of the session and was more spontaneous in her sharing. She denied current or past suicidal or homicidal ideation.

Health and Medical Status

Adriana has no known health concerns beyond the bed wetting and has met developmental milestones regarding physical, emotional, and cognitive development.

Legal Status

Adriana's sexual assaults have been reported to local authorities and her parents are working with a lawyer and local prosecutor in the process of pressing charges against the perpetrator who assaulted Adriana. Adriana has met with the police, a victim advocate, and the lawyer. She described those meetings as "scary" but was glad that her parents could be with her for many of the meetings.

Bronfenbrenner's Ecological Systems Model

Table 11.1

Microsystem: Mother, father, grandmother, neighbors, friends, classmates at school, teachers and staff at school, lawyer, police officers, victim advocate.

Mesosystem: Frequent interactions between school, family, and legal professionals.

Exosystem: School follows traditional hours and scheduling. Mother and father work schedules that conflict with school schedules and are often unavailable to participate in school events. School has standardized expectations for achievement that are linked to public education curricula. Expectations and values at school align with values within the home.

Macrosystem: Some presence of Catholic values and practices, working class socioeconomic status.

Chronosystem: Middle childhood with some regression to earlier stages of development. Career exploration process is normative for a nine-year old child. Client is at expected stages of racial identity development.

Client's Reported Treatment Goals

Adriana stated that she wants "home to feel normal again" in regard to the tensions between her mom, dad, and grandmother. She also said she wants to be able to hang out with her friends without feeling "weird." She said she sometimes feels like she can't concentrate at school. Lastly, she said she wants to "keep exploring outside" because she has been scared that the boy who assaulted her is hiding in the woods and has been hesitant to spend time alone outside. She said she wants to be a science teacher and that is important to her to "keep being in nature" because that is how she learns about biology.

Dialogue: First Session Following the Intake

COUNSELOR: It's nice to see you again Adriana. How are you doing today?
ADRIANA: (softly) Hi. I'm good, thank you.
COUNSELOR: Do you want to color while we talk today?
ADRIANA: Sure.

[*Counselor and Adriana sit down at a table and leaf through coloring pages and select some markers and pages to color. They sit quietly and begin coloring for a few minutes.*]

COUNSELOR: What would you like to talk about today?
ADRIANA: Hmmm, I don't know. [*Adriana looks out the window for a little while.*]
COUNSELOR: There's no rush to figure it out. We can talk about whatever you like, whenever you like.
ADRIANA: Okay.

[*Counselor and Adriana continue coloring in silence for several minutes.*]

ADRIANA: So, we're going to have a science fair at school.
COUNSELOR: Oh wow, tell me about that!

ADRIANA: I don't know much but my teacher said we can do an experiment and show it off to the other students and teachers and our parents can come too. There is going to be a prize for the best experiment. Kids from the junior high school are going to come be the judges. I don't know if my dad would be able to come because he might be on the road when it happens. My mom might be able to come though since she could take off work. I hope she could.

COUNSELOR: That sounds like something you might like. How are you feeling about it?

ADRIANA: Well, at first, I was excited because I have already been doing some experiments at home with pond water. I've been looking at the pond water under my microscope and drawing pictures of what I see. I'm trying to compare the water in the big pond to the water in puddles. I don't know how to make that an experiment though.

COUNSELOR: It sounds like you have an idea that you're happy with but feel like you need to figure out a bit more?

ADRIANA: Yeah, I was thinking maybe I could talk to my teacher about my idea.

COUNSELOR: That sounds like a good idea. She will probably be helpful.

ADRIANA: Yeah, I don't know though. I'm still not sure if I want to do it.

COUNSELOR: I see, you're interested but not sure yet. Sounds like you're feeling a little hesitant? You mentioned that junior high school kids will be judging the competition. How do you feel about that?

ADRIANA: That's what I'm scared about. (long pause) What if *he* is there?

COUNSELOR: The boy who hurt you?

ADRIANA: [*Nodding head and looking down.*]

COUNSELOR: That would be very scary. If you knew he wouldn't be there would you want to participate?

ADRIANA: Yeah, I think so.

COUNSELOR: I noticed you stopped coloring. How are you feeling right now as we talk about this?

ADRIANA: This makes my stomach hurt. Sometimes I wish we could just move and then I wouldn't haven't to think about him anymore. I wish I could go with my dad to work and travel with him and see the country and be far away from here.

COUNSELOR: Yeah, these emotions feel yucky, huh? It makes you want to get away from it all.

ADRIANA: Hmmhmm. Sometimes my stomach feels so bad that I don't even want to eat the dinner that Gramma Lynn makes. Sometimes she has to make me frybread to eat because that's all that sounds good to me.

Dialogue Analysis

- What are specific aspects of this dialogue that seem culturally responsive? What aspects seem trauma-informed?
- What are some other, equally responsive, ways the counselor might interact and respond to Adriana?
- How might the counselor's non-verbal and paraverbal behavior impact Adriana?
- How might you respond to Adrianna given what she stated in the final line of dialogue?

Case and Self-Reflection Questions

- What aspects of Adriana's Ecological Systems Model support her clinical goals? Which aspects might present a barrier?
- What aspects of Adriana's experiences and identities are familiar to you, and which are not? How might this impact your preconceived views of her?
- How does her referral from her parents impact your perceptions of the treatment goals?
- What aspects of her identities and history would you want to know more about to effectively work with her? (Consider the ADDRESSING acronym).
- What does it look like to work with Adriana in a trauma-informed manner?

India

Presenting Concern

India is a single, Black, straight and cisgender woman who is 29 years old. She has been referred to counseling by her faculty advisor because she has been struggling academically with the final requirements of her Ph.D. program in cellular and molecular biology. Her advisor suggested that she seek counseling because he wasn't sure how to encourage and motivate her after a series of missed deadlines in the past 1.5 years. India entered her graduate program immediately after completing her undergraduate degree in biology but is the only member of her original cohort that has not graduated yet. The past two years of India's schooling have been difficult for her because India has become the primary caretaker for her mother, who developed a severe autoimmune disorder two years ago. India assists her mother with bathing and dressing, along with doing the majority of the cooking, cleaning, and household managements tasks (e.g., paying bills, interior and exterior maintenance of the home).

Patient History

India is the younger of two children in her family of origin. She lives with her mother and older sister Renee, who is five years older. Both her mother and sister are nurses, although her mother had to retire two years ago when she became ill. India's father died in a car accident shortly after India was born, when Renee was five, and she has very minimal contact with her paternal family throughout her childhood. India does have a large extended family in the area, and most of her socializing is with family and friends from her mosque. She is very popular and active in her mosque community. She is in her seventh year of her Ph.D. program. She has maintained high grades throughout her entire program but she has struggled to make adequate progress on her dissertation in the past two years.

India describes her sister Renee as being dominant and critical. Throughout their lives, Renee has seemed to have critical and unkind things to say to India about all aspects of her life: her appearance, her educational choices, and her choice of friends. Although their mother observes these interactions, she has never intervened, and in many respects, it feels more like Renee is the head of the household. Renee interacts similarly with their mother, and India experiences her sister as a "bully." She has felt unable to defend herself emotionally, while her mother offers no solace or protection from Renee's verbal assaults. India's mother is passive and unwilling to express disagreement or make requests of Renee to help with tasks around the house. Renee argues that she is "working in the real world" and that the household and caretaking duties for their mother should be India's responsibility since India is "only in school."

India was employed as a Research Assistant for most of her Ph.D. program thus far but funding cuts in the department led her contract to not be renewed for the most recent academic year. Since the non-renewal of her contract, she has been working as a biology tutor for high school students, but the work is time consuming and low-paying. Socially, she has a circle of five close friends, mostly from her graduate program. They have lots of contact on social media and go out for meals, concerts, and movies. She experiences them as her "friend family," and they offer her unconditional support. Several of these friends will be graduating this year though, and are likely to accept jobs in different states.

In the first session, India was candid about feeling dubious as to whether counseling would do anything to help. The goal-setting conversation focused not specifically on her struggle with completing her dissertation, but rather on aspects of her functioning and life where some adjustments could be made to support her improved mental and emotional health. She recognizes that the increased care taking responsibilities have severely impacted her productivity, but holds the view that she "should" be able to manage everything, without much help from others.

Objective Assessment and Level of Functioning

She appeared well-groomed and with appropriate hygiene. She has been able to establish and maintain meaningful long-term relationships with peers. Her work performance and academic performance have historically been above average, except for the past two years when she has failed to meet deadlines with her dissertation work. All of this information is self-report from the client or made from observations from the provider.

Subjective Assessment

By self-report, India expressed a range of emotions about her stagnation in her academic progress. Those feelings encompassed fear that she would never graduate, fear about not being competitive for post-doctoral positions and jobs, and hopelessness about her ability to take steps that would improve the circumstances. She was highly aware of Renee's criticisms and had internalized negative messages about many aspects of her ability to juggle home and school. She also expressed yearning for someone to date, while also feeling hopeless about ever finding a partner who would be loving, reliable, and treat her well, as both her mother and sister had very negative experiences in their own intimate relationships, and both spoke globally and negatively about all men.

Mental Status

India was oriented to person, place, and time. Her paraverbal and non-verbal behaviors were consistent with her self-report of feelings of hopelessness and apathy. She was easily forthcoming with information and was a reflective responder, meaning that she took time to reflect on the assessment questions before answering. Her range of affect was broad and appropriate; she was tearful when discussing some past and current events, and her demeanor brightened as she disclosed about her friends, working with high school students in her tutoring job, and wishes for her career.

Health and Medical Status

India reported that her mother's autoimmune disease may be heritable and she worries for her own future health, but that currently she is focused on caring for her mother and tries to "push off" worries about her future health. India has been without health insurance for several years. She had been on her mother's insurance but when her mother took early retirement, she was no longer eligible for coverage. India hasn't seen her primary care physician for two years and is slightly worried because she was pre-hypertensive two years ago but hasn't received any monitoring or follow-up care since then. The recommendation from her doctor at that time was to take a blood pressure medicine, increase her exercise, lower her stress, and improve her diet. India reported that her stress has increased since then, and that she hasn't had time to maintain a regular exercise routine or "healthy" diet. Also, her prescription for her blood pressure medicine expired and she has not had it renewed.

Substance Use

India reported that she would very occasionally have a glass of wine with dinner, but otherwise had no history of consuming psychoactive substances of any kind.

Legal Status

India has had no history of interaction with the legal system.

Bronfenbrenner's Ecological Systems Model

Table 11.2

Microsystem: Mother, sister, friends, classmates at school, professors and staff at school, children at work, mosque members.
Mesosystem: Minimal interactions between home, work, school, and friendship realms. Some connections between mosque community and family relationships.
Exosystem: Work and school structures follow traditional working hours and scheduling. School has standardized expectations for achievement. Expectations and values at work and school align with values within the home and religious expectations.
Macrosystem: Islamic-linked values and practices, middle class.
Chronosystem: Early adulthood with some mismatch between desires for independence and resources to access independence. Career development process feels congruent with her desires but progression feels stalled. Client is at expected stages of racial identity development.

Client's Reported Treatment Goals

The client reported three goals for treatment as: 1) "Feel better and be less stressed"; 2) "Stand up to my sister"; and 3) "Get back on track with the dissertation." These goals were operationalized and resulted in the following:

1. Decrease depressive symptoms, including apathy, difficulties concentrating, and sleep disturbances.
2. Increase use of healthy coping skills for managing stressful situations.

3   Increase assertiveness in relationship with sister.
4   Develop and execute plan for making progress on dissertation.

Dialogue: First Session Following the Intake

COUNSELOR: [*Smiling*] Nice to see you here today! I know that when we did your intake last week, we touched on a number of issues and concerns that were pretty upsetting for you, but toward the end when we closed the session by identifying goals you expressed maybe a little bit more hope than when we had started the session. How are you feeling about those goals now that you've had some time to sit with them?

INDIA: I feel mixed. Like I know I need to take better care of myself, I know I need to do something about my relationship with my sister, but I can't imagine what to do, and standing up to Renee is literally impossible. She's already run right over my mother, so she'll definitely keep having her way with me...but I'm really starting to feel resentful. When my mom was first diagnosed, it made sense that I took over a lot of the caretaking stuff, because I have the flexible schedule. But it's really getting to the point where I can't get my own work done now. Renee doesn't seem to care, and part of me feels like it's sabotage, she's jealous of me getting my Ph.D.

COUNSELOR: I hear your ambivalence. Renee has been so much this way, and for so long, it's hard to have a mental picture of how it could ever be different. At the same time, you recognize that figuring out how to navigate this will give you skills that can help you as you move forward with your life.

INDIA: Exactly! [*sigh*] So which one of those goals do we start with?

COUNSELOR: Actually India, as I think about your family system with Mom and Renee, I see a couple of your goals as being sort of connected.

INDIA: What do you mean?

COUNSELOR: Well, you said you've struggled with prioritizing parts of your own life, like your schooling and your health. It sounds like you wish you could lighten the load of your caretaking responsibilities with your mom and the house, but the dynamic with Renee seems like a barrier to that. I'm thinking that developing healthier ways to cope with stress and increasing your assertiveness with your sister are connected, and could results in freeing up time and energy to take care of yourself, which would include your dissertation.

INDIA: That makes sense. Yeah, I'm good with that since it seems like it's all related.

COUNSELOR: Let's start by talking about your history with trying to change patterns in your life. I'd like to go into a bit more detail than last week about your previous efforts to make changes in your relationship with your sister. I want to hear about what you tried, what parts of your effort worked and especially explore what prevented you from being successful.

INDIA: Well, to be honest, I've never really tried to change things with her. I've just tolerated her. I'm afraid that if I show that I'm struggling, she'll use it against me and paint me as "weak" and incapable.

COUNSELOR: I see, so it's hard to know how to even start because you fear that you will be seen in negative way in her eyes. It sounds like you want her to see you a certain type of way, as a strong and capable person who doesn't complain?

INDIA: Yes, although I don't always like the way she treats people, she doesn't ever seem to be emotionally hurt and sensitive herself. She tries to paint me as the "sensitive and weak" one. Sometimes I don't want to give her a single reason to think of me that way. My friends have really helped me see though that part of the way that she treats me might be that she is jealous of my accomplishments, and maybe feels threatened by me.

COUNSELOR: [*nodding*] Part of you admires her steely nature and part of you recognizes that maybe she has her own insecurities underneath.

INDIA: Yup, exactly. Are you familiar with the "strong Black woman" concept? She really subscribes to that. Sometimes it feels like the core of our struggle is that I did subscribe to that idea, in the past, but I'm starting to realize how that can be really detrimental for my own health.

Session 5 (7 weeks later)

COUNSELOR: I'm so glad to see you today!

INDIA: Well I'm glad to be here. It's been a couple weeks and so much has happened I couldn't wait to tell you....

COUNSELOR: Wow. What's been going on?

INDIA: Two days ago, my sister and I had a huge fight. I really tried to use the assertiveness skills we discussed but she kept fighting back in her usual ways. I held the line though. I repeated myself and made it clear what I needed to change. And then, get this, she started to cry. I haven't seen her cry since...since we were kids. She started to talk about how hard it was to see mom struggle and that she thought mom was going to get better, faster. It did feel a bit like she was deflecting what I said and making herself the center of the conversation, but it felt like progress to see her express some real emotion.

COUNSELOR: That is shocking! You must have been completely bowled over by her response.

INDIA: I was completely blown away. I still don't know what to think or feel about it.

COUNSELOR: From what we have talked about the last couple sessions, it is very complicated emotionally. You have wanted to see Renee acknowledge how the stress of your mom's illness is affecting her too, so that she could develop empathy for the situation that you're in given all your caretaking responsibilities. So, in a way it feels like progress. I hear that you still want her to acknowledge that she could be doing more for your family and that her own emotional avoidance is likely the reason she isn't, not because she's simply "too busy." It sounds like you want to give her some credit for opening up to you but you still want her to come along further.

INDIA: That's it. I feel so overwhelmed with all these feelings. Tell me what to do.

COUNSELOR: India, I'm so honored that you would value my opinion that much, thank you. I think the best way for me to help you is to support you working through all these feelings so that you can clear out some space inside to figure out for yourself what you want to do.

INDIA: [*quietly crying*] I know, it's almost like I want you to tell me what to do. Just in the same way I let Renee tell me what to do for all these years.

COUNSELOR: [*Prolonged silence until India's crying began to stop.*] This is so overwhelming and scary for you. For much of your life you've wanted to have more power and control over your life, and it's starting to feel like you could gain some of that. It's also overwhelming to recognize the implications of having to be more outspoken, and in a way, more vulnerable.

INDIA: I feel squeezed and like I can't get my breath. Like, really truly, it feels hard to breathe.

COUNSELOR: I want to take a time out to focus on your difficulty breathing right now. Considering the squeeze you feel emotionally, your struggle with your breath makes total sense. Let's take a couple minutes and do some four-square breathing before moving on. Get both of your feet flat on the ground and rest your hands on your lap. Close your eyes and inhale through your nose for a count of 4, then we will hold for 4, and exhale through your mouth for a count of 4.

Dialogue Analysis

- What are specific aspects of this dialogue that seem culturally responsive?
- What are some other, equally responsive, ways the counselor might interact and respond to India?

Alternative Dialogue

Session 2 (first session after intake)

COUNSELOR: I'm glad you followed through with your advisor's recommendation to come here; it is going to be really important for you to make progress on your dissertation.

INDIA: Yeah, I suppose. I'm afraid I'm going to be put on academic probation if I don't meet another writing deadline.

COUNSELOR: The way I like to work with people on this is to teach them some lifestyle and psychology tricks because a lot of time people just need to learn how to start asking for more help, and then things get easier.

INDIA: What do you mean?

COUNSELOR: So, let's talk first about how you could start asking a bunch of people in your life to pitch in and help out more. I mean you've got friends at your church right? At my church there are things called "meal trains" where people cook when someone dies or if someone in their family is really sick.

INDIA: Yeah, I'm familiar with the concept. We've done stuff like that at my mosque but it doesn't feel like it applies here. My mom isn't dying though, and she's been struggling for years, so it seems like the window of time for asking for that type of help has passed.

COUNSELOR: Church communities are supposed to help people in need.

INDIA: Oh, yeah, of course. It's just that I'm usually the person who is helping others there. It would be totally out of character if suddenly I requested that I was the one who needed help at home.

COUNSELOR: Well, sometimes change is hard.

INDIA: MmHm.

COUNSELOR: So, what about sending a text tonight to someone at church to ask if someone can make some meals for you guys? We could write up the text right now in session together. Why don't you pull out your phone and let's do it.

Dialogue Analysis

- What are specific aspects of this dialogue that seem culturally responsive?
- What components of the dialogue are problematic?
- What are some other ways the counselor might interact and respond to India?

Case and Self-Reflection Questions

- What aspects of India's Ecological Systems Model support her clinical goals? Which aspects might present a barrier?

- What aspects of India's experiences and identities are familiar to you, and which are not? How might this impact your preconceived views of her?
- How does her referral from her advisor impact your perceptions of the treatment goals?
- What aspects of her identities and history would you want to know more about to effectively work with her? (Consider the ADDRESSING acronym).
- What does it look like to work with India in a trauma-informed manner?

John

Presenting Concern

John is a 71-year-old cisgender White man who identifies as bisexual and recently separated from his partner of 20 years. He was referred to counseling by his daughter who has been increasingly concerned about John's social withdrawal and other depressive behaviors. These problems began when his partner left the household to relocate to the other side of the country.

Patient History

John is the elder of two boys in his family of origin. His father was an electrician and his mother did not work outside the home. John's brother is seven years younger and they have not had contact more than once a year for many decades.

John grew up during the 1960s, and although his father was continuously employed, there were significant financial struggles. This had the result of John becoming extremely frugal and uncomfortable spending money, even in his later career when he had attained an upper middle-class level of income. John grew up in a small community in a rural area, and his parents were quite religious and active in the church. His younger brother was often ill and often had the parents' doting attention, while John, as the eldest son, felt somewhat invisible.

John attended college away from home, and he was out to a very small group of romantic partners but otherwise was not out among most friends and family. After graduation, John married a woman, Terri, and they had two children. John and Terri maintained a consensually open relationship for much of their marriage, and their arrangements worked well for the first ten years of the marriage. John was employed as an administrator of a community college and would sometimes travel out of town on business trips, during which time he would date and socialize with other men.

Although John would have continued with the marriage, Terri grew dissatisfied and she chose to leave the marriage to begin a new life after fifteen years of marriage. John seized the opportunity, and increasing societal openness to LGBTQ+ people in the mid-1990s to more fully come out to most family and friends.

After several years of casual dating John found a partner, Marcos, with whom he wanted to get serious, and Marcos moved in with John. They had a stable, compatible relationship for 20 years. Immediately following John's retirement, they moved to Florida and were happy and active there, until John experienced a stroke that left him unable to walk by himself or care for his own physical needs. John's demeanor changed with the illness, and after 12 months of physical and occupational therapy, it was becoming apparent that John was very unlikely to return to the activities and level of functioning he enjoyed before the stroke, and Marcos no longer wanted to maintain the relationship. About six months prior to John's counseling referral, Marcos announced that he was leaving and in the space of two days, left all his belongings in the house to move across the country with no contact information. This decision came as a complete shock to John and others who knew them, so the rapidity of the separation added substantially to the stress. John's daughters suspect that Marcos had been unhappy for some time and that some of John's depressive symptoms existed prior to the stroke, and that the stroke and recovery exacerbated his social withdrawal. Since the separation, John's daughters have been doing their best to provide care by having home health care, in addition to they themselves, taking care of John in an emotional and physical sense.

Subjective Assessment

John denies that he feels depressed and denies that he feels anything whatsoever about Marcos leaving. His main emotional complaint is anger over his lack of independence. John expresses frustration over the lack of control he has in many aspects of his life. For example, John can no longer drive and relies on grocery delivery services and others to complete errands and tasks for him. He reports that these services are expensive and "don't do a good job."

Objective Assessment and Level of Functioning

John's objective level of functioning is atypical and more dependent in comparison to his age peers who are generally still independent, as a result of the stroke. Where he was previously an avid car traveler, he can no longer drive. John lives in an assisted living apartment with a full kitchen and bathroom, and he is able to cook and shower mostly independently. His activities of daily living consist of maintaining his hygiene with occasional assistance, maintaining some social contact with his daughters, watching movies and television, and reading. John was previously active in a pickleball league but no longer participates, owing to balance and strength challenges.

The depressive behavior observed by his daughters includes rarely smiling or laughing, eating very small amounts of food, extreme irritability, sleep disruption in the form of sleeping all afternoon and staying awake until 3 or 4 in the morning, and declining invitations to socialize. Most of John's friends in Florida were linked to Marcos and John has felt alienated from the group after the separation. John's daughters understand his hesitancy to socialize with that friend group but also express frustration that John is not making efforts to build new friendships.

Bronfenbrenner's Ecological Systems Model

Table 11.3

Microsystem: Daughters, neighbors, healthcare providers and caretakers. Mostly estranged relationship with brother, parents, and former friends. Minimal contact with ex-wife and former work friends. No contact with Marcos.

Mesosystem: Consistent contact between daughters, neighbors, healthcare providers, and staff at assisted living apartment. This group agrees on their assessment of John's functioning and needs.

Exosystem: No workplace or school schedules to structure days. Interactions with healthcare systems and providers are the only reoccurring demands of John's time.

Macrosystem: Agnostic, middle-class.

Chronosystem: Older adulthood with notable mismatch between desires for independence and ability to have independence. Career development process feels concluded. Client has low racial identity development and a normative level of sexual orientation identity development. Client has dissonance regarding potential identity of being a person with a disability.

Mental Status

John presented for this interview appropriately groomed and with seasonally appropriate clothing. His gait was slow, and he walked with a cane in one hand. During the interview, John was oriented to person, place, and time. He denied anxiety or depression, but his affect was flat. While describing his activities and his grandchildren, there was minimal pleasure evident, despite his describing honors and successes his children and grandchildren had achieved. He denied current or past suicidal or homicidal ideation.

Health and Medical Status

John's health status currently is stable. He takes medication for high blood pressure, high cholesterol, and multivitamins. He has lingering cognitive and physical impacts of the stroke.

Legal Status

John has no history of contact with the legal system. There were some issues around finances and potential bankruptcy when Marcos left the relationship. John was unable to keep making the mortgage payments and sold their home.

Treatment Goals

John flatly states that he has no goals other than for his daughter to quit worrying about him and quit haranguing him about going for counseling. In light of the information John shared in the intake interview, the counselor generated some treatment goal ideas to be discussed with John. The counselor's suggested short-term treatment goals included managing his physical symptoms of depression, namely increasing his appetite, regulating his sleep/wake cycles through better sleep hygiene, and increasing his patience. Several long-term treatment goals were also identified. These include metabolizing the loss and grief about Marcos leaving and the impact of his stroke on his life, expanding his social network of friends who are developmental peers and share some common interests, and exploring other potential interests in which he might engage.

Dialogue: Session 2

COUNSELOR: I'm glad to see you today, John. How have things been going this week?

JOHN: [*Raised eyebrows, clipped voice*] Fine.

COUNSELOR: I wondered if you had any ideas of things we would talk about today.

JOHN: Not really.

COUNSELOR: I know you expressed the last time your annoyance at needing to chat with me, and I do want to respect your feelings about that. So, I thought perhaps we could keep our visits as brief as possible until you think you'd benefit from having more time. Is this okay?

JOHN: Yes. But my daughter took time out of her day to drive me here so we better not end too quickly or she might be annoyed that she drove me here just for a short time.

COUNSELOR: So maybe we could start today with your goal about eating better. Would that be okay with you?
JOHN: Why not? I have to be here so we might as well make the best of it.
COUNSELOR: I do want to acknowledge that you don't *have* to be here. I know you want your daughters not to worry about you but ultimately, you don't have to attend counseling. I do appreciate your willingness to talk with me even when you feel ambivalent. So, I think I recall you mentioning that part of you not wanting to eat was because of you said most food has become dull and tasteless to you?
JOHN: Yes, I was never the cook in any of my relationships and now that I cook for myself, I'm not very good at it. Even when I make something that should be good though, it doesn't taste very good to me. I also don't have much energy to be in the kitchen for very long.
COUNSELOR: If you could have anything you wanted to eat, what would sound good to you?
JOHN: It's hard to say. I really miss Marcos' cooking. I mostly eat prepared foods now. He used to make 'ropa vieja', and that was my favorite. He also would make a roasted pork dish that I loved.
COUNSELOR: I'm curious about whether you have made any of these things for yourself since you've been in the new apartment.
JOHN: No, I guess it just seems like way too much work. I don't have any idea how he even made those. I think he followed recipes that he knew by heart.
COUNSELOR: When in the past have you cooked for yourself?
JOHN: Only when Marcos would travel which wasn't often. I don't really mind doing it if I can get organized to order the groceries.
COUNSELOR: So I know your daughter Anna has expressed interest in helping you get feeling better. I wonder about enlisting her to come to your place and prepare some of those meals with you?
JOHN: Huh. I never thought about that.
COUNSELOR: Perhaps you and she could make a large batch of those dishes that could be frozen and reheated easily.
JOHN: Yes. I think we could do that. I'm going to ask her. So are we good now or do we need to schedule another appointment?
COUNSELOR: Well, I'd like to do at least one more to hear about how our plan worked for you. If it works well, maybe we could tackle another one?
JOHN: Ok, fine.
COUNSELOR: Did you want to discuss other things today? I know you said you didn't want the appointment to be too short.
JOHN: Hmm, let me think about what else has been going on lately...

Dialogue Analysis

- What may have been the rationale for prioritizing the eating focused goals? Conducting a brief session?
- Where do you see missed opportunities for responsiveness to his identities and experiences?
- How would you have used the skills differently to encourage John to lead the session?

Continued Dialogue: Session 4

COUNSELOR: Thanks for coming in today, John. How have things been going?

JOHN: I'm actually doing a little better. We, that is, Anna and me, have actually been working on a monthly menu and then going grocery shopping together, instead of using those grocery shopping services. I like it a lot more because I have more control over what we're buying. It makes Anna happy to see me getting out of the apartment too. We made a big lasagna last week and froze most of it. It's been nice to be eating things that I actually enjoy.

COUNSELOR: That's wonderful to hear. I notice too that you look well-rested compared to a month ago. How has your sleep been going?

JOHN: I talked to my neurologist and he adjusted my medicine so I don't get so sleepy in the afternoon, and since I'm not napping anymore I tend to fall asleep easier in the evenings. I haven't been staying up so late, only a few times in the last month.

COUNSELOR: How about your sleeping through the night? I know you were struggling with waking up at 2 or 3 am.

JOHN: I'm not having that problem now, yeah, I'm sleeping a lot more soundly.

COUNSELOR: So this is our fourth meeting and it seems you feel better physically. I'm wondering how you're feeling about continuing to work with me on some of the more emotionally related concerns we touched on in your first session.

JOHN: What exactly would we be talking about?

COUNSELOR: Well, a couple of things come to mind. Maybe we could talk about how your life and lifestyle have shifted now that Marcos is gone. Sometimes people find it helpful just to put feelings about loss and changes into words. Maybe we could talk about things you might want to add, or change, that could help your life feel more satisfying and rewarding than it has been.

JOHN: With all due respect, I don't see how I can have a more rewarding life. My best years are behind me. I'm living in an assisted living apartment complex at 71. How is that ever going to be rewarding?

COUNSELOR: I hear you, it feels like you'll never feel fulfilled in this living situation, and it all looks hopeless.
JOHN: It doesn't just feel hopeless, it actually is.
COUNSELOR: Describe for me what a hopeful situation would be.
JOHN: Somewhere I could be around other people like me, maybe?
COUNSELOR: Like you? In what way?
JOHN: I don't know, I don't want to be around a bunch of *old people* but I would appreciate spending time with people who understand what it's like at this stage of life.
COUNSELOR: Well, I wonder how would you feel about maybe meeting some people like you, online or maybe through other ways?
JOHN: Do you mean to date?
COUNSELOR: No, not necessarily, just other people to talk to, and maybe make plans to socialize like sharing a meal or going to the movies.
JOHN: Oh I don't know. That sounds like a lot of work.
COUNSELOR: I just want to point out to you that when we first started talking, and we discussed cooking, you said you hadn't done it because it seemed like too much work.
JOHN: Good point. Point well taken.
COUNSELOR: What if you and I agreed to continue meeting for a couple more sessions to look more at this social connection thing? Then we can re-visit if you want to quit.
JOHN: Yes, I think that sounds fine.
COUNSELOR: Maybe before our next session you could look at a website or two. I'd like to show you the website for the local LGBT+ Community Center. You can take a look around yourself outside of session. If you see anything that looks like it might be good, maybe we could talk about getting connected with some of the groups they have. I believe they have a series of recurring activities for folks in the SAGE organization. SAGE is a group for LGBTQ+ people who are older adults.

Dialogue Analysis

- What aspects of this dialogue represent cultural responsiveness?
- What missed opportunities did you observe, and what was the nature of the opportunity?

Case and Self-Reflection Questions

- What aspects of John's Ecological Systems Model support his clinical goals? Which aspects might present a barrier?
- What aspects of John's experiences and identities are familiar to you, and which are not? How might this impact your preconceived views of him?

- How does his referral from his children impact your perceptions of the treatment goals?
- What aspects of his identities and history would you want to know more about to effectively work with him? (Consider the ADDRESSING acronym).
- What does it look like to work with John in a trauma-informed manner?

Challenges to Using Intentional, Multiculturally Informed Helping Skills

No matter how well-intentioned we may be as we work to provide the best services to our patients and clients, there are a number of challenges that may arise which impede our ability to do that. We touch on them here to raise awareness in the hope that they can be ameliorated or avoided.

Time Restrictions

One such circumstance is time restriction. Some clients and patients may have insurance coverage that limits the amount of time a provider can treat the patient. In addition, some agencies or practices may require attainment of particular treatment goals in a specified period of time. These time restrictions may create a sense of urgency and time pressure for a counselor, which then drives them to be more directive and outcome focused than is needed. A client might benefit from ample time to build rapport and trust with a provider though. Thus, if agencies and providers are indeed going to be trauma-informed and culturally responsive, it will be necessary for increased time allowances to support relationship development.

Implicit Bias

If we ourselves have not done our personal work around understanding our own intersecting cultural and social identities, and of people and communities different from our own, we run the risk of making assumptions about others. We cannot overemphasize the urgency of providers engaging in honest, sincere, introspection about their feelings and perceptions toward groups of people who are different from themselves in some demographically relevant way. There are a number of avenues and ways we can work on expanding our consciousness about other cultural and social groups. For example, in one of India's sessions, a therapist made the recommendation to simply ask for more help from her religious community. This request seemed to bypass the presence of a long-standing family dynamic in which India didn't ask for help. It also failed to acknowledge the presence of the "strong Black woman" concept that was a prevailing norm in their home. That assumption results in a series of directive statements that probably have little likelihood of inspiring follow-through from India. Similarly, if the counselor working with John in the example was a straight, cisgender woman, whose religious beliefs were critical of same-sex relationships, she would have not been willing or able to guide him on making connections with the LGBTQ+ senior organization.

Provider Burn-out

Lastly but certainly not least is the possibility of being burned out and having that exhaustion impact the capacity to be culturally responsive. When we become burned out, we have no emotional energy to bring to our client interactions, and we have little ability to bring enthusiasm, commitment, and authenticity to the work. We may be responding to ongoing, demanding, levels of work production or number of billable contact hours we are required to generate. A person who is burned out is significantly hampered in their ability to experience empathy, compassion, or unconditional positive regard. A burned-out clinician is also unlikely to engage in the type of introspection and critical thinking needed when working with a client who could be harmed by operating from ethnocentric treatment assumptions. While other conditions in addition to these are useful in helping, we do believe they are essential foundational aspects of an effective helping relationship.

Conclusion

In this chapter, we have explored several dialogue sequences. Some of these dialogue sequences reflected culturally attuned and trauma-informed helping skills, whereas other dialogue reflected rigid and non-responsive ways of interacting. The case and self-reflection questions may have generated some new awareness of how you might have gone about working with the patient. We hope that you recognize that there is no singularly "correct" way to engage with a patient. Rather, each provider can bring their own unique experiences, personality, and knowledge to the interaction and can respond thoughtfully and compassionately. We won't get it right every single time, but with a focus on the relationship and the larger social context, we are much more likely to build the type of healing relationship that the patient needs.

Index

Page numbers in italics refer to figures. Page numbers in bold refer to tables.

access, healthcare 51, 53, 186
accuracy checks: in emotion reflection 135, 136, 138; in paraphrasing 117, 122
ACES Aware 176
active listening 17, 61, 103, 125, 140
activities of daily living (ADLs) 174
ADDRESSING framework 41–43
adolescents: psychosocial stages of development 65, **66**; verbal communication of 120
adverse childhood experiences (ACEs) 32–33, 54–55, 63, 176
Adverse Childhood Experiences Questionnaire 176
affect, definition of 126
affect circumplex 130, *131*
African Americans: healthcare abuse of 51–52; infant mortality rate 11; and medical mistrust 52; Tuskegee Syphilis study 11, 51–52
Agency for Healthcare Research and Quality (AHRQ) 12
ambivalent emotions 130–131
American Personnel and Guidance Association 28
American Psychiatric Association (APA) 173
American Psychological Association (APA) 197, 199, 204, 205
Americans with Disabilities Act 39
appointments, mental health assessment 168, 171
Arnold, M. 129
Association of Counselor Educators and Supervisors 28

attending behaviors *see* nonverbal behaviors; paraverbal behaviors
authentic connection with patients 10, 19, 20, 99
autonomy 9–10, 21, 30–31, 35, 81, 162; case example 31; of minors 30

Beck, A.T. 141
Beck Anxiety Inventory (BAI) 170
bedwetting 62
behavior(s) 16; child, and developmental norms 62; and cultural responsiveness 17; ethical 35–36; expectations, and culture 60; interpersonal 13, 14; interpretation of 5; pathologizing 10; patient readiness to change 68–70; self-monitoring 90–91; unhelpful communication behaviors 18–19; *see also* nonverbal behaviors; paraverbal behaviors; questioning; suicide risk assessment; violence risk assessment
beneficence 31
Bertrand, M. 44
bias(es) 23, 38, 40, 50; implicit 13–14, 162–163, 230–231; and mental health diagnosis 173–174; of patients 92
big T trauma 55
bipolar I disorder 175
body language 89, 93, 98; *see also* nonverbal behaviors
body movement 95–96
body posture 95, 96
brain development 64

Index 233

Bronfenbrenner, Urie 14, *15*, 47–49, *48*, 55, 61–62, 77, 81, 142, 212, 218, 225
Brown, J.S. 80
burn-out, provider 29, 231

Chambless, D.L. 198
children 61, 65; adverse childhood experiences 32–33, 54–55, 63, 176; asking "why" questions to 157; autonomy of minors 30; behavior, and developmental norms 62; and collateral information 180; self-disclosure of 107–108
chronosystem 15, **213**, **218**, **225**
clarifying questions 159–160
clinical documentation 82, 103–104, 170, 190–192
clinical expertise of providers 198–199, 204–205, 206–207
clinical judgement 21–22, 23, 193
closed questions 152, 156
codes of ethics 8, 9, 21, 28–30; autonomy 30–31; beneficence 31; congruence of counselors 29; justice 32; non-maleficence 31–32, 33; veracity 32
cognitive appraisals 129, 139, 140
cognitive behavioral therapy (CBT) 6
cognitive development 64
cognitive distortions, awareness of 6
cognitive processing therapy (CPT) 206
cognitive triad 141, 143
collaborative documentation *see* concurrent documentation
collateral data sources of mental health assessment 178, 180–181, 193
communication 115, 147; approaches 16; of children 107–108; and culture 108–109; influence of time on 109; overt/covert 145–147; patient-centered 13; with patients, purpose of 20–24; for reducing medical mistrust 52–53; skills 18–19, 20, 50; of trustworthiness 68; unhelpful behaviors 18–19; *see also* nonverbal behaviors; paraverbal behaviors
concurrent documentation 82, 103–104
confidentiality 21, 24, 35, 71
confirmation from patients, and leading questions 163–164

consultation 82, 189–190, 203, 207
context 10, 61, 66, 76; and ambivalent emotions 130; of helping relationship, and self-disclosure 108; and human development 15–16; and meaning making 140
continuing education 82, 207
Cook 44
Council for the Accreditation of Counseling and Related Educational Programs 28
counseling 70–71, 74; for academic performance 215–223; client working 156; crisis counseling 75; expectations of clients 155–156; factors that inhibit people seeking 76–77; homeostasis 77–78; as a process of re-parenting 80–81; questioning for beginning a counseling session 159; referral source 75; for relationship issues 223–230; for sexual assault 210–215; termination stage 73–74, 79–81; warm-up stage 71–73, 75–77; working stage 73, 78–79, 82
counselor congruence 29
Covid-19 pandemic 82
Crenshaw, K. 43
crisis counseling 75
cultural display rules (CDRs) 131–133
cultural mistrust 53
cultural responsiveness 16–17, 78
culture 76; commonalities in human development across 65–67; cultural identities 41–43; definition of 41; and definition of unhealthy behavior 173; and evidence-based practice 202; and eye contact 94; and human development 60–61, 62–63; intersectionality 43–44; and nonverbal behavior 93; and paraverbal behaviors 98–101; and perspective on time 109; and self-disclosure 108–109; and silence 111, 113; and social development 64
curiosity of providers 4, 16, 46, 96, 100, 122, 123, 138, 179

Davis, W. 10
dehumanization 51
demand characteristics 5
developmental crisis 126–127

diagnosis 172; mental health 173–174; patients with terminal diagnoses 9
Diagnostic and Statistical Manual of Mental Disorders (DSM-5-TR) 173
dialectical behavior therapy 9, 104
DiAngelo, R. 44
DiClemente, C.C. 127
directive counseling 71, 150
disabilities, people with 38–39, 52, 62–63, 163
discrimination of cultural/social groups 10–14, 54
distress 172–173, 174–176
diversity *see* pluralistic society, helping in
Doan, S.N. 126
documentation, clinical 82, 103–104, 170, 190–192
Dupree, D. 61

ecological systems theory (Bronfenbrenner) 14–15, *15*, 47–49, *48*, 55, 61, 81, 142–144, 212, 218, 225
Edinburgh Postnatal Depression Scale (EPDS) 170
Ekman, P. 94, 131, 132
emerging adulthood 65
Emery, G. 141
emic perspective 9–10
emotional development 64
emotional vocabulary 133, 134
emotion reflection 125, 126–127, 145–146, 154, 164, 170; components of 135; empathy 127–129; skill 135–136, 138–139; *see also* meaning reflection
emotions 9, 90; affect circumplex 130, *131*; ambivalent 130–131; bracketing of 104, 105; cognitive appraisal approach 129; and communication 19; and cultural display rules 131–133; definition of 126; emotional state of providers 104–105; emotional tracking 101–102, 114; emotion wheel 134–135, *134*; and growth 126, 127; and human needs 135; identification and categorization of 133–135; incongruent, expressing 18, 19; labeling of 133–134; recognition of 133; regulation of 104, 177; satisfied *136*; universal 94, 95, 131; unsatisfied *137*; *see also* nonverbal behaviors; paraverbal behaviors
empathy 9, 10, 18, 108, 122, 127–129, 170, 177
empirically supported relationship (ESR) 202
empirically supported treatment (EST) 198, 201, 202, 205–206, 207
Erikson, E. 126
ethics 27; codes of 8, 9, 21, 28–32; ethical behavior 35–36; impact of ethnocentric care 34; and interpersonal relationships 8–10; licensure 27–28; program accreditation 28; risk assessment 183; and trauma-informed care 32–34
ethnocentrism 10, 34, 40, 139
evidence-based practice (EBP) 196; adapting ESTs 206; benefits of 201; clinical expertise 198–199; competency development 206–207; components of 197–201, *198*; critiques of 201–202; definition of 197; knowledge, sources of 205–206; movement, history of 196–197; patient variables 199–201; randomized controlled trials 201–202; research evidence 197–198; symptom reduction *vs.* patient functionality 202; terminology 197–199; treatment planning 202–205
exosystem 14, 48, 143, 144, 213, 218, 225
eye contact 94–95, 103, 111

facial expressions 94–95, 96, 131, 132
family system 67, 77
feedback 3, 21, 205
feelings, definition of 126; *see also* emotions
feeling wheel 134–135, *134*
flat affect 98
forced sterilization 52
friendships 8, 18
Friesen, W.V. 94, 131, 132

Gamble, V.N. 51
Gardiner, H.W. 66
Gawande, Atul 9
Geertz, C. 41
Gestalt counseling 71–72

Index   235

gesticulations 95–96
Gordon, K.H. 80

Haggård-Grann, U. 193
Hall, G.C.N. 17
Hampden-Turner, C. 109
Harkness, S. 61
Hartmann, T. 61
healthcare abuse 51–52
healthcare disparities 12–13, 34; definition of 12; interpersonal factors of 13; intrapersonal factors of 13; systemic factors of 13
healthcare systems 10–11, 40, 50–51
health insurance 12, 51, 230
helicopter parenting 67
helping skills 3–5, 19, 20, 65; building effective interpersonal relationships 7–16; case descriptions 210–230; challenges to 230–231; helping relationship development 67–69, 171, 230; microskills model 4, 17, 18, 19; self-awareness 5–7; see also interpersonal relationships
high-context (HC) communication 109
Hill, C.E. 74, 79
Historical, Clinical, and Risk Management Violence Risk Assessment Scheme (HCR-20) 193
historical trauma 55
Hofmann, S.G. 126
Hofstede, G. 111
holarchy 47
Hollon, S.D. 198
homeostasis 77–78
homicide risk assessment see violence risk assessment
hope 20, 171–172
human development 14–16, 60; commonalities across cultures in 65–67; and culture 60–61, 62–63; helping relationship development 67–69; lifespan development 60–63; realms of lifespan development 63–65; research, limitations of 61; trauma-informed 63
human existence, definition of 47
human needs 135, 200

ideation, suicide 187
impairment 174

implicit bias 230–231; and healthcare disparities 13–14; and leading questions 162–163
individual level trauma 55
infant mortality rate of African Americans 11
internal development processes 64
International Classification of Diseases – 11th Revision (ICD-11) 173
interpersonal conflicts 162
interpersonal relationships 7–8; diversity 10–14; ethics 8–10; in healthcare 8–9; human development 14–16
intersectionality 43–44
intonation (speech) 97, 101, 102, 153
Ivey, Allen 17, 89
Ivey, M.B. 89

Jakobsons, L.J. 80
Joiner, T.E. 80
justice 32

Kessler, R.C. 54
key word repetitions 115, 116

Larson, L. 76
leading questions 161; assumption of solution 161–162; desire for confirmation 163–164; reflection of implicit bias 162–163
licensure 27–28
life roles, and impairment 174
lifespan: development 60–63; development, realms of 63–65; and patient self-disclosure 107–108, 120
Linehan, M. 104
little t trauma 55
location of provider's practice 203
low-context (LC) communication 109

macrosystem 15, 48, 49, 143, 213, 218, 225
Manning, K. 52
marginalization 44, 45; definition of 43; systemic nature of 43, 45
meaning making 139–140, 141–144
meaning reflection 125, 139–140, 154, 170; schemas 140–141; skill 141, 144–147; see also emotion reflection
medical mistrust 52–53, 98–99, 150

mental health assessment 167; appointments 158–159, 168; approaches to 176–177; areas of 170; building rapport 168; classification system of mental health disorders 173; collateral data sources 178, 180–181, 193; distress 174–176; formal 169–170; goals 167–172; impairment 174; instilling hope 171–172; mental status exam 181–183, **182**; objective data sources 178, 179–180; presenting concern 172; psychopathology 172–174; semi-structured interviews 178; structured interviews 177; subjective data sources 178–179; suicide risk assessment 183–192; targeted assessment 168–169; timing 167–169; unstructured interviews 178, 192; violence risk assessment 183, 192–193

mental status exam (MSE) 181–183, **182**

mesosystem 14, 48, 142–143, 144, 213, 218, 225

microaggressions 12, 44

microskills model 4, 17, 18, 19, 65

microsystem 14, 48, 49, 142, 144, 213, 218, 225

minimal encouragers 113–114, 115–116

minor assent 30

minority groups/communities 11, 12; medical mistrust of 52–53; and mental health diagnosis 173–174; minority cultural groups 40; stressors of 53–554

minority stress model (MSM) 53–54

minors, autonomy of 30

motivational interviewing (MI) 70

motor development 60–61

Mullainathan, S. 44

multicultural competence 35, 39, 49–50, 205; awareness 49; knowledge 49; skills 49

multiple-choice questions 156–157

National Center for PTSD 176

nondirective counseling 71

non-judgmental attitude of providers 4, 21, 100

non-maleficence 31–32, 33

non-suicidal self-injury (NSSI) 184

nonverbal behaviors 89, 93, 110, 111, 145, 146, 158; body posture and movement 95–96; and breaking silence 113; and concurrent documentation 103–104; and emotional state of providers 104–105; facial expressions 94–95, 96; as minimal encouragers 113–114; observation of 93–96, 111, 113; of patients 72, 89; of providers 89–90, 96, 104–105; use with restatements, paraphrases, and summaries 120–123; *see also* paraverbal behaviors

Norcross, J.C. 20, 127

objective data sources of mental health assessment 178, 179–180

observation 5, 72, 89; of nonverbal behaviors 93–96, 111, 113; of paraverbal behaviors 98, 99–100; self-observation 5, 69, 91, 114, 133; of time boundary 74

openness to correction of providers 135, 138, 146

open questions 152–153, 155, 156, 157–158, **158**, 159

oppression 45; of cultural/social groups 10–14, 38; racism 11, 43–44; systemic 50

paralinguistics *see* paraverbal behaviors

paraphrasing 114–115, 117–119, 120–123, 144–145, 154, 160, 164, 170

paraverbal behaviors 89, 97–98, 138, 145, 158; and concurrent documentation 103–104; cultural considerations 98–101; and emotional state of providers 104–105; mirroring of 101–102; of patients 72, 89, 97–98, 130; of providers 89–90, 101–103, 104–105; and questioning 153; use with restatements, paraphrases, and summaries 120–123; *see also* nonverbal behaviors

personal judgement 21, 23–24

phenomenological variants of ecological systems theory (PVEST) 62

physical development 64

pitch (speech) 97, 101

pluralistic society, helping in 9, 10, 38; consciousness raising 44–47; counseling process 70–81; ecological model of human development (Bronfenbrenner) 47–49, *48*; establishing trust 39–41; foundational concepts 41–44; healthcare abuse 51–52; healthcare disparities 12–13; healthcare systems 50–51; helping relationship development 67–69; historical and individual level trauma 55; implicit bias 13–14; medical mistrust 52–55, 98–99; minority stress model 53–54; multicultural competence 49–50; patient readiness to change 68–70; pervasive and multifaceted nature of oppression 11–12; privilege and marginalization 44–47
post-traumatic stress disorder (PTSD) 33, 54, 55, 206
power: dynamic, in therapeutic relationship 4, 6, 35, 68, 117, 150, 163; empowerment of patients 151, 171–172; and minority cultural groups 40; and oppression 11
privilege 42–43, 44, 45; definition of 43; socioeconomic 47; systemic nature of 43, 45; White 44
Prochaska, J. 69, 127
productive silences 112
professional codes of ethics *see* codes of ethics
professional organizations 28, 207
program accreditation 28
prosody (speech) 97, 101, 102
psychopathology 172–174; *see also* distress
psychosocial model of human development 126

qualifiers: in emotion reflection 135–136, 138; in paraphrasing 117, 122
questioning 150–151; acknowledging client's response 154; avoiding rapid-fire questions 153–154; beginning a counseling session 159; clarification of patient's statement 159–160; developing good questioning habits 161–164; dialogue examples 158–161; effective 152; gathering information at intake/assessment appointment 158–159; ineffective behaviors 155–158; mechanical aspects of 153–155; in mental health assessment 171; open and closed questions 152–153; overt and covert messages 153; for sharpening the focus 160–161; timing of 161; from trauma-informed perspective 151–152; "why" questions 157–158, **158**

racial trauma 55
racism 11, 43–44
randomized controlled trials (RCTs) 201–202
rapport 8, 20, 21, 65, 99, 108, 114, 167, 168, 177, 230
readiness to change, patient 68–70
relapse prevention plan 70
release of information 35, 180
research evidence 197–198
restatements 114–117, 120–123
risk assessment: myths and facts 184–185; suicide 183–192; violence 183, 192–193
Rush, A.J. 141

Sackett, D. 196, 205
safety, sense of 7, 12, 35, 39, 55, 68, 71, 151
Savickas, M.L. 64
schemas 140–141
schizophrenia 38–39
scholarly journals 205
scope of practice of providers 28, 36, 67, 167, 169, 203, 204–205
self, levels of *200*
self-awareness 4, 5–7, 9, 16, 40, 50, 92, 117, 119
self-care 74, 105
self-concept 62
self-disclosure 162; patient 107–109; of personal life circumstances 18
self-esteem 30, 61, 96
self-fulfilling prophecy 6
self-monitoring 90–91, 93
self-perception 47, 49, 61, 142
self-reflection 4–5, 19, 111, 114
self-report, patient 107, 169, 178–179, 180–181
semi-structured interviews 178

sequential cultures, communication in 109
Shaw, G.F. 141
shell-shock syndrome *see* post-traumatic stress disorder (PTSD)
silence 110–111, 153; and anxiety-driven talking 113; breaking 113; and faulty beliefs 113; not allowing for 18–19; times for 111–112; types of 113–114
small talk 71
SMART (Specific, Measurable, Achievable, Relevant, and Time-bound) goals 203–204
social anxiety 21–24
social determinants of health 39
social development 64
social stimulus value 91–93
Society of Clinical Child and Adolescent Psychology (APA) 205–206
Society of Clinical Psychology (APA) 205–206
socioeconomic status 44, 46, 51
speed (speech) 97, 101
Spencer, M.B. 15, 61, 62
stereotypes 13, 162–163; microaggressions 12, 44; social stimulus value 91–93
stressors of minority populations 53–54
Structured Clinical Interview for DSM-5 (SCID-5) 177
structured interviews 177
subjective data sources of mental health assessment 178–179
Substance Abuse and Mental Health Services Administration (SAMHSA) 7, 33, 39, 151, 176, 206
Sue, D.W. 199, 201
suicidal tendencies 184
suicide risk assessment 183, 186–189; clinical terminology 183–184; consultation 189–190; documentation 190–192; myths and facts about suicide 184–185; protective factors 185–186, 189; risk factors 185–186, **186**, 189; suicidal ideation 187–188, 191; suicidal intent 188–189, 191; suicide plan 188; warning signs 185–186, **187**
summaries/summarization 104, 114–115, 119–123
Super, M.C. 61, 64

supervision 35, 82, 189–190, 203, 207
synchronic cultures, communication in 109

Tarasoff case (1976) 192
technological developments 81–82
terminal diagnoses, patients with 9
termination stage (counseling) 73–74, 79–81
Terry, M. 48
Test of Memory Malingering (TOMM) 179–180
time: boundary, observation of 74; influence on communication 109; restrictions 230
timing: mental health assessment 167–169; questioning 161
Tolin, D.F. 198, 202
transgender patients, oppression experienced by 12
transparency 151–152, 168
transtheoretical treatment model (TTM) 69–70, 127
trauma: Big T/little t 55; historical 55; and human development 61; individual level 55; -informed human development 63; screening tools 176
trauma-informed care 4, 7, 35, 39, 54, 55–56, 167, 205; and ethics 32–34; four Rs of 33, 151, 176; and mental health assessment 170, 176–177; questioning 151–152
treatment planning 202–203; clinical needs of patients 203, 204; goal creation 203–204; integration of EBP 204–205; location of a provider's practice 203; maps 202
triangulated data 180
Trompenaars, F. 109
trust 20, 21, 24, 68, 230; communication of trustworthiness 68; establishing 39–41, 170; medical mistrust 52–53, 98–99, 150; and patient self-report 179
Tuskegee Syphilis study 11, 51–52

uncertainty avoidance 111
unconditional positive regard 36
unhealthy behaviors 68–69, 173
United Nations Educational, Scientific and Cultural Organization 41
universal facial expressions 94, 95, 131

unproductive silences 113
unstructured interviews 178, 192
upspeak 102, 115, 122

validation of patients 17, 110, 168, 177, 190
values clarification exercises 141
veracity 32
verbal skills 107, 125; emotion reflection 125, 126–129, 135–136, 138–139; impact of being understood 109–110; influences on patient self-disclosure 107–109; meaning reflection 125, 139–141; minimal encouragers 113–114, 115–116; paraphrasing 114–115, 117–119, 120–123; restatements 114–117, 120–123; silence 110–113; summarizing 114–115, 119–123; *see also* questioning
verbal utterances 113–114, 116
Veterans Administration 54

violence risk assessment 183, 192–193; *see also* suicide risk assessment
Vogel, S. 76, 77
volume (speech) 97, 101

warm-up stage (counseling) 71–73, 75–77
Wester, S. 76
White fragility 44
White privilege 44
"why" questions 157–158, **158**
Wiseman, T. 127
wise mind (dialectical behavior therapy) 9
women: Black, oppression of 43; with intellectual disabilities, forced sterilization of 52
working stage (counseling) 73, 78–79, 82
World Health Organization (WHO) 173